The Human Side
of Factory Automation

ANN MAJCHRZAK

The Human Side
of Factory Automation

MANAGERIAL AND HUMAN RESOURCE
STRATEGIES FOR MAKING
AUTOMATION SUCCEED

Jossey-Bass Publishers

San Francisco • London • 1988

THE HUMAN SIDE OF FACTORY AUTOMATION
Managerial and Human Resource Strategies for Making Automation Succeed
by Ann Majchrzak

Copyright © 1988 by: Jossey-Bass Inc., Publishers
350 Sansome Street
San Francisco, California 94104

&

Jossey-Bass Limited
28 Banner Street
London EC1Y 8QE

HD
6331
1 M2253
1988

Library of Congress Cataloging-in-Publication Data

Majchrzak, Ann.
    The human side of factory automation.

    (The Jossey-Bass management series)
    Bibliography: p.
    Includes index.
    1. Labor supply—Effect of automation on. 2. Job satisfaction. 3. Measuring instrument. I. Title.
II. Series.
HD6331.M2253   1988   658.3   87-45505
ISBN 1-55542-050-8 (alk. paper)

Manufactured in the United States of America

The paper in this book meets the guidelines for permanence and durability of the Committee on Production Guidelines for Book Longevity of the Council on Library Resources.

JACKET DESIGN BY WILLI BAUM

FIRST EDITION

Code 8757

The Jossey-Bass
Management Series

Contents

Preface

Manufacturing companies in the United States are facing severe difficulties in today's marketplace. Foreign competition, a strong dollar, changing consumer tastes, poor worker productivity, old factories, and an unrelenting recession in the manufacturing sector create an unprecedented array of challenges.

Many companies are turning to factory automation to meet these challenges. Company managers have invested in such advanced manufacturing technologies as computer-automated manufacturing, flexible manufacturing systems, and computer-numerical control machine tools, in the belief that they will reduce lead time, reduce in-process inventory, improve quality control, reduce space requirements, increase productivity, and more.

In spite of the clear urgency to update manufacturing methods, however, U.S. firms are currently experiencing an estimated 50 to 75 percent failure rate when implementing advanced manufacturing technology (Ettlie, 1986a; Hwang and Salvendy, 1985; Jaikumar, 1986). What accounts for this shocking lack of success? Research results discussed throughout this book point to management practices: human resource issues have been identified as crucial factors in the successful, effective implementation of advanced technology. The purpose of this book is to describe and explain methods managers can use in organizing, motivating, and directing the people involved in designing, implementing, and using the new technology. It shows why an understanding of how to create an effective human infrastructure is essential to the success of any company's automation effort.

Who Should Read This Book?

This book has been written for two audiences: professionals and academics. Professionals and managers in manufacturing industries are confronted daily with talk of the need to modernize. However, they have few resources to aid them in preparing their human infrastructures for the modernization effort. For factory managers, this book is designed to provide (1) convincing data and discussion showing that managers need to engage in long-range planning for organizational and human resources when considering flexible factory automation; (2) information about the important body of state-of-the-art research on the consequences to the human infrastructure that can be expected with advanced manufacturing technology; and (3) specific suggestions and a useful tool—the Human Infrastructure Impact Statement—to help managers apply research findings for long-range planning.

This book is not a "how-to" manual for job analyses, organizational climate assessment, or training. It is intended to illuminate the full range of issues related to the human infrastructure that are encountered with flexible factory automation and to advise the reader on applications when research has been sufficient to indicate applications. After reading this book, managers may want to review some of the better-known "how-to" sources on various topics. The bibliography at the end of this book includes such sources and many other categories of selected readings.

For scholars in departments of industrial engineering, psychology, sociology, or management, this book presents a review of the empirical literature on the impact of advanced manufacturing technology on the workplace. In addition, important research questions yet to be adequately analyzed are identified. This book lends itself to use in introductory courses on managing and researching new technology, as well as in the development of inductive theories on individual and organizational adjustment and adaptation to technological change.

Overview of the Contents

The book consists of four parts. In Part One, "Understanding the Human Infrastructure in Factories," basic arguments and research are presented supporting the important role that the human infrastructure plays in determining how successfully advanced manufacturing technology (AMT) will be implemented. The research is so conclusive, in fact, that the analogy to an infrastructure of highways is drawn: just as a planned sequence of roads is necessary to provide supplies between cities, a planned series of management strategies is needed to integrate technological change into the organizational setting. Part One also includes a discussion of the basic framework for the remainder of the book. This framework poses an open systems, staged model for understanding the impacts of AMT on the human infrastructure. Specific elements of the human infrastructure are identified that must be analyzed when automation is being considered. These are grouped into first- and second-order effects of AMT to underscore the interdependent nature of the different human infrastructure options and decisions to be made by the manager of tomorrow's flexible factory.

Part Two is titled "First-Order Effects: How Job Tasks Change." It describes changes to the jobs of AMT operators, technical support and administrative staff, and supervisors and managers. These first-order effects are identified based on the research literature to date; thus, the reader is spared unfounded speculations. Moreover, critical to the discussion of each first-order impact is an identification of the variety of options that factories with AMT have used to manage the impacts. Finally, where research literature is available, the variety of options are compared and contrasted to determine which ones are most likely to work for a particular factory setting.

The third part of the book, "Second-Order Effects: Organizational Adaptations to Job Changes," examines the identification of new skills needed with AMT; selection procedures and delineation of the recruiting pool for finding personnel with the right skills; setting up AMT training programs, including specific examples of curricula currently used by AMT plants; changes in such personnel policies as job classifications, pay, career development, job security, shift work, and union-management relations; and modifications to an organization's structure and climate that are often necessary when AMT is installed. Again, as with the first-order effects, research-based information is the primary focus here, not idle speculation. Moreover, options for effectively managing second-order effects are identified, accompanied by a discussion of their relative merits and appropriateness for different situations.

The final part of the book, "Implementing Factory Automation Successfully," discusses the issues involved in effectively assimilating AMT into the organization. Such issues include ways to overcome resistance to factory automation among organizational members, structuring the automation project team to effectively manage the equipment selection and implementation process, and an overview of critical concerns for preparing organizational members for a change from the status quo to a new environment. This part of the book closes with a chapter on the management implications of planning for the human infrastructure. Critical decisions that managers must make to effectively achieve the potential yields of AMT are summarized, ending with a list of do's and don'ts in making these decisions.

Critical to implementing the suggestions presented in this book is the Human Infrastructure Impact Statement (HIIS), a tool for evaluating an organization's propensity to effectively integrate the technology and its human infrastructure. This instrument appears in the Appendix, along with instructions and a glossary of terms. Finally, the book includes a list of references to selected empirical literature on the impact of AMT. This list, included for both the researcher and the manager interested in purveying original sources, is categorized by case studies, quantitative data analyses, and research reviews.

It is a difficult task to write a book for both academic and managerial audiences. Academics generally prefer lengthy descriptions with substantial supporting evidence; moreover, for them the processes by which conclusions are derived are in many ways more important than the conclusions themselves. Managers, however, want brevity, prescriptions, and conclusions—with as little rationale and background discussion as possible. Despite these different preferences, there is a common ground shared by the two audiences: they both want to know what conclusions about the human infrastructure with flexible factory automation can be made from the existing empirical research.

In response to this shared concern, this is not a book of speculation, personal forecasts, or isolated experiences. Rather, my discussion remains intentionally close to the data; empirical case studies, surveys, and interviews provide the evidence for the conclusions I draw. Given this orientation, however, the reader needs to remember that the advanced manufacturing technologies on which the data were compiled are infinitely varied. Moreover, the technology is constantly changing, as are companies' efforts to implement it. Thus, in drawing inferences from the research data, I have made some assumptions about the likelihood that the findings will apply to other technologies not directly tested. In doing so, I have relied on knowledge derived from the combination of my experiences working directly with managers implementing advanced technologies as well as doing research in the area. Finally, in deference to the brevity preferred by managers, much of the research evidence supporting conclusions presented throughout the book has been relegated to simple citations. While for some academic readers this may create some frustration in learning about the details of the studies that form the basis of each conclusion, interested readers are provided full bibliographical information and are encouraged to read the original sources. The Selected Guide to the Empirical Literature Technology lists empirical studies categorized by major types of case studies, quantitative analyses, and research reviews.

Acknowledgments

I would like to acknowledge several individuals who have helped me throughout the preparation of the book. Dale Romine was exceptionally helpful as a practicing manager willing to closely and critically review the manuscript, share insights, and encourage me about the need for such a book. Janice Klein and Frederick Krantz also provided quite helpful and insightful comments on an earlier draft. Expressing my appreciation here for such careful reading seems hardly enough for their efforts. In addition, I would like to gratefully acknowledge the support of the National Science

Foundation whose funding (ISI-841724 and ISI-8696111) provided me the opportunity to prepare this manuscript. Finally, behind every completed project there is a champion; for this project, that champion is my husband, Peter Niemiec. It was he who had the foresight to appreciate the need for the book and the conviction to accept the sacrifices that the preparation of a book such as this entails.

Venice, California   Ann Majchrzak
December 1987

The Author

Ann Majchrzak is associate professor of human factors at the University of Southern California. She received her B.A. degree (1976) from Pitzer College in psychology and her M.A. (1977) and Ph.D. (1980) degrees from the University of California at Los Angeles in social psychology. Before joining the faculty at USC, Majchrzak was an organizational and management consultant and contract researcher in Washington, D.C., and then served for several years as a faculty member in the Krannert Graduate School of Management at Purdue University.

Majchrzak has been actively involved in research and consulting on the design and assimilation of advanced manufacturing technology (AMT) for the past seven years. Her studies have included several surveys of plants with computer-automated manufacturing and computer-integrated manufacturing equipment, indepth case studies of job changes when computer-aided design and computer-automated manufacturing are introduced, interviews with managers responsible for the selection and implementation of AMT, and "reverse engineering" analyses on military weapon systems to identify areas of improvement in the system development process. In these efforts, her focus has consistently been on identifying ways in which new complex hardware systems can be introduced into the workplace with minimal production disruption and maximum utilization of the technology's full capabilities. Sponsors for Majchrzak's research and consulting include the National Science Foundation, the Congressional Office of Technology Assessment, several manufacturing companies, and the Rand Corporation.

Majchrzak has spoken and written extensively on the design and implementation of AMT, for both practitioner and academic audiences. She has presented papers at the Society of Manufacturing Engineers' AUTOFACT and American Institute of Industrial Engineers (AIIE) conferences, and has served as a panelist in several workshops and conferences that were specifically focused on explaining human infrastructure issues in AMT. The workshops have been sponsored by such groups as USC's Center for Effective Organizations and Center for Operations Management Education and Research; the Industrial Technology Institute; American Productivity Center; the large Japanese conglomerate, NEC Corporation; and the Indiana Economic Development Council. She has made numerous presentations at the annual meetings of the Academy of Management, American Psychological Association, American Institute of Decision Sciences, Human Factors Society, and American Society for Engineering Education. Majchrzak has published articles in *IEEE Transactions on Engineering Management, Behavior and Information Technology, Journal of Manufacturing Systems, Journal of Occupational Psychology,* and *Journal of Technology Transfer,* as well as in the 1987 edition of the *Handbook of Human Factors.* In addition to several book chapters, she has recently co-authored a book entitled *Human Aspects of CAD* (with others, 1987).

The Human Side
of Factory Automation

1

The Clear Links Between Proper Human Resource Planning and Successful Automation

In the past, the implementation of new conventional equipment resulted in little change to the human infrastructure. The installation of new equipment only slightly modified direct labor jobs or training activities. Substantial preplanning of broad-based changes was rarely necessary. With the implementation of advanced manufacturing technology, however, such a strategy regarding the human infrastructure is inadequate. This chapter describes the managerial problems created by a strategy in which little preplanning is undertaken. An alternative approach is then briefly presented. This approach, the open systems framework, illustrates the need not only to preplan for changes to the human infrastructure but also to consider in those plans the interactive effects of changes in equipment, tasks, structure, and people. An example of an open systems approach applied to the implementation of advanced manufacturing technology is presented. Finally, the chapter clarifies the technologies encompassed by flexible factory automation.

Current Approach to Planning for the Human Infrastructure

A recent trade journal article titled "No Automation Additives" recently asked the manager: "How many times have we been told recently that you can't just plunk a robot down, can't just add a vision system, can't just jump into CAD [computer-aided design], can't just stick a sensor wherever it seems convenient? The frequency of, and the consistency of, this [question] indicates that it probably stems from a long rehearsed set of habits built up

1

around the means by which we were able to improve or fix mechanical manufacturing technology: add a little oil, file a flange, reset a gasket, or go so far as to add another lathe and operator to the shop floor" (1985, p. 2). In the past, managers applied only simple implementation strategies to the installation of new equipment. They concentrated on technical interfaces and paid little attention to the human beings who would work with and around the new equipment.

Paying little attention to human resources in planning for new technology has led to a series of assumptions about the human infrastructure. These assumptions include the following:

- Optimal technical utilization can be achieved primarily through technical factors.
- People are more flexible than equipment.
- Human resource issues for new technology can be narrowly defined around personnel policies of rewriting job descriptions and training; other effects of new technology are unknown or too difficult to predict.

In many ways, these assumptions were correct for the purchase of conventional equipment. In the past, implementing the technology was often a relatively simple affair. Equipment reliability was predictable, roles for operating and managing the new equipment were well defined, and major human resource changes, such as information exchange and departmental coordination, rarely changed with the new technology. Thus, technology problems were primarily seen as needing technical solutions. Often the only type of human resource solution considered was the elimination of direct cost. Because the equipment purchase process allowed for little change once the purchase decision had been made, changes in people were expected to occur more easily than changes in equipment. Thus, advance planning for effects on the human infrastructure seemed much less important than planning for the technology. Moreover, because the greatest flexibility in human resource adaptation is achieved by rewriting job descriptions and training personnel, adjusting these human factors to the technology became the focus of human resource change, if any occurred at all.

As the implementation of conventional equipment has given way to the implementation of flexible factory automation, many companies have continued to ignore the human infrastructure until after the technological plan was in place. For example, in one series of nineteen case studies of automated equipment implemented in different manufacturing environments worldwide, most managers reported a lack of initial structured consideration of the human consequences of automation (Butera, 1984). The managers indicated that human resources were considered only a remedial action to counteract problems as they occurred. Other recent studies in multiple manufacturing industries have also documented the lack of initial consideration given to the human infrastructure when computerized technology is installed (Bishop, 1984; Blumberg and Gerwin, 1985; Manufacturing Studies Board, 1986; Walton and Vittori, 1983). Moreover, when the human consequences of new flexible technology are considered, often only the reduced labor costs are examined (Ayres and Miller, 1983). This is in spite of numerous admonitions in the practical literature that flexible automation must be purchased for total cost reduction, which involves far more than direct labor cost reductions (Goldhar and Jelinek, 1983).

Failing to preplan for the human infrastructure in as much depth as for technology has been shown to be a flawed approach. It results in several problems. First, this approach assumes that optimal technical utilization can be achieved primarily through technical factors. This assumption has not been supported by the research evidence. The Congressional Office of Technology Assessment conducted a 1984 study involving surveys and case studies on the implementation of flexible automation. The study concluded that "the main stumbling blocks in the near future for implementation of programmable automation technology are not technical, but rather are barriers of cost, organization of the factory, availability of appropriate skills, and social effects of these technologies" (Office of Technology Assessment, 1984, p. 94). In a recent study by the National Academy of Sciences in which twenty-four plants implementing flexible automation were visited, the conclusions were similar: Nontechnical change with new technology often poses greater problems than the technology itself (Manufacturing Studies Board, 1986).

Digital Equipment Corporation (DEC) provides an example that supports these conclusions. DEC installed a flexible manufacturing system (FMS) and reported that the technical issues were the easy ones to work out. The major problems were human resource issues. Employees at every level lacked awareness of new technology and its implications, feared newness, and relied on getting the product out and not using the FMS effectively. In addition, engineering "superstars" responsible for installing the equipment believed that people in the plant could not possibly understand the new technology and thought that educating them would be a waste of time. The DEC people called this latter problem "technological superstar mentality" and found it to be particularly influential in inducing resistance to the FMS.

A second flaw in the status quo approach is that it focuses on reductions in direct labor costs as the rationale for new technology. This flaw often results in ignoring the role of people in the operations of the new technology. However, despite talk of unmanned factories, few flexible automation systems achieve unmanned status. Although some FMSs are specifically designed not to need people, few of the current systems operate totally unmanned for prolonged periods of time (Hwang and Salvendy, 1985). People are needed to inspect incoming materials, determine if the production process is operating effectively, intervene before dangerous situations are created or excessive scrap is generated when the process goes awry, check computer instructions, communicate to others for diagnosing machine problems, identify process improvements, and so on.

One example of the need for people is in the making of silicon chips at Harris Corporation's semiconductor plant in Melbourne, Florida. In the clean room two robots service a machine that imprints electronic circuits on the chips. One robot feeds the silicon wafers into the circuit-printing machine and the other removes and washes finished parts. "But while demonstrating the system, an operator occasionally had to tap a wafer with a pen to push it along a conveyor because the robot couldn't detect or correct hang-ups. And one of the robots botched the wafer-washing process because of bugs in the programming" (Stricharchuk and Winter, 1985, p. 14C). In another example, at Husqvarna AB in Sweden, two robots were purchased to handle the enameling of ovens to be installed in household stoves. "But these robots cannot [operate] entirely independently. A couple of persons work in the immediate vicinity, one of whom welds ovens that will then be enameled, and the other keeps a check on how well the robots are doing their enameling work" (Aguren and Edgren, 1980, p. 44).

A third flaw in the status quo approach is that it emphasizes narrowly defined human resource issues, such as job descriptions or training. This often results in the neglect of many available options for managing the human infrastructure with flexible factory automation. For example, job designs are not necessarily constrained by the new technology. When implementing a computer-numerical control (CNC) machine, a firm could expand or limit operators' job responsibilities. For example, Butera (1984) reports from his nineteen case studies that the variations of job designs and compensation plans were as numerous as the organizations and not constrained by the technologies. Wilkinson (1983) studied four firms with CNC machines and found that two of the four firms had redesigned operators' jobs for the CNCs in one way and the other two firms had redesigned operators' jobs in a completely opposite way. The first two firms had reduced the tasks of machine operators to loading and unloading and monitoring. Programming of the CNCs was carried out by managers or by a separate department for programming. In the other two firms, the CNC operators were responsible for programming as well as verifying the computer programs once written. Clearly these two strategies are sufficiently different not to be a function of the technology.

A fourth flaw in the status quo approach is that failure to preplan for the human infrastructure can create obstacles on the shopfloor that may prevent or slow utilization of new technology over the short run. These obstacles may range from shopfloor personnel lacking motivation to stop machines that aren't working properly, to sabotage, or even to strikes that necessitate unplanned downtime and expenses. Harley Shaiken (1984) describes a firm implementing a CNC machine tool that was initially intended to replace the machinist. However, in the process of implementing the CNC, the firm found that the part programs rarely worked the first time, necessitating the machinist's intervention during the first few production runs. Moreover, it was discovered that the programs could be substantially optimized by having the machinist advise the programmer about better cutters, faster cutter paths, and why some problems in cutting might have occurred. Finally, the firm found that it needed to modify certain technical CNC features after installation because of a failure to consider the role of operators during equipment selection. The technical feature modified was the addition of an override switch so that the operator could adjust the programmed feed of the machine to actual cutting conditions. Without the override switch, hard spots on the metal shattered the cutter and damaged the machine tools. In sum, failing to plan for these human resource issues prior to selecting the technical features of the machine delayed effective utilization of the new equipment.

Westinghouse provides another example of the short-term effects on the shopfloor of ignoring human resource issues until the equipment is installed (Knight, 1985). In this case, a Fanuc robot was designed to user specifications but never used. Case analysis revealed the following sequence of events. A project team began design of the robot at the request of upper-level manufacturing managers. Shopfloor supervisors were not consulted during the design'work. When the robot arrived, several technical problems needed to be worked out during production runs, but shopfloor personnel helped as little as possible and essentially circumvented the efforts of the project team staff. In the end, production lagged so far behind the delivery schedule that some of the work was subcontracted out. As the technical problems continued, the entire process originally intended to be performed by the robot was subcontracted without union information or approval. This is a strike issue for most unions!

Ignoring human resource issues until the technology arrives or until human resource problems present themselves creates problems *off* the shopfloor as well as on. If support staff are not properly informed, if managers' jobs are not redefined, or if management involvement is not sufficiently considered in advance, full utilization of the new equipment may be inhibited. In one example, a firm redesigned CNC operators' jobs giving them a higher job classification with more pay and operator training (Butera, 1984). Production began on schedule; however, the system soon failed because management refused to specify precise decision-making and problem-solving responsibilities for operators. Management claimed that only they—the management—should have responsibility for certain decisions despite the recommendation of system designers that the operators needed discretion over these decisions to effectively operate the equipment.

In another example, Majchrzak (1985b) describes a plant in which new manufacturing cells were created with old equipment to cut capital investment costs. To encourage a higher machine utilization rate through proper motivation of cell operators, management began a new policy whereby cell operators were encouraged to suggest process improvements to manufacturing engineers. Engineers were never independently and personally informed of this policy and thus had neither the desire nor the training to respond to semiskilled workers telling them how to do their jobs. As a result, the program of process improvement suggestions not only failed to increase machine utilization rates but backfired and generated more hostility and sabotage than before.

A fifth flaw in the status quo approach is that it assumes that the human infrastructure can adjust to changes rapidly. Thus, for example, training-dependent estimates of project completion dates and costs often turn out to be seriously wrong during implementation. Thompson and Scalpone (1983) have examined FMS implementations and found that firms commonly estimated training needs at 1 percent of the total system cost and expected to require one part-time trainer. However, experience from these same firms proved that training costs typically amounted to 5 to 10 percent of total system cost and that two full-time trainers were usually needed.

Ignoring human resource issues until after the technology has been selected or implemented creates the potential for human resource problems that are so severe that the capital investment for an expensive FMS or other flexible automation system may be completely negated. Wilkinson (1983, pp. 35–36) describes a small, privately owned plating company unhappy with the waste of material and time on its conventional plating line. Management blamed platers for the inefficiencies because they controlled the movements and timing of carriages containing the steel components to be plated. Platers would often increase the amount of time carriages were left in various solutions—a strategy that would make the platers' work easier but wasted time and plating materials. So the company automated two of its five plating lines by installing computerized control panels. The control panels preset the movements and timing of the carriages and thus usurped the control that platers had previously exercised over the carriages' movements. "Going automatic was to be the answer to our problems: the platers would no longer control the process, for the control system would be completely in the hands of management." The control panels were installed behind a wall to prevent workers from tampering with the controls, and semiskilled workers replaced the more skilled platers. "We want the operator to just stand there and watch, and stop it if things go wrong," one manager said.

Did the company achieve its objectives of decreasing waste and time on the plating lines? The results can be briefly summarized as follows:

- When something went wrong on the line, the whole batch would have to be scrapped since the plater no longer had control of the carriages.
- Because semiskilled workers were watching the plating lines, slight deviations in the process that might have been spotted by more-experienced or better-trained workers were not noted.
- During the first few months of automation, a manual override was made accessible to workers for use when programs were tried out; however, the platers were not motivated to use it.
- Occasionally a carriage would miss components and carry thin air. This resulted in either components being in a solution too long or carriages colliding, causing a dangerous accident. Unmotivated platers failed to prevent such accidents.
- Platers tended to use the override not to prevent accidents or to prove programs but to achieve exactly the finish they considered constituted a good job. This use of the override was done despite

(or in spite of) management's attempts to convince the platers that the finish achieved by the automatic process was sufficient.

Management intended the automation to increase process speed and reduce waste by decreasing the unreliability factor of humans involved in the process, but those objectives were not achieved. Regardless of where the blame lies, the capital investment of automating the plating lines was to naught.

Another example of human resource issues negating the capital investment strategy of a firm can be found in a study by Love and Walker (1986), who interviewed managers and workers at eight printing firms. They found that in three of the eight firms, the implementation of new equipment in the typesetting area created disputes between union and management about increases in rates of pay for the operators. The union became so hostile over what they perceived as the intransigence of management that strikes, blacking of the equipment, and an escalation of union demands ensued. In order to resolve the issue, management finally had to approve a rate increase for all workers, not just those affected by the new technology. Clearly, the amount of money management expected to save by reducing labor costs with the new equipment was lessened by management's failure to consider human resource issues.

A final flaw in the status quo approach is that the failure to consider the human infrastructure can be directly linked to a failure on the part of management to understand that value judgments are embedded in the implementation and use of new technology. Several studies have found that managers' value judgments about quality of work correspond to the amount of control and discretion workers have with the new technology (Hedberg and Mumford, 1975; Taylor, 1979; Zuboff, 1982). The manager who ignores the issue of values may be one who mistakenly believes that the capital investment decision ensures proper implementation. A system designer who believes that workers do not value job challenge may create a system that is very different from the one workers envision. Moreover, system design decisions that fail to share in and explicate value judgments may convey expectations and messages to workers that engender hostility. Contradictions in the organizational culture are rarely maliciously intended; yet workers perceive the hypocrisy and respond angrily.

In sum, companies cannot effectively implement flexible automation with little planning for the human infrastructure. An alternative approach is needed.

Open Systems Approach to Human Infrastructure Planning with New Technology

A model of an open systems orientation—and one adopted throughout this book—is depicted in Figure 1-1. Developed by David Nadler and Michael Tushman (1980), scholars of organizational change, this model presents any organization as comprising a set of four components: the task, the individuals, the formal organizational structure, and the informal organization. The task component of the model is the basic and inherent work to be done by the organization; this component includes skill and knowledge demands, types of intrinsic rewards of work, degree of uncertainty in work, and constraints on performance demands. The individual component refers to the characteristics of individuals in the organization, and includes employees' knowledge and skills, needs and preferences, perceptions and expectations. The formal organizational structure includes the organizational and job designs that have been formally created to facilitate individuals' successfully performing their tasks. Finally, the informal organizational component consists of the emerging arrangements, such as leader behavior, intra- and intergroup relations, and communication and influence patterns.

While it is important that management recognize the existence of each of these four components, to consider each one individually is not enough. As Nadler and Tushman argue, "in any system, the critical question is not what the components are, but what the nature of their interaction is" (p. 161). The question the manager should address, then, is, What are the dynamics of the relationships among the components and are these dynamics conducive to organizational effectiveness? Moreover, it is the *fit* between the various components that determines organizational effectiveness. The manager must determine whether individual

Figure 1-1. Open Systems Model for Diagnosing the Human Infrastructure.

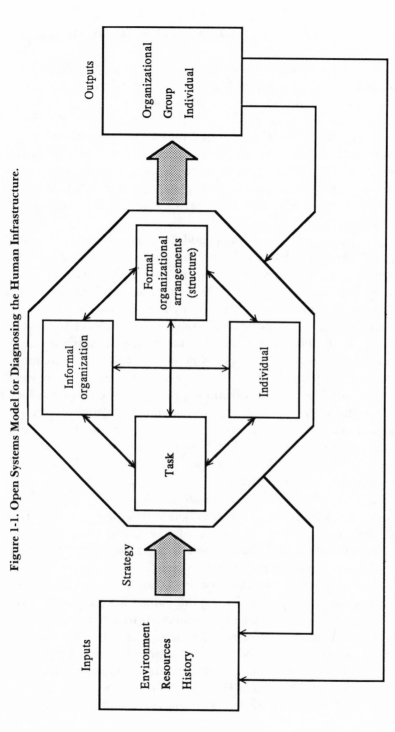

Source: D. A. Nadler and M. L. Tushman, "A Congruence Model for Diagnosing Organizational Behavior," in *Organizational Psychology* (3rd ed.), edited by David Kolb, Irwin Rubin, and James McIntyre. New York: Prentice-Hall, 1980, p. 451. Used by permission.

needs are met by the formal organizational structure or whether effective task performance is enhanced through informal communication channels. These questions constitute the essence of human infrastructure planning as a determinant of organizational effectiveness. Therefore, the manager or human resource professional implementing technological change needs to ask not only What is the correct job design? but also, more precisely, How do we match the job design, equipment, organizational structure, and people to achieve the objectives initially desired by our capital investment strategy?

Critical then to the Nadler and Tushman model, as to most open systems models, is the notion that the organization is composed of multiple components, and that the interrelationships among those components determine organizational effectiveness. In addition, this model suggests that there is no one best way of managing; that is, no one combination of components constitutes the best fit. Rather the question for managers, particularly as they implement flexible automation, is how to find effective combinations of components that will lead to congruent fits for the organization. As a result, this book presents different options for each of the different components of the human resource aspects of the organization. In addition, since the important question is not what the components are but how they interrelate, empirical research that describes how these options interrelate to other aspects of the organization are described.

This model, with its open systems orientation, is not easy to implement. Multiple aspects of the organization must be considered in ways not yet well understood, based on hypotheses that have yet to be empirically tested. How different components of an organization interact is also difficult to understand, let alone communicate. Because open systems are complex, identification of precise causes when things go wrong (or right) is difficult, at best. Although it is difficult to implement an open systems orientation to human infrastructure planning for new technology, it is not impossible. One firm adapting the open systems approach was a 350-person manufacturer of optical lenses that also made spectacles to prescription (Wilkinson, 1983). The company implemented a computer that essentially selected the tools and machine settings for each lens prescription, a task that was previously done by the machine setters themselves. With the computer, an accurate lens could be produced in one cut, yielding faster production runs. Moreover, guesswork could be removed from the production process, yielding a lower scrap rate.

With new technology that could perform all the setups, an obvious human resource choice was available to management—to completely deskill machine setters' jobs. Then management could have structured the jobs to maintain control over quantity, quality, and task assignments. Instead, in this firm, management reviewed how the different organizational components interacted with each other and determined that a deskilling of the setters' jobs would not be congruent with either the employees' backgrounds or the informal organization that had evolved over the years. Forcing a match would have led to less effective rather than more effective performance. Thus, management planned for the following five changes to the human infrastructure when the technology arrived:

1. Machine setters' group bonus pay was maintained with pay related to the number of lenses turned out by the group in a week; efforts were made to ensure that the section supervisor liaised between the computer programmer and the machine setters in such a way as to facilitate group performance.
2. Production pace was not controlled mechanically; instead, the pace was determined informally by the workers themselves.
3. Individual and group effort could have been monitored by the computer; instead, effort was judged solely on final output and not machine utilization rates.
4. Setters were persuaded to do some of their own computing, with consideration given to installing the computing facilities in the surfacing room itself.
5. A compulsory job rotation within the surfacing room was implemented including rotation into the programming job.

This organization's approach to its implementation of new technology exemplifies an open systems approach because before the equipment was installed the organization took a step back and reflected on the question, How will all this fit together when the equipment is installed? Management determined that an alternative to deskilling—an alternative involving more changes to more aspects of the organization—would better serve the objectives of the organization and its capital investment strategy. It is this pause, questioning, and commitment—even given the short-term costs of time and resistance—that is necessary if success is to be achieved with an open systems framework to planning the human infrastructure for advanced manufacturing technology. And it is the open systems framework that is necessary if advanced manufacturing technology is to be successfully implemented.

Brief Description of Flexible Automation

Throughout this chapter and for the remainder of the book, the terms flexible factory automation, advanced manufacturing technology (AMT), flexible automation (FA), and computer automated manufacturing (CAM) are used. A brief description of the technologies encompassed by these terms is necessary to ensure a common understanding.

There are many types of flexible automation equipment. Moreover, there are many different ways organizations use the same type of equipment. Flexible automation can be used solely in the production process, such as in early robotic applications of the "three *d*'s" (dangerous, dirty, or dull). Or it can be used solely for materials handling or materials storage and retrieval. Flexible automation can also be used in the production planning, inspection, testing, and design stages of manufacturing. Finally, flexible automation can be a new philosophy of management, such as a "systems approach" to managing the internal and external environment of the shopfloor. In short, there is no singular profile of the automated factory. For example, in one worldwide survey of different flexible manufacturing systems, as many configurations of equipment were found as there were different systems (Dupont-Gatelmand, 1981). Thus, in examining the human resource implications of flexible automation, the specific technical features of the adopted equipment must be considered. For this reason, the different equipment and technical features are briefly discussed below and become part of the framework presented in Chapter Two.

Flexible automation comprises a range of different technologies that have evolved over time. Figure 1-2 portrays this evolution. Examining this evolution indicates that one of the earliest forms of flexible automation was the numerical control (NC) machine. NC machines were developed after World War II to do metal-cutting operations for the production of jet aircraft. The development of computer-numerical control (CNC) machines replaced the hard-wired control units of the NC machines with minicomputers. As early as the 1950s, machining centers were found in which several machines were combined, usually involving at least one CNC. The capability to connect these computerized machine tools to a central computer, referred to as distributed numerical control (DNC), became commercially available around the late 1960s.

In the late 1960s, other technological advances for the manufacturing environment began their slow diffusion to the shopfloor. These advances included computer-controlled material handling systems that integrate machining centers by automating the movement of work pieces from one machine or machining center to another; computer-controlled storage that provides for the automatic selection of work pieces from storage; robots (reprogrammable manipulative devices) for picking, placing, welding, painting, assembly, or other similar operations; and computer-aided design (CAD), which is the process of electronically drafting and designing engineering drawings.

The introduction of flexible manufacturing systems began slowly in the 1970s. FMSs are computer-automated machining work cells or centers that combine DNCs and automated materials handling systems. In addition to DNCs and materials handling, FMSs might also contain automatic inspection equipment, or adaptive controls that sense such performance factors as heat, torque, or vibration. An essential component in the evolution of FMSs and other flexible automation systems has been group technology (GT). Group technology is the segregation of parts according to their design or manufacturing characteristics. With similar parts grouped together, production costs are reduced since each group of parts can share setups and machine tools. Finally, the development of manufacturing resource planning systems (MRPs)

Figure 1-2. The Evolution of Flexible Automation.

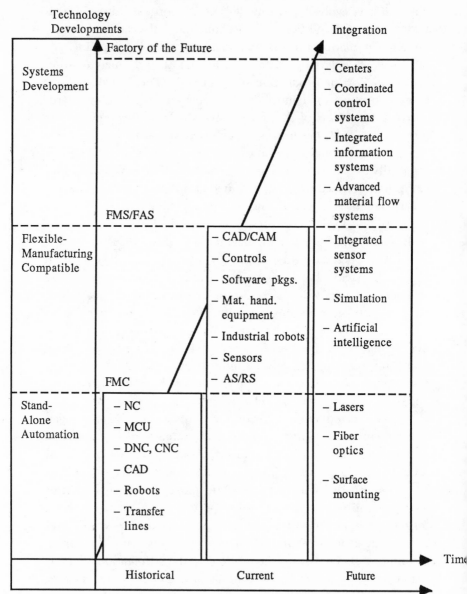

Source: Teresko, 1986, p. 48. Used by permission.

has provided for more efficient manufacturing capabilities by computerizing the inventory and scheduling functions.

These technologies are being purchased at ever-increasing rates. In a June, 1986, *Business Week* article, Dataquest Inc., a San Jose market research company, estimated that purchases of factory automation systems doubled to $18.1 billion from 1980 to 1985 ("High Tech to the Rescue," 1986). As of 1986, U.S. industry had purchased 100,000 numerical control machines (Sharit, Chang, and Salvendy, 1987), 15,000 robots (Stricharchuk and Winter, 1985) and at least thirty flexible manufacturing systems (Bylinsky, 1983). Indeed, the implementation of advanced manufacturing technology is growing enormously. Dataquest Inc. estimates that factory automation will double by 1990.

While each of these technologies independently promises some increment in productivity over conventional equipment, their greatest gains to the organization are achieved only when they differ from conventional machining technologies in three important ways: integration, intelligence, and immediacy (Graham and Rosenthal, 1985).

First, flexible automation is far superior to conventional equipment when it is *integrated*. The concept of integration, or computer-integrated manufacturing (CIM), is one of the most technologically sophisticated gains over conventional equipment. CIM is a closed-loop feedback system, with prime inputs as product requirements and product concepts, prime outputs as finished products, and processes as a combination of software and hardware, that incorporates functions of product design, production planning, production control, production equipment, and production processes (Schaffer, 1981). The degree to which CIM equipment is integrated can vary dramatically. A CAD/CAM system may integrate only CAD drawings with CNC machine tools, while a true CIM system like that at Ingersoll-Rand ties suppliers, inventory, scheduling, design, and production into a common data base.

Intelligence is another characteristic that makes flexible automation qualitatively different from conventional machining. Intelligence is the software that provides for communication, feedback, and correction between system users and machines as well as between machines and machines. The more "intelligent" the system, the greater the potential for performance gains.

Finally, *immediacy* is a third characteristic that distinguishes flexible automation from conventional machining. Immediacy refers to the speed of response delivered by the system and the speed with which response by system users and information sources is required. With computer automation, the system has the capability for almost instantaneous response. In turn, such quick equipment response demands that users constantly input as well as monitor the equipment.

In sum, flexible factory automation is distinguished from conventional equipment because it integrates functions of processes, people, and equipment; it has the ability to adjust to feedback; and it provides and demands immediate response. Note that these are characteristics that demand people: to aid the integration process, to ensure appropriate equipment reactions to feedback, and to respond immediately to unpredictable events. Thus, the human infrastructure is an essential element of flexible factory automation. This infrastructure is examined closely in the next chapter.

Assessing Automation's Impact on People in Organizations: A Framework

Chapter One argued that an approach that broadly defines and considers the human infrastructure prior to technical selection is needed when flexible automation is implemented in today's manufacturing plants. In this chapter, a framework for such an approach is presented. The framework is based on the supposition that it is important to understand the precise ways in which the human infrastructure is affected by AMT and how these affects influence the extent to which organizational goals are achieved by the new technology. The framework then identifies those components of the human infrastructure that need to be analyzed when considering the implementation of AMT. These components include job designs, personnel policies, management responsibilities, and organizational structure. The components are grouped into first- and second-order effects to underscore the interdependent nature of the decisions made with regard to the different facets of the human infrastructure. Constraints on human infrastructure decisions are then identified to clarify when certain human resource options may not be available for a plant. Finally, the chapter closes with a discussion of the instrument for operationalizing these concepts—the Human Infrastructure Impact Statement (HIIS), which appears as Appendix A at the end of this book. The HIIS is a tool for analyzing an organization's human infrastructure prior to equipment selection to determine what impacts are likely to occur and therefore what human infrastructure and equipment choices are in the best interest of achieving the desired outcomes.

Outcomes of AMT

AMT is purchased to achieve two types of benefits: (1) ultimate organizational survival and (2) changes in the production process expected to maintain organizational survival and growth. Organizational survival benefits may include growth in share of an existing market, entrance in new markets, or just "staying even" (Kaplan, 1983). Benefits of changes in the production process include reduced scrap, work-in-process and end-product inventory, high machine utilization, reduced changeover times, and increased throughput. Mariann Jelinek and Joel Goldhar (in press) describe several examples of achieving these benefits. At Ingersoll Milling Machine's Rockford, Illinois, plant, a CIM system has produced 25,000 different parts—half of which will never again be manufactured and 70 percent of which are made in lots of one. At Hughes Aircraft's El Segundo, California, facility, nine integrated FMS centers do the work previously done by twenty-five stand-alone dedicated machining centers. At Vought Corporation's Dallas plant, the CIM equipment has provided a savings of $25 million in machining costs over that of conventional methods. In addition to these types of benefits, AMT may have other benefits as well, benefits to the human infrastructure. Such benefits include personnel satisfaction, reduced absenteeism and turnover, and fewer grievances and accidents. An FMS that increases worker commitment because the workers now see a future in the company is an unequivocal benefit of the new equipment.

As the research results discussed in Chapter One attest, these benefits do not happen automatically. They happen through a process of changes in the human infrastructure: Management may pay more attention to quality in departmental performance reviews, operators may work more collaboratively with maintenance to fix equipment breakdowns, design and manufacturing engineers may overcome their traditional disciplinary barriers and together "design for manufacturability." Thus, in understanding if, when, and how AMT benefits are to be achieved, the changes to the human infrastructure necessary to achieve those benefits must be understood as well. Such an analysis is essential for at least two reasons. First, not all benefits may be achieved by making the same human infrastructural changes. For example, in a survey of human resource practices in high- and low-performing manufacturers with CIM equipment, human resource practices leading to low scrap rates were found to be different from practices leading to high met delivery schedules. Ensuring that operators focused their attention on machine operation, not maintenance tasks, seemed to help increase met delivery schedules while, in contrast, having a clearly defined reward system helped to keep scrap rates down (Majchrzak and Paris, 1986).

A second reason for the importance of an analysis of the human infrastructure is that a benefit initially expected may prove, upon close scrutiny from a human resource perspective, to be of little utility to the organization. For example, analysis may reveal that the espoused benefit of increased production with reduced direct labor costs will not materialize because direct labor constitutes such a small portion of product cost. In fact, several studies have found direct labor to constitute less than 10 percent of the total cost in some industries (see, for example, Hayes and Clark, 1985). Moreover, since personnel are often unexpectedly needed for indirect support as well as machine unpredictability, the benefit of reduced labor may conflict with a successful human infrastructure. An analysis of the human infrastructure needed to achieve the expected benefits would identify such a conflict. In sum, the benefits desired of AMT are numerous and depend on an entire pattern of activities being in place for the company. One of these sets of activities that must be in place is the human infrastructure. We now turn our attention to the components of that human infrastructure.

Components of the Human Infrastructure

A portion of a model describing the six major components of the human infrastructure is presented in Figure 2-1. The four components represented here have been arranged as stages to signify the fact that earlier decisions affect later options. The stages include (1) the consideration of equipment features (parameters) and selection of equipment, (2) effects that decisions about equipment features could have on jobs (first-order effects), (3) effects that the decisions about jobs can have on personnel training, selection, and

Figure 2-1. Staged Model for Identifying Human Resource Impacts
of New Manufacturing Technology.

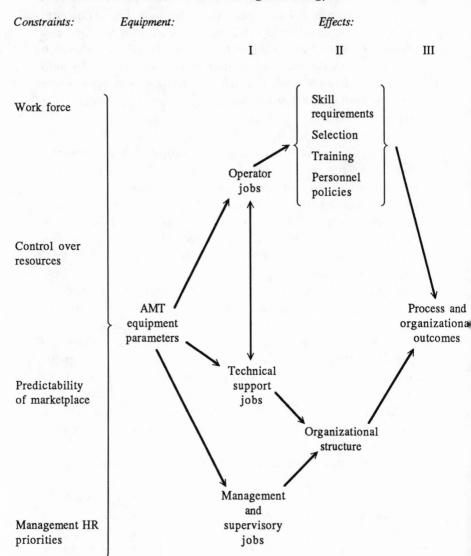

other related policies, and on organizational structure (second-order effects), and (4) the ultimate significance of the equipment for the production process, human infrastructure benefits, and organizational survival. The two remaining components of the model are the planned change process for implementing the decisions, and constraints on the human infrastructure decisions. Each of these components (with the exception of outcomes that have already been discussed) is described here.

Selection of Equipment Parameters

A fundamental tenet of the open systems approach to human infrastructure planning is that choices about the human infrastructure must be congruent with equipment parameters to achieve optimal use of the new technology. To aid the reader in understanding how equipment parameters can be congruent (or incongruent) with the human infrastructure, I have developed a typology of equipment parameters, which follows. This typology describes parameters—not technical specifications—that make the human infrastructure effects more apparent. Taking the complete typology into consideration when implementing AMT will help readers overcome a mistake commonly made by automation project teams and AMT researchers: failure to consider the separate impacts of different equipment parameters. For example, consideration of the impact of one equipment parameter—the system's sophisticated internal feedback system—might lead to the conclusion that the operators need not be involved in maintenance or repair work. But a different equipment parameter—the unproven reliability of the equipment in comparable production settings—would indicate a different conclusion: that operators need to be involved to immediately detect problems as they occur. Ignoring the impacts of either parameter would lead either to ignorance of the conflicting impacts of the different parameters or to an emphasis on the impacts of one parameter, to the detriment of the other. One result could be an organization choosing less integrated technology when the problem actually lies with the technology's unproven reliability.

Six equipment parameters have been identified as having important and independent effects on human resources: integration, rigidity, reliability, workflow unpredictability, feedback, and safety.

Integration. Most manufacturers have been found to purchase automated equipment piece by piece (Goldhar and Jelinek, 1983; Office of Technology Assessment, 1984). When those manufacturers go on to connect their islands of automation, they find a qualitative leap in complexity from stand-alone machines to integrated systems. Far more involved than simply intersecting or interfacing different types of equipment, integration actually involves linking the production process and support functions in such a way that the process is inextricably intertwined. This leap in complexity creates new human infrastructure needs (see Gerwin, 1982). For example, in a survey of CAM plants, the more integrated the equipment, the larger the training needs (Majchrzak, 1986b). In another study, forty-four discrete parts manufacturing plants—half with stand-alone CAM equipment and half with integrated CIM equipment—were surveyed (Majchrzak and Paris, 1986). The plant managers were asked about human resource choices made and measures of recent performance (met delivery schedules, scrap, work-in-process inventory, and machine uptime). Survey results indicated that the human resource choices of successful plants with stand-alone equipment were dramatically and statistically significantly different from the choices made by successful plants with integrated equipment. One difference was in what operators do, especially in terms of their involvement in process improvement. Successful plants with integrated CIM equipment had CIM operators spend, on the average, 12 percent of their workweek identifying process improvements. In contrast, successful plants with stand-alone CAM equipment had operators spend, on the average, only 4 percent of their workweek identifying process improvements. In sum, the level of integration of the new manufacturing technology will be an important parameter in assessing the impact of the technology on human resource issues.

Reliability. When we install new equipment, we always hope that it will perform reliably to our expectations and those of the vendor. Unfortunately, we are often disappointed. In part, this is because reliability of a flexible automation system involves not only the equipment but also the knowledge and activities of operators, support functions, and managers responsible for the equipment. The greater their collective experience and knowledge, the more reliable the machine.

Unreliability of the new technology can affect human resource issues in multiple ways. First, the degree of unreliability has a proportional effect on the jobs of operators, support personnel, and managers since less reliable systems demand more attention. Unreliable systems also necessitate either having a well-trained staff of operators, capable of and responsible for getting the machine restarted or helping maintenance to do so, or designing operators' jobs in such a way as to give them more independence from the machine to feel productive and motivated despite the breakdowns.

The extent of unreliability can also determine what information should be disseminated during the planned change process of implementing the new technology. In a study of robot implementation at one plant, the workers felt increasingly frustrated that their early expectations about the reliability of the robot operations were not met (Argote, Goodman, and Schkade, 1983). Plant managers who expect some unreliability in the machine should inform workers of that expectation.

Finally, unreliable equipment may necessitate reorganizing the reporting arrangements of maintenance personnel to ensure that equipment repair of the flexible automation system is a priority. This reorganization may take the form of having maintenance report to a flexible automation department in the production division or changing the performance appraisal criteria of maintenance workers to emphasize the new equipment over the old.

Rigidity. A critical component of flexible automation in terms of its impact on human resource issues is whether the production process can reroute around the new equipment if equipment breakdowns occur. Referred to as rigidity, this parameter concerns whether there are alternative paths for products to go or if, during equipment breakdowns, the equipment becomes a bottleneck in the production process. Rigidity, a concept used in the organizational literature for years, has been found to be related to the structure of the production department (see, for example, research by Pugh and Hickson, 1976; and Child, 1973). Organizations with a more rigid technological system have production departments structured in more rigid, bureaucratic fashions.

In addition to the implications of these early findings for the structure of the organization, the rigidity of the new technology would also be expected to affect the job tasks and priorities of people involved with the new equipment. A more rigid work flow process would necessitate that operators of the new equipment be able to quickly fix equipment or effectively communicate to the maintenance people what the problem might be, or that maintenance staff be assigned specifically to the new equipment. Human resource effects of the rigidity of the system must also be considered in light of the other equipment parameters. For example, a highly unreliable new system installed as a central bottleneck in a rigid production flow process may be asking for trouble unless a human infrastructure (for example, operators, managers, and maintenance) has been established to encourage giving the equipment the priority it needs.

Work Flow Unpredictability. The inputs, processes, and outputs of the work flow of any human-machine system vary in their degree of predictability. Work flow predictability is a concept that has been researched and reported on in the organizational behavior and design literature (see, for example, work by Thompson, 1967; Perrow, 1967; and Rousseau, 1979). This research has found that work flow unpredictability is directly related to the job tasks of workers involved with the equipment; that is, the more unpredictable the work flow, the greater the variety and challenge people perceive in their jobs. In addition, this research has found unpredictability to be related to the organization's structure; that is, increased unpredictability necessitates that those directly involved in the production process have greater discretion over work decisions and have more informal ways to communicate with others.

Turning specifically to flexible automation, work flow unpredictability is particularly important as it relates to batch size and input material—density, timing, source, variety, and especially quality. The greater the unpredictability, the more that is demanded from the equipment: Tools need to be changed more often, setups are more frequent, chemical solutions need to be changed, feedback systems need to detect and adjust to variations, operators need to monitor the process more closely, and equipment breakdowns are more difficult to diagnose because many different combinations of inputs and processes may be the cause of the problem.

With greater degrees of unpredictability, there is a need for a human infrastructure that promotes sufficient knowledge and abilities, flexibility, decision-making discretion, and responsibility to cope with unpredictable change. Such an infrastructure may be achieved by having technical support staff (scheduling, maintenance, quality control for suppliers) essentially control the variations. Or operators' jobs could be redesigned and operators retrained to keep production flowing given the unpredictability. Or the organization may need to be restructured to create an elite group of managers, technical support, and operators with sole responsibility for handling only those production processes that are particularly unpredictable.

Feedback. A fifth parameter is the feedback system designed for the equipment. Flexible automation necessitates feedback on a variety of different factors: tolerance, temperature, tool wear, distance, cycle time, density, and so on. The equipment needs to receive this information at critical junctures and have the capability to adjust its processes accordingly.

Feedback affects the human infrastructure by the role the operator plays in the feedback loop. While some flexible automation is purchased with the intention to keep the operator out of the feedback loop, no system is fail-safe (Hirschhorn, 1984; Perrow, 1984). We are not at a point on our technological learning curve (and may never be) where the equipment can be assumed to be able to generate accurate feedback and always respond appropriately. As such, then, the operator needs to have a role in the feedback loop.

The human infrastructure comes to bear then when considering how to structure the feedback so that the operator is effectively included in that loop. Ignoring such operator issues as perceptual biases in the ways information is perceived, certain information-processing limitations, and biases toward certain problem-solving strategies for diagnosing when and why equipment failure has occurred will lead to ineffective, if not dangerous, control panels.

Safety. A final parameter to consider in planning for human resources with new technology is the accident proneness (or lack thereof) of the equipment. Some equipment is more likely to be accident prone than others. For example, robot-welding equipment is quite dangerous if programmed incorrectly, while a CAD terminal that malfunctions is much less dangerous.

The safety issue involves, assuredly, training employees in safety regulations and accident prevention. Most plants implementing flexible automation apparently understand this since, in a survey of plants implementing CAM, 92 percent offered training in the safety issues surrounding the new equipment (Majchrzak, 1986a). However, there is a broader issue around safety that concerns structuring the entire human infrastructure to ensure that accidents do not occur. With flexible automation, work speeds far in excess of less automated equipment are found; yet the equipment is far more complex. Thus, when the equipment fails to operate at the expected levels, workers involved in the equipment are put under excessive pressure to push the equipment. This excessive pressure often leads not to decreased efficiency but to the type of anxiety that creates faulty attention to detail and the likelihood of accidents. The solution may be to slow down the production line. Or the solution may be more managerial. For example, departmental performance ratings could be prioritized around quality rather than quantity. Or a culture could be established whereby workers are encouraged to put accident prevention as a higher priority than speed. Or supervisors could be made more directly responsible for the safety record of their departments and are backed up for it in their performance appraisals, even if it means lower production rates. Of course, not all equipment is prone to major, serious accidents. Not all plants run the risk of a Bhopal or Chernobyl. However, an analysis of the impact that safety as an equipment parameter has on human resource issues (and on the outcomes of the organization and new technology) can help to make the organization more safe than sorry.

As we continue our discussion of the impacts of AMT (especially in terms of first- and second-order effects), we need to recognize that the degree of impact will vary with the parameters of the equipment selected. For the researcher, this suggests measuring equipment parameters in studies of technological change. For the manager, this means an understanding of the independent and cumulative effects of the different parameters and the smug feeling knowing that the parameters could be changed if the analysis of the impacts is not done too late.

First-Order Effects on Human Infrastructure

First-order effects are those that are most directly affected by the equipment parameters. As originally depicted in Figure 2-1, the effects (and decisions that must be made as part of the effects) include the jobs of the equipment operators, technical and administrative support personnel, managers, and supervisors. Since each of these first-order effects are described at length in their own chapters, effects and decisions are only briefly presented here.

Machine Operators' Jobs. Job activities can be analyzed in many different ways, using different forms of task analyses, time motion studies, ergonomic principles, or motivational principles (see review by Campion and Thayer, 1985). From the perspective of changes brought about by flexible automation, four dimensions of machine operators' jobs are most likely to be directly affected by the implementation of flexible automation. The first dimension, *coordination needs,* refers to the extent to which operators must work, and with whom they must work, to obtain the necessary information to perform their jobs. With integrated equipment, the need to coordinate with others often increases. The second dimension, *information needs,* flows from identified coordination needs and refers to the type, source, and amount of information the operator must have to effectively operate the new equipment. Information may be needed to carry out identified areas of discretion, undertake machine-redundant tasks, meet output priorities, and monitor the production process. *Human-machine redundancy* is the third dimension and refers to the extent to which operators should be involved as a redundant check on machine operations. Examples of redundant operator tasks with flexible automation include stopping and starting cycles using override buttons, as necessary; undertaking tasks in response to digital readouts about the production process or tool wear; and checking for errors in computer programs. The fourth dimension is *areas and degree of discretion*, which refers to the broad category of autonomy: how much, over what, and how manifested. For example, with flexible automation, an operator may have sole discretion to perform a maintenance task, discretion in consultation with peers, or discretion in consultation with technical experts, such as engineers, supervisors, or maintenance personnel.

These four dimensions of machine operators' jobs identify areas likely to be affected by flexible automation. Precisely how they are affected and the impact these effects have on decisions about operators' job designs are discussed in Chapter Three.

Technical Support Functions. Flexible automation often affects functions other than those of the operator; for example, the technical support positions of skilled trades, quality and production control, programming, engineering, and accounting and marketing. The quality control function may change dramatically if quality becomes an output priority of the operator and an area over which the operator has substantial discretion. Under this scenario, quality control experts might become trainers, diagnosticians, or inspectors for suppliers' deliveries only. The technical support functions are evaluated along the same dimensions as those of the operators' jobs, including information and coordination needs and areas of discretion. The specific effects of flexible factory automation on these functions are discussed in Chapter Four.

Management and Supervisory Functions. The effects of flexible automation are very different for higher-level managers than for production and first-line supervisors. The former group must typically worry about how to manage from a systems perspective, while the latter group worries about a major redefinition of their jobs. For example, with higher-level managers, flexible automation may allow the manager the time needed to identify opportunities for growth or development, such as exploring ways to involve operators in the bidding-for-contract process. First-line production supervisor's jobs, on the other hand, have been found to change with flexible automation in terms of an increased need to liaison with other departments, undergo technical training, facilitate group activities, and closely observe workers to ensure that they perceive that they are appropriately rewarded for their performance. Chapter Five discusses these effects in more detail.

In summary, the delineation of these first-order effects on factory jobs identifies job responsibilities that must change if at least this portion of the human infrastructure is to be congruent with the needs of the new equipment and the benefits expected to be achieved. Once these areas of job change are identified for a particular configuration of equipment parameters, decisions can be made about new job designs. It is this set of decisions that then influences the second-order effects—not equipment parameters. Thus, the choice of a job design has ramifications that reverberate beyond the immediate personnel affected. These choices help to define the remaining shape and congruency of the human infrastructure for the flexible automated factory.

Second-Order Effects on Human Infrastructure

Second-order effects are changes in the human infrastructure that result from changes in jobs and technology. Five second-order effects on the human infrastructure of the implementation of flexible automation are identified in the model depicted in Figure 2-1: skill requirements, selection, training, personnel policies, and organizational structure. (Since these effects are discussed separately in the chapters that follow, I will describe them only briefly here.)

Skill requirements refer to the skills that operators, technical support, managers, and supervisors need to carry out their job duties as defined by the tasks identified for them. Five skill areas needed with AMT for various occupational groups are identified in Chapter Six. These skill areas include perceptual (for example, vigilance, concentration, and attention), conceptual, manual dexterity, discretionary (such as imagination and judgment), and human relations. To meet these five skill needs, an effective human infrastructure has both a selection process to identify appropriate people and a training program to prepare the workers. *Selection* issues for AMT include knowing the numbers of people needed to staff positions, criteria for selection, formality of the selection process, who has control over the selection process, and whether workers are to be recruited from in-house or outside. The selection issues are discussed in Chapter Six along with the skill issues. *Training* for AMT includes identifying the course content, amount of training needed, formality of training (for example, courses or on-the-job training), and source of training (for example, vendor or in-house). These issues are discussed in Chapter Seven. A fourth second-order effect is *personnel policies*. These policies, which include job descriptions, career development, pay systems, job security, and labor relations, are discussed in Chapter Eight. Finally, *organizational structure* is another second-order human resource issue to consider when implementing flexible automation. Changes to decision-making authority and the manner in which departments are differentiated have already been briefly identified in case studies presented earlier. In addition, organizational structure may change in terms of coordination mechanisms or the way in which the organizational departments are integrated, and the climate or informal organizational structure. These changes are discussed as part of Chapter Nine.

In accordance with the open systems model, decisions about second-order effects must be made to be congruent with each other as well as with other human infrastructure decisions. It is only with this congruency that successful outcomes with flexible automation can be achieved.

Planned Change Process

Although equipment parameters may be selected with the human infrastructure in mind, first- and second-order effects understood, and decisions made to ensure congruency, all is to naught without appropriate attention to the planned change process. Since most professional managers and researchers have some understanding of the process to be considered when initiating change in an organization, general techniques for planned change are not described here. What is of concern is how the changes to the human infrastructure attributable to the new flexible automation system affect this planned change process.

For flexible automation (FA), four issues are particularly important in the planned change process. *Resistance to change*, as the first planned change process issue, refers to the natural response most people have to a change in their status quo. Since FA demands a change in both technology and the human infrastructure, resistance is a virtual certainty. A second process issue is *counterresistance acts* that serve to manage the inevitable resistance. Counterresistance actions include education, persuasion, participation, and empathy. The third process issue is the *management of automation project teams*. Automation project teams are work groups responsible for the selection of the new technology and planning for its implementation. Recent research has identified the management techniques that help to explain why some automation project teams fulfill their responsibilities more successfully than others. Finally, the planned change process for flexible automation involves *implementation steps*. Adopting a model originally developed by Kurt Lewin (1951), successful implementation of flexible automation is only possible provided that the organization "unfreezes" the workers' preference for the status quo, then involves the workers in "moving forward" while the equipment is installed and the human infrastructure modified, and finally "refreezes" the organization into the new procedures and processes of the flexible automated factory.

Organizational Constraints

A final component of the human infrastructure is that set of factors that constrain infrastructure decisions. No organization operates in a vacuum; thus it is erroneous to analyze the human infrastructure effects and options without taking these constraints into account. Four constraints are identified as having particularly important effects on human infrastructure choices:

1. Work force factors such as the experience base of the operators
2. The plant's control over its resources, such as is derived from supplier agreements on quality
3. Marketplace predictability, such as the mix of customer needs
4. Management human resource (HR) philosophy, such as the priority that top-level managers assign to training.

These constraints delimit those alternatives—both technical and human—that can be considered for the existing and future organization. Note that, with greenfield sites, the constraints are typically not as severe as when introducing new technology in existing plants. However, since few organizations can afford to close old plants and build new ones, redesign of existing facilities is far more common. Thus, this framework is concerned in many ways primarily with the modernization of conventional factories. Since these constraints may have serious consequences for the human infrastructure preplanning process, the influence of each constraint on human infrastructural effects and options is discussed here.

Work Force Factors. When retrofitting existing plants, the work force presents a substantial constraint on how the technology will affect human resource issues. A plant with a work force in which job challenge and management trust is an accepted part of the organizational culture will be able to engage in an open dialogue and learning process between workers and managers as the new technology is implemented. In contrast, a work force that mistrusts management and has traditionally worked at semiskilled jobs with conventional equipment will necessitate a very different implementation strategy and job design.

The impact of work force constraints on technological impacts can be assessed by examining the following four characteristics of the existing work force: (1) preferred job challenge, (2) work force trust of management, (3) union status, and (4) level of skill and experience.

Preferred job challenge refers to the fact that different people prefer different levels of challenge in their jobs. Research evidence to be discussed in Chapter Three on operator job design strongly indicates that not everyone wants more variety or autonomy or stress in a job, even if it leads to more pay, responsibility, and promotions. Since people differ on the extent to which they prefer challenge in their jobs, it is necessary to know if major subgroups in the existing work force can be characterized as preferring more or less job challenge. If the semiskilled work force as a whole can be fairly characterized as not preferring challenge while the skilled labor work force does, then expecting skilled labor to attend to the new machines may be more appropriate than retraining the semiskilled work force. The key here is to systematically identify subgroups of workers who prefer challenge, and to do so before decisions about job designs are made.

A second characteristic of the work force that constrains human infrastructure planning for AMT is the degree to which employees *trust* the intentions and competence of plant management. If the work force feels that plant management will "burn them any chance they can get," a stated policy of no layoffs will probably not be believed and will therefore be of little help in motivating workers to quickly get the new equipment operational. A different work force may feel that while plant management has good intentions, they have neither the willingness nor competence to follow through on their intentions. Such a work force might view the purchase of an FMS as a way for management to enter into another fad until something better comes along. A management confronted by such a work force will need to devote substantially more time to education, information sharing, and the planned change process than would be needed with a more trusting work force.

Unionization is the third work force characteristic. The human infrastructure planning strategy for a unionized plant will differ from that for a nonunionized plant in two important respects: In unionized plants, (1) the planned change process must take into consideration both local and national representation, and (2) new personnel policies and job designs must be renegotiated within the clauses provided by the union contract. Despite these complexities introduced by unionization, there are as many differences among unionized plants in their support of new technology as there are between union and nonunion plants.

Another constraint of the work force is the average *skill level* of the workers. The skill level of the work force not only affects the job tasks that workers will be expected to perform but also constrains new organizational arrangements that involve restructuring the decision-making authority in the plant. A more highly skilled work force will create problems if relegated to monotonous jobs that involve little discretion. On the other hand, a work force that has previously had very narrowly defined jobs may need too much training to be able to initially perform well in jobs with substantial responsibility and decision-making authority. Skill level also pertains to managers. Managers who have had little experience in group process or human relations may have difficulty managing AMT operators. Inadequate skills in these areas will necessitate carefully planned training programs. Finally, included in the skill-level issue is the amount of previous experience employees have had in dealing with technological change in general and flexible automation in particular. Workers and managers with little previous experience with complex technological systems may need the new technology and human infrastructure introduced slowly to build the necessary experience base.

Plant Control over Resources. In addition to work force constraints, there are constraints posed by the degree of control that plant management has over its critical resources. Three constraints in degree of control are identified: (1) plant's degree of autonomy, (2) supplier agreements, and (3) labor force mobility.

Many plants function as part of a larger corporate structure. As such, the *plant's degree of autonomy* over decisions involving such in-house resources as personnel, capital expenditures, research and development (R&D), financing, and so on may vary from total control to little control. For example, a nonunion electronics manufacturing plant of a large machine tool corporation was in the process of purchasing AMT. After reviewing their plans for implementing the new technology, plant management determined that a group compensation plan (paying people by group, not individual, performance) was necessary in order to match the reward system with the particular equipment and desired job design. Planning for the new compensation system proceeded until the plant manager was called into the corporate offices one day and informed that changing compensation systems was not within his discretion and that a group compensation plan was not considered an option for this corporation.

Optimal use of integrated flexible automation also demands that certain *agreements with suppliers* be in place on the quality and timing of material provided. The more that suppliers meet just-in-time delivery and 0 percent reject rates, the greater the likelihood that manufacturers can achieve higher levels of performance from their equipment. The extent to which a plant is large enough or carries enough clout to insist on high supplier standards varies. A plant needing to accept poorer supplier performance will need to compensate by having more inspectors, greater attention to production planning, and more discretion provided to operators to spot raw material problems as they arise.

Finally, *labor force mobility*, or the availability of alternative jobs, is another constraint on human infrastructure decisions. Occupations and industries in which workers have many job alternatives create little plant control over the work force. Such a plant may either need to expect high turnover rates (and thus reconsider major training investments in short-term employees) or attend much more carefully to the human infrastructure to induce workers to stay.

Marketplace Factors. In addition to constraints posed by the work force and limits on control of resources, marketplace factors present major constraints for many plants. The plant may not be able to easily enter new markets, accurately predict customer needs, or correctly anticipate economic downturns. Thus, the purchase of a new flexible automation system may be undertaken with assumptions about the marketplace that may very well be wrong. In one plant, management predicted that it would find new markets for its newly automated gear line. In fact, management was so convinced that it would find these new markets that it promised the union, in writing, that job security at all costs would be maintained. Unfortunately, new markets were not identified and plant management had to quickly turn to its lawyers to figure out how to get out of its written promise of job security. Obviously, deterioration of trust between the company and the union was only one of the deleterious results of this misconception of marketplace factors.

In determining how the marketplace influences the effect of technology on the human infrastructure, three aspects of the marketplace need to be considered: (1) the company's ability to enter into new markets, (2) recent "performance gaps," and (3) market growth predictability.

Organizations able to *enter new markets rapidly* will be able to implement new technology with an atmosphere of optimism and efficient utilization of human as well as technical resources. However, plant management may not always be cognizant of precisely how it will use its newly found production capacity, as the case example just cited illustrates. Clearly, different strategies are needed for planned change and possibly for job designs when new markets are known, not simply suspected, to exist. *Performance gaps* are situations in which the organization's recent performance fails to meet the expectations of management, customers, or stockholders. Performance gaps often create a sense of urgency about the need for new technology. When the performance gaps are adequately conveyed to the workers during the planned change process—for example, by visits to customer organizations or competitors—that urgency may help to encourage ready acceptance of change. Finally, predictability of *market growth* constrains what promises can be made and what long-term expectations can be established about job security, pay, and other personnel policies. In a stable marketplace that has been experiencing slow but steady growth, it seems quite reasonable for the plant to undertake an evolutionary implementation of the new technology. Such an implementation would involve gradually retraining the work force and designing jobs to gradually give workers more responsibility.

However, such a long-term growth strategy may be too slow or inappropriate when customer demand, dollar, trade, competition, interest rates, and other economic indicators begin to fluctuate unpredictably. In such situations, a human infrastructure that promotes flexibility and quick change may be needed.

Management Human Resource Philosophy. A final constraint to consider for its influence on the human infrastructure is the human resource philosophy of top-level management. Three aspects of management's human resource (HR) philosophy seem to exert substantial influence: (1) its model of worker motivation, (2) decision-making style, and (3) human resource priorities.

Running the risk of oversimplifying the concept of *worker motivation*, key managers in the organization may espouse a view of the worker that may vary along a continuum from Theory X to Theory Y (MacGregor, 1960). Managers who espouse a Theory X view frequently dislike technological designs that allow workers substantial freedom and discretion in their jobs. Such managers are also likely to question the competence of labor representatives to set aside personal agendas and accurately represent the work force. With such managers, informal agreements with labor may be difficult to uphold.

Decision-making style is management's preferred method for making decisions in the organization. Decision-making styles include consultative, consensus, delegative, or authoritarian. Top management in a plant preferring an authoritarian style, for example, will have difficulty giving up discretion to first-line supervisors.

Human resource priorities are top management's attitudes about the importance of training and group process skills. Priorities can often be placed along a continuum characterized by two extremes. At one extreme are managers who feel that everyone needs to be trained on a wide range of human relations and technical issues (for example, team building, knowledge of the manufacturing process). At the other extreme are managers who feel that training should be kept to a bare minimum, administered only to those who absolutely need it. Clearly, where plant management falls on this continuum has an important effect on the human infrastructure decisions to be made.

In conclusion, in preplanning the human infrastructure for flexible automation, each of the constraints just discussed must be considered. However, each constraint is not equally important for a particular configuration of human infrastructure decisions, nor are the constraints unchangeable. Management philosophy can be changed, control over resources can be negotiated, and major organizational efforts to reestablish management trust among workers can be undertaken. Thus, for the manager, these constraints may not need to be accepted as given. In planning for the change, the constraints might be the first aspect of the organization to change, prior to selection of the equipment and deciding on the human infrastructure. For the researcher, any study of the effects of technological change cannot proceed without an understanding of the role these constraints have played on the human infrastructure options available and choices made.

Human Infrastructure Impact Statement (HIIS)

The Human Infrastructure Impact Statement (HIIS), which appears as Appendix A, is a tool for operationalizing the issues discussed in this chapter. It is intended to be completed when conversion to AMT is being considered. The instrument is designed to yield insight about the extent of change needed in the human infrastructure and thus to guide the user's choice of AMT equipment and estimation of timing for implementation. If a technology plan is in place before the HIIS is used, the results may or may not indicate a need to change the plan; in any case, the HIIS should be helpful in identifying areas of the human infrastructure that will need to be changed to create a congruent open system.*

*I am certainly not the first to recommend a systematic assessment of the human resource effects that introducing a new technology may have on the organization. Boynton's (1979) assessment emphasizes the employment effects in terms of distribution of people and skills. Walton and Vittori (1983) describe first-order effects as employment and information, with second-order effects as human reactions, such as feelings of autonomy.

The basic framework of the HIIS is presented in Exhibit 2-1. The different elements of the human infrastructure identified in the model at the beginning of the chapter are presented along the left-hand column, with the assessments to be made listed as the remaining column headings. Four assessments are to be made for each element of the human infrastructure:

1. What are the *existing conditions* in the organization for each element of the human infrastructure? For example, what are the existing information needs of machine operator's jobs in the production area receiving the new technology?
2. What are the effects of *different equipment parameters* on each element of the human infrastructure? For example, what change to information needs of machine operators' jobs will be created by equipment that has a high breakdown rate?
3. What influence, if any, do *organizational constraints* have on the effects identified in response to question 2? For example, given a work force demanding job challenge, will a reduced information need in the job design of machine operators create a problem?
4. How will the effects identified in question 2 directly *influence other elements* of the human infrastructure? For example, given decreased information needs of machine operators, will skill requirements for the new job be affected?

The HIIS delineates the specific assessments to be made for each element of the human infrastructure (for example, the six equipment parameters and four operator job dimensions). To make each assessment, the manager will find it necessary to use a combination of different data bases: vendor promises, experience

---

Margulies and Colflesh (1985) recommend a needs analysis of the human resource system in any technological planning model. Schreiber (1982) describes General Electric's systematic examination of how external conditions are projected to impact on human resources. Globerson and Salvendy (1984) focus on costs and benefits of different job designs. Finally, Corlett and Coates (1976) describe a conceptual model for conducting cost-benefit analyses of alternative ergonomic designs.

Exhibit 2-1. Structure of the Human Infrastructure Impact Statement.

Assessments

Elements of Human Infrastructure	1. Existing state	2. Impact of equipment parameters	3. Constraints on Impacts				4. Impact on other elements
			Work force	Plant resource control	Market predictability	Mgt HR philosophy	
I. Machine Operator Job Activities							
II. Technical Support Functions							
III. Management Functions							
IV. Supervisory Functions							
V. Skill Requirements							
VI. Selection							
VII. Training							
VIII. Personnel Policies							
IX. Organizational Structure							
X. Outcomes							
XI. Planned Change Process							

with currently proven technology, experience with the use of similar technologies, and estimates provided by company personnel.

It is not my intention to specify a particular way to conduct the assessments. Methods will vary depending on the organizations' circumstances and resources. Instead, this book identifies the specific issues managers need to consider in making the assessments and the options they need to consider for implementing the results.

Keeping Machine Operators Involved: Nine Options

Although direct labor constitutes less than 10 percent of most manufac-turing operations, research clearly indicates that we are not yet at a point technologically where we can ignore the important role of AMT operators. Indeed, the need to have operators involved in flexible factory automation is so significant that this entire chapter is devoted to this topic and to an examination of the research on effects of AMT on operators' jobs. This research identifies such effects as the need for increased coordination and information, increased discretion over certain produc-tion tasks, and the need to create human redundancy in the system. The chapter goes on to discuss the various job design options that may best serve these new needs. Nine options are presented, along with the idea that different options are appropriate to different organizations. Across all organizations, however, the research clearly discredits the utility of the scientific management approach for AMT jobs. More flexible designs, such as synergistic human-machine systems and work teams, are much better suited for the flexible automated factory.

Is Direct Labor Needed with Flexible Automation?

In a survey by Ayres and Miller (1983), robot users frequently reported reduction or elimination of direct labor as a reason for purchasing flexible automation. Does this finding imply that direct labor is not needed when AMT is installed?

Despite flexible automation users' intentions to reduce direct labor costs, evidence from numerous case examples indicates that direct labor is still needed after the technology arrives. In a case study of the modernization of Ford Motor Company's Dearborn engine plant, managers were asked why workers were needed to tend the computer-automated machining process (Chen, Eisley, Liker, Rothman, and Thomas, 1984). Their answers: "Tools must be checked and changed, the grinding wheels must be 'dressed' periodically so they are the right width and 'dressed' evenly, new grinding wheels must be manually installed periodically, quality control checks must be performed, including checking parts with manual gauges to be sure the automatic gauges are functioning properly, and, in the case of machine breakdowns, a skilled tradesperson must be called while crankshafts are manually unloaded to be run on a different line or stacked on pallets" (p. 50). In short, direct labor is needed. Other studies with the same conclusion abound (see, for example, work by Blumberg and Alber, 1982, and Fadem, 1984).

These studies suggest that direct labor is needed to serve a variety of different functions. One function that machine operators need to perform is the modification of work instructions developed by process planners, since at least half of the instructions issued must be modified (Schaffer, 1981). Other functions machine operators need to perform are quality checks and troubleshooting. These include checking operations for tool wear, maintaining the equipment, and preparing the equipment for variations in inputs that would otherwise cause machine malfunction or poor processing of materials. Case examples of the need for machine operators to carry out these functions include a company installing material-handling robots (Ayres and Miller, 1983), an automated pulp factory (Hirschhorn, 1984), and at Avco Lycoming (Kinnucan, 1983).

Thus, contrary to initial intentions of some companies, direct labor, in combination with flexible automation, is here to stay—for quite some time. Given the importance of direct labor, what do we know about the effect that flexible automation has on the content of jobs?

Research on Effects of Flexible Automation
on Machine Operators' Jobs

A machinist working at a conventional machine tool appears, visually, to be doing something very different from what an operator at a computer-controlled machine tool does. Precisely how the conventional machine operator's job differs from that of the job with AMT varies tremendously from organization to organization. Studies of the direct labor effects of flexible automation have found that in some companies the jobs of AMT operators are far worse than the jobs of their conventional counterparts; the jobs offer less autonomy, task identity, and motivation to perform well (Gerwin, 1982); involve more stress, pressure, and isolation (Argote, Goodman, and Schkade, 1983); and yield less job satisfaction because there is less challenge and variety (Gent and Weinstein, 1985).

In other organizations, however, studies show that the jobs of AMT machine operators are far better than they were with conventional equipment in that they involve greater skill than was needed prior to automation (so much so that some jobs were reclassified from unskilled to skilled labor categories) and yield more satisfaction because many difficult, dangerous, or unpleasant tasks have been removed (Ayres and Miller, 1983; Kolodny and Stjernberg, 1986).

Thus, it is not the case that flexible automation will necessarily affect the jobs of direct labor negatively. However, it is also not the case that the new technology will necessarily have positive consequences for direct labor. Moreover, it is possible that the change from nonautomated to automated machining cells may have no effect on job satisfaction at all, as was found in a study by Huber and Hyer (1985).

Part of the reason consequences of new technology for machine operators may be good, bad, or equal is that organizations may implement the same technology in such different ways that very different job designs result. For example, Wilkinson (1983) examined two different companies, both of which purchased the same type of CNC machine. In the first company, the owner-manager of the small machine shop wished to use the CNC to expand his control over that of the skilled labor. "He talked about the 'illiterate and innumerate [sic] kids' on the labor market today: 'They're no use to me, so I get CNC instead.'" (p. 29). In this organization the CNC operators' jobs consisted exclusively of machine tending, with no troubleshooting or programming required. At the opposite extreme was the other company where CNC operators were highly trained and expected to set up their own machinery, including correcting CNC programs if necessary. Similar such differences between organizations with the same equipment have been found by Hyer (1984), Gerwin and Tarondeau (1982), Butera (1984), and Graham and Rosenthal (1985).

Thus, the findings of this research suggest that effects of flexible automation on the content and design of direct labor jobs are not equivalent across different organizations. This implies that, although a new flexible machine may create similar changes to machine operators' job tasks, different organizations may not directly translate these changes into the same job designs. If a piece of equipment demands substantial monitoring, a single operator need not do it all; a team could rotate the responsibility. Thus, the effects of flexible automation on machine operators' job tasks and content need to be distinguished from the implications of these effects for job design.

To avoid further confusion regarding the effects of new technology on job content as opposed to job design, this chapter is divided into two main sections: (1) analysis of technological effects on different dimensions of machine operators' jobs and (2) options for job designs. The chapter closes with a reminder of the open systems perspective on human infrastructure planning: any job design chosen must be matched to the technical system, the individual, and the organizational structure.

Technological Effects on Machine Operators' Jobs

There are four dimensions of machine operators' jobs that are affected by flexible factory automation. These four dimensions summarize several other classifications of different aspects of a job (Amber and Amber, 1962; U.S. General Accounting Office, 1976; Davis and Taylor, 1979; Turner and Karasek, 1984). The four dimensions particularly pertinent to the effects of flexible automation are (1) coordination and interdependence needs, (2) information needs, (3) human-machine redundancy, and (4) discretion and responsibility.

Coordination and Interdependence Needs. The introduction of flexible automation has a profound effect on the coordination requirements of direct labor jobs. In all the studies reported to date, AMT has increased operators' needs to coordinate with others (Argote and Goodman, 1986; Mann, 1962; Shaiken, 1983). However, AMT operators do not have to coordinate more with *all* personnel. The research indicates that most of the increased coordination is done with other operators in order to share information about system experiences, as well as with such technical support personnel as engineers and maintenance. Coordination with supervisors may or may not increase.

Coordination may increase not only with specific personnel but also for particular purposes. Coordination can be classified by direction (initiated versus received) and focus (exchange of resources, information, or tasks) (Kiggundu, 1983). A coordination effort may be initiated toward others, as when it involves, say, informing maintenance personnel of machine problems. In contrast, coordination may be received from others, as when operators receive the help of maintenance people who repair the machine. Coordination purposes also vary in whether they involve the exchange of resources, critical information, or critical tasks. Although evidence is scarce on the specific coordination purposes affected by AMT, the studies that have examined coordination appear to suggest that much of the increased coordination that AMT generates involves increased *information* exchange *initiated* by the operator toward others (such as telling engineers about machine flaws) and increased *task* exchange *received* from others (such as relying on maintenance to fix the complex equipment when it breaks down). If this tentative conclusion is supported by further research, it is important to note that Kiggundu (1983) found people to be more satisfied with initiated coordination in general and to prefer exchange of resources rather than exchange of information. Thus, job designs that avoid an abundance of information exchange and received coordination might prove invaluable for the future flexible automated factory.

Information Needs. Flexible automation has been found to have a substantial effect on the information needs of people in direct labor jobs. Studies have found increased information needed concerning quality control, machine "personalities" (that is, how machines react to different raw material inputs), scheduling requirements to enable maximum use of the operator's and machine's time, and events leading up to machine breakdowns (Davis and Wacker, 1987; Roitman, Liker, and Roskies, 1987; and Shaiken, 1984).

While AMT generally increases information needs of operators, the introduction of AMT may inadvertently disrupt important existing information flows. In one pet food manufacturing plant, new automated process equipment was laid out expansively; but the spacious arrangement impaired communication and interaction among the relatively small numbers of employees working with the new equipment (Dickson, 1981). Extensive intercom and video systems were needed to rectify the problem. In another company, thirty-six automatic mail carriers were installed, but the machines undermined major organizational values sustained by the humans who formerly had covered the pickup circuits. Corporate communications were no longer provided firsthand, and private arrangements for transfer of special messages was no longer possible (Harris, 1985, p. 187).

While on the one hand flexible automation may interrupt essential communication patterns, on the other, it can introduce information overload (Chervany and Dickson, 1974). Information overload creates "cognitive lockup" and "cognitive narrowing" (Sheridan, 1981). *Lockup* and *narrowing* refer to the tendency for operators to focus on only one or two displays (or controls) rather than monitor the complete array of incoming information. These problems can be so severe as to cause disasters like the Three Mile Island accident. Operators at Three Mile Island formed an initial impression that a problem with pressure buildup had developed. As a result of "locking-in" on this definition of the problem, they focused solely on the pressurizer throughout the accident, despite accumulating evidence that the structure and direction of the accident had changed over time (Hirschhorn, 1984).

To protect against problems induced by information overload, job designs are needed that limit the rate of appearance of new tasks, ensure that information pertaining to a difficult task is not presented too quickly, help operators to distinguish irrelevant or redundant information, and, since optimizing multiple criteria in solving a difficult problem encourages overload, prioritize multiple problem-solving criteria so that the operator can safely focus on only one aspect of the problem at a time (Sheridan, 1981; Salvendy, 1983; Sharit, 1984).

Human-Machine Redundancy. Anyone attempting to understand the impact of flexible automation on machine operators' jobs needs to consider the amount of redundancy that must be built into the human-machine system. An unreliable and technically complex system necessitates more redundancy than a reliable or less complex system. In terms of the machine operators' job, the issue is not redundancy alone, but rather the role of the operator in that redundancy. As the research evidence graphed in Figure 3-1 indicates, systems in which humans have a part outperform systems in which the redundancy is completely technically determined (Chapanis, 1965). Management at Harris Corporation's semiconductor plant in Melbourne, Florida, failed to provide for human redundancy when two robots were installed in the clean room. As a result, the robotized system sometimes poured out defective parts undetected for as long as two hours before a correction was ordered (Stricharchuk and Winter, 1985).

In human-machine redundant systems, the human redundancy may be manifested in multiple ways. Often redundancy is exercised by operators responsible for monitoring equipment operations. With flexible factory automation, such a change in job activities—from physically performing production operations to watching a machine perform the same operations—is quite common (Office of Technology Assessment, 1984; Argote and Goodman, 1986).

Designing a system whereby human redundancy is manifested by operators monitoring machine activities limits somewhat

Figure 3-1. Advantages of Human-Machine Redundancy.

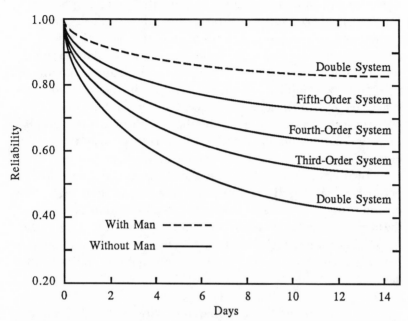

The reliability of a double redundant navigation system in which one of the redundant components is a man (dashed line) as compared with the reliability of systems with various orders of redundancy in which all components are machines (solid lines).

Source: Chapanis, 1965, p. 9. Used by permission.

the effectiveness of that redundancy, however. As evidenced by Salvendy's (1983) research results, the relation of performance effectiveness to arousal can be described as a U-shaped curve: ineffective response occurs when arousal is too low because of errors of omission, while ineffective response also occurs when arousal is too high because of errors of commission and fatigue. This curve suggests that if operators are expected to be attentive monitors their jobs must be structured for an optimal degree of arousal. Thus, a job that demands little physical activity most of the time is not one in which operators can legitimately be expected to be attentive to equipment problems.

Human redundancy does not necessarily have to be manifested by operator monitoring. Having the operator physically involved in the production process through statistical sampling, setups, and maintenance and troubleshooting are other ways to create system redundancy. Regardless of the particular manifestation, consideration must be given to human error and variability in designing the complete system. For example, including humans as system-redundant elements introduces the fact that humans can not only fix technical errors caused by the machine but they can also create technical errors and then fix the errors they cause. Thus, a job design that inadvertently eliminates operators' chances of correcting their own errors would be a mistake. Moreover, humans do not perform equally well throughout a day. As research originally described by Dudley (1968) indicates, operator output drops off at the beginning and at the end of the workday. Thus, job designs need to take into consideration that the effectiveness of the human as a redundant system may fall off dramatically at certain points in the day.

Discretion and Scope of Responsibility. With AMT, changes often occur in the degree and type of discretion the operator exerts over the job. However, the precise pattern of these changes varies across organizations. In some organizations, operators report less or little control over their jobs (Blumberg and Gerwin, 1985). For example, Zuboff (1982) found that when a computer-controlled monitoring system in the Kalmar Volvo plant was installed, workers felt their discretion was taken away in terms of how defects were defined. Previously, supervisors determined when a part was of sufficiently poor quality to be returned to the workers; this procedure allowed the workers some room to negotiate with the supervisor. With the new system, a red light flashed when a defect was detected, allowing workers little opportunity for discussion or discretion. The introduction of AMT has also been reported to increase discretion in some organizations, notably in the area of quality inspections (Manufacturing Studies Board, 1986).

For example, in a survey of ninety-nine manufacturing cells by Pullen (1976), 76 percent of them had operators responsible for their own quality inspections. Increased discretion over quality is often necessary with AMT because of the strategic shift in management's output priorities from quantity to quality production. Operator discretion over quality may be manifested in many different ways, such as statistical process control, individual inspection gauges, or the right to stop the line (the Japanese Jidoka principle). At Ford's Dearborn plant, the implementation of automated equipment caused management to refocus its effort toward quality. This effort was manifested by management providing workers with control charts and additional gauging equipment for use in determining whether they were producing good-quality parts. In addition, workers had the right to refuse to run bad parts, even if their supervisors suggested otherwise. The possibility of refusing to do poor-quality work was created by the installation of a phone line throughout the plant that workers could use to anonymously identify supervisors who ordered them to run bad parts (Chen and others, 1984).

In addition to discretion over quality, studies have found other areas of increased discretion with AMT to include responsibility to debug programs for CNC machine tools (Aguren and Edgren, 1980; Manufacturing Studies Board, 1986; Hartmann, Nicholas, Sorge, and Warner, 1983), control over the paperwork of cell operations (Pullen, 1976), responsibility for improvements in production processes (Majchrzak and Paris, 1986), as well as increased responsibility for machine uptime, for example, through routine maintenance, simple troubleshooting, and scheduling of maintenance (Argote and Goodman, 1986). In addition, when operators are organized into work teams, additional responsibilities may include job assignments, selection of co-workers, and selection of team leaders (Gulowsen, 1979).

These case studies indicate that areas and amounts of discretion will change with the introduction of flexible automation. The precise nature of the change appears to depend as much on such nontechnical factors as management's human resource philosophy as on features of the new equipment. Nevertheless, an interesting conclusion of a study by Graham and Rosenthal (1985) of eight firms implementing FMSs seems appropriate here: most managers of the eight companies concluded, after implementation, that they underestimated the level of operator responsibility required to keep the equipment running.

Implications for Operators' Job Design

This review of the research on the effects of AMT on operators' job tasks has identified several issues that must be considered in the redesign of the operator's job. First, the AMT operator will need to have a job that is designed to facilitate coordination with other operators and technical support. Given that much of this coordination will focus on information exchange—information to be received from others as well as initiated to others—and given that such forms of coordination may be less satisfying than others, the operator's job will need to be designed to counteract these prevailing negative reactions. Such job designs might profitably ensure that coordination responsibilities are shared with others or that the types of coordination needed are balanced. In any case, increased coordination and interdependence bring with them increased emphasis on group performance, which makes the monitoring and evaluation of individual performance (called "task visibility") more difficult (Jones, 1984). Decreased task visibility may reduce the motivation of certain individuals because their contributions are not as easily recognized or rewarded as before. Thus, jobs must be designed and rewarded to promote not only coordination but individual effort as well.

In addition to coordination issues, the operator's job must be designed to meet the operator's needs for information about quality, machine idiosyncrasies, schedules, and events leading to machine breakdowns. With so much information, the danger of information overload is ever present. While some precautions to reduce the risk of overload can be achieved through training and system design (incorporating gauges, for example), the job design must also confront this risk. As I mentioned earlier, designs are needed that limit the speed with which new tasks are required and new information presented, that help the operator to distinguish irrelevant and redundant information, and that prioritize problem-solving criteria.

As the examples given earlier demonstrate, job designs of AMT operators must also provide for human-machine redundancies. Redundancy based solely on operators monitoring machine operations may provide insufficient operator arousal to ensure effective monitoring performance. Thus, additional redundancy mechanisms must be considered. Moreover, job designs must give the operators the opportunity to fix not only technically created errors but also errors they introduce themselves.

While there are cases of AMT operators having less discretion than conventional equipment operators, as we have seen, increased operator discretion in certain areas is often needed with AMT and should be provided for in job designs. Increased operator responsibility may be needed in such areas as quality, NC programming, debugging, paperwork, maintenance, troubleshooting, scheduling, and process improvements.

Job Design Options for the Machine Operator

The previous section described the ways in which operators' tasks may change with AMT and the issues raised for redesigning operators' jobs. With these task changes and issues in mind, we are now ready to consider the different options for redesigning operators' jobs. It is important to note that task changes and issues do not determine which job redesign option should be chosen; they only establish the minimal criteria to be met by any of the options. The choice of the correct approach will depend on the organizational constraints discussed in Chapter Two (for example, management human resource philosophy) and the match of the job design to the equipment, individuals in the organization, and organizational structure, according to the open systems approach. In this section of the chapter, then, nine different options for redesigning AMT operators' jobs are presented. Listed in Table 3-1, the nine options differ by values, focus, level of analysis, and strategies for implementation. For example, the *sociotechnical systems* approach to job design focuses primarily on involving the operators in the generation of the job design rather than on the specific design itself. In contrast, the *ergonomics* approach to job design assumes one

Table 3-1. Options for Job Designs.

Approaches	Level of Analysis	Job Design Strategy
Scientific management	Individual jobs	Job fragmentation; increase management control
Job enrichment	Human	Vertically or horizontally enlarged jobs; task variety
Job rotation	Human	Horizontally increase task variety
Sociotechnical systems (STS)	Process	Options identified by STS design group
Work teams	Group	Group responsibilities and individuals' contributions
Ergonomics	Human-computer interface	Optimize ergonomic environment
Task allocation	Tasks	Human versus machine capabilities
Fault detection	Human-computer interface	Enhance human capability to detect technical system errors
Synergism	Human-machine system	Principles of open system organizations designed into job and technology

operator for each (or multiple) machine, and therefore its focus is on how to optimize the ergonomics of the human-machine environment.

The characterizations of the nine approaches to job design options have relied primarily on their more popularly practiced operating principles rather than on theory. Thus, for example, most *task allocation* approaches, as currently practiced, tend to allocate tasks by pitting the capabilities of humans against the capabilities of the machine, although more system-oriented task allocation approaches have been suggested (Ghosh and Helander, 1986). In addition, the approaches are not necessarily mutually exclusive. For example, a *synergistic* approach, when appropriately executed, would yield an adequate fault detection system, proper ergonomics, optimal task allocation, and enriched jobs. While not mutually exclusive, though, the different approaches serve to provide distinctions in focus and limitations. Thus, an *ergonomics* approach would not focus on the open system, and a *fault detection* approach would not consider other factors than those that influence the detection of potential system errors. Finally, since not all options are equally effective under all circumstances, the situational constraints and research evidence on the effectiveness of each option are reviewed.

Scientific Management

Most managers attending a basic education class on organizational behavior are aware of the scientific management approach to job design. In this approach, the focus is on individual jobs with an effort to identify the simplest group of tasks that optimize management control and worker efficiency. As such, the scientific management approach leads to job fragmentation; the old auto assembly production lines are classic examples.

The scientific management approach to operator job design tends to be frequently used by U.S. manufacturers implementing AMT. For example, an Air Force study on the metalworking industry (cited by Shaiken, 1984) views production gains as most likely to occur when the technology is designed to minimize the need for skills and to diminish worker decision making. A Numerical Control Society publication, also cited by Shaiken, maintained that a central advantage of computerization is more direct control over decisions that affect accuracy of unit cost, delivery dates, quality, and repeatability. Shaiken states that these examples are proof that the new manufacturing technology is a vehicle to exercise Taylorism; that is, to take control of the machine shop out of the hands of the workers and into the hands of management. The frequent use of the scientific management approach is perhaps due to the fact that it succeeds at increasing efficiency by reducing both the training time for particular jobs and the number of people needed to perform the job (Campion and Thayer, 1985).

Despite the frequency of its use, case examples are beginning to indicate that the scientific management approach to operator job design may not be the best approach for flexible automation. A classic example of problems that occur when scientific management is applied to jobs of workers who need discretion, redundancy, coordination, and information is the "Strike in Space," described by Schoonhoven (1986). In 1973, *Apollo 3* astronauts conducted the first day long sit-down strike in space, closing down communication with mission control for twenty-four hours. An examination of the reasons for the strike indicated that the blame was attributable to a scientific management approach to the astronauts' work schedule while in space. "To accomplish all planned activities, ground control shortened the times allowed for meals and setting up experiments and made no allowance for unsystematically stowed equipment. Favorite leisure activities—watching the sun and earth—were forbidden . . . . The Skylab crew members had zero autonomy and discretion in determining the pace and sequence of their work, with no local control over the conditions of work" (p. 273). The cost of the one-day strike to the National Aeronautics and Space Administration (NASA) was $2,520,000!

Similar antagonism over the scientific management approach has occurred among CNC operators. A scientific management approach to CNC operators' jobs typically results in the fragmenting of programming and machine operator tasks into two separate jobs. However, such a delineation is often ineffective, since, according to vendor recommendations, CNC programmers should have a working knowledge of machine shop practices, blueprint reading, tool design, and sheet metal fabrication techniques. Few programmers are skilled in so many noncomputer areas; consequently, the programs they create tend to be inefficient in the use of materials and contribute to expensive scrap rates (Nulty, 1982).

Perhaps most defeating to the scientific management approach for AMT operators is a recent review of nineteen case studies of firms implementing flexible automation (Butera, 1984). The review found that in all those companies where jobs were designed according to scientific management principles (that is, where the companies used unskilled labor and specialized jobs focused primarily on monitoring activities), operators experienced increased stress and the system was less cost-effective.

Job Enlargement and Enrichment

Job enlargement refers to adding tasks of similar skill levels to workers' jobs. Job enlargement also usually involves giving workers increased responsibility for controlling their own work pace (Griffin, 1982). Table 3-2 presents examples of enlarged jobs in the production environment. In all these examples, the worker is given more responsibility for tasks of similar skill levels. In contrast, job enrichment refers to the job design strategy in which workers are not simply given more of the same tasks to perform, but are given tasks that represent greater skills, such as tasks previously held by the supervisor. Examples of job enrichment tasks include having the CNC operator do programming, or having FMS cell operators coordinate directly with maintenance or perform some maintenance operations themselves.

Job enrichment, more than job enlargement, has been used by some firms for the design of operators' jobs with flexible automation. In one small company implementing CIM, a job enrichment strategy was applied in which the operator, referred to as the "cell manager" was responsible for programming, operations, and maintenance of the FMS cell (Roitman, Liker, and Roskies, 1987). At Ford's Dearborn engine plant, in which $600 million worth of flexible automation was installed from 1979 to 1981, a new job classification was created called "automation equipment operators—set own machines" (Chen and others, 1984). The automation equipment operators were responsible for inspection, machine setups, troubleshooting, and minor maintenance. In an aerospace manufacturing plant, job enrichment provided operators with the extra responsibilities of preventive equipment maintenance, minor machine adjustments and repairs, and debugging new as well as troubleshooting existing tapes, tools, and fixtures (Fadem, 1984).

Research on the effectiveness of the job enlargement/job enrichment approach to job design is fairly conclusive about its positive effect on job satisfaction (Campion and Thayer, 1985; Griffin, 1982). The effect of this approach on productivity, however, seems far less clear. While the aerospace manufacturer just mentioned found significant increases in machine utilization and group productivity, a recent review of job enrichment studies found that only 12 percent

Table 3-2. Enlargement of Simplified Jobs: A Sample of Typical Changes.

Job Category	Simplified	Enlarged
Spot Welding	Operator inserts wires to jig and spot welds shelves; stores welded shelves on rack.	In addition to the simplified job, operator is also responsible for filing electrodes, adjusting the speed of machines, adjusting the voltage of spot welding generators and fits jigs.
Power Press	Operator inserts items to power press, activates the power press, and removes the pressed item.	In addition to the simplified job content, the operator is responsible for bringing the material to the power press workstation and removing the pressed items from the workstation.
Metal Platers	Each worker is responsible for only one job. For example, one worker's job is only to mix chemicals for plating; another operator only puts items on a conveyor line that travels through plating. A total of three operators works at each machine.	Each of the three workers arranges his own work; rotation from job to job occurs.
Wire Cutters	Workers align machines, insert wires, and empty bins.	Work content exactly the same but workers can choose their own working hours, providing the machines are manned a total of at least twenty-three hours a day.
Time Study Engineer	Documents current methods and establishes time standards, using stopwatch.	In addition to documenting current methods and establishing time standards, he is responsible for developing improved methods (previously done by production engineer) and handling time study grievances (previously handled by personnel manager).

Source: Salvendy, 1978a, p. 469. Used by permission.

of such job redesigns improved productivity outcomes (Roitman and Gottschalk, 1984). Of most importance in understanding the effectiveness of this approach appears to be whether or not the individual worker wants an enriched job. For example, studies have found some shopfloor workers do not want enriched jobs (Salvendy, 1978b; Hackman, Pierce, and Wolfe, 1978). Clearly, then, individual differences need to be taken into account when enriched jobs are to be used as a strategy for job design.

Job Rotation

Job rotation has been found to be a popular approach to operator job design (Smyth, 1982). Job rotation defines specific tasks for different jobs and then, to provide the variety that workers need in their jobs, workers rotate among the different jobs. In organizations with such job rotation strategies, workers tend not to think of the job as a steady state of preidentified tasks, but rather as a series of different tasks through which they rotate either on a predetermined or apparently random basis.

Many firms implementing AMT have used job rotation as the solution to potentially boring operator jobs that otherwise might only involve monitoring activities (see cases by Clutterbuck and Hill, 1981; Mann, 1962; and Saari, 1985). For example, in a study of eight firms implementing FMSs, all eight companies moved to job rotation within the FMS cell allowing the operators to rotate through preventive maintenance tasks (Graham and Rosenthal, 1985). Job rotation was felt to be necessary not only to reduce the boredom but because the FMS was too small to need dedicated maintenance people.

There are many alternative forms of job rotation. Operators have been reported to rotate across different functions (preventive maintenance, operations, and so on) (Graham and Rosenthal, 1985), between conventional and the CNC machine tools (Shaiken, 1983), and across different machine tools (Kohler and Schultz-Wild, 1983). Figure 3-2 presents an example of the latter rotation strategy.

Since there are so many different forms of job rotation, it is difficult to assess the general effectiveness of job rotation for system performance. In a review of the literature by Griffin (1982), job rotation did appear to increase worker flexibility. However, job rotation also seems to decrease efficiency because workers constantly do jobs with which they are not completely familiar. Nevertheless, it may not be meaningful to attempt to assess the effectiveness of job rotation strategies given how many different ones are used and the different contexts in which they are implemented. A job rotation

Figure 3-2. Example of a Job Rotation Scheme.

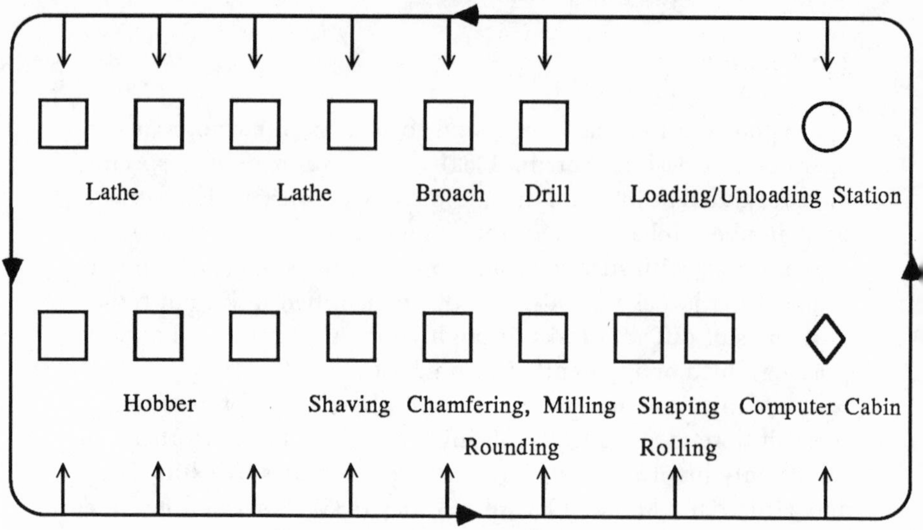

Rotation of (six) operators (per shift) between all tasks
- systems control: according to a fixed plan (change in position after several weeks)
- all other tasks: according to operational requirements and decisions within the team

Source: Kohler and Schultz-Wild, 1983, p. 11. Reprinted courtesy of the Society of Manufacturing Engineers. Copyright 1983, from the Proceedings of the World Congress on the Human Aspects of Automation.

strategy for AMT operators that involves some enriching tasks, such as maintenance or programming, has the potential to yield more positive results than a job rotation scheme that involves nothing more than having operators monitor different but very similar machines.

Sociotechnical Systems Approach

The Sociotechnical Systems (STS) approach is based on the tenet that those affected by the technology must be involved in the development of job design options. Thus, of all the approaches presented here, the STS approach is the most process oriented. No single job design option is recommended at the outset by STS designers; rather, their orientation is that the option should develop from a systematic analysis of the job and social dimensions followed by a consensus-development process among members of the STS design group. The STS design group consists of between six to twelve people from different levels, functions, and departments in the organization affected by the new technology. For AMT operator job design, the group would consist of future AMT operators and those with whom they would need to work closely (for example, maintenance and engineers). In addition to this focus on process, STS advances certain principles as to what defines a "better" job: more autonomy, minimum of coercion, opportunity to learn, variety, identity with completed product, and ability to control critical variances that impact on work outcomes.

Given its primary focus on process, the STS approach typically considers a range of specific job design options. For example, an STS design group for a maker of baby care products generated the nine separate job designs listed in Table 3-3.

Not only do STS design groups generate a range of job design options, but, in analyzing the outcomes of different job design options, the STS design group may actually take a step back and reevaluate the appropriateness of the chosen technical system. In a major oil refinery, for example, the STS approach led to a counterintuitive choice of a less advanced computerized control technology (Pava, 1983). From a purely technical standpoint, it was possible to fully automate many procedures, but this would have eliminated an on-going need for operators to have discretion over operations. In Table 3-3, the reader will note that several of the job design options are much less automated than others.

Since STS is more a process approach than an actual job design option, it is difficult to judge its effectiveness for system performance. Some examples of increases in productivity can be found (National Center for Productivity . . . , 1977; Davis and Trist, 1974). Moreover, cases of increases in job satisfaction with no increase in productivity are also frequently reported. Therefore, the choice of the STS approach should not be based on its proven effectiveness. Rather, it should be based on whether management and workers can comfortably adhere to the STS process, tenets, and outcomes, no matter what they are.

Table 3-3. Examples of Alternative STS Options.

1. T3.	Mechanically paced line with buffer stocks. +		**6.** T5.	Individual workstations with no mechanical pacing. +
S2.	Line-type work organization. Each worker does a number of operations.		S3.	Group given responsibility for allocating tasks.
2. T3.	Mechanically paced line with buffer stocks. +		**7.** T5.	Individual workstations with no mechanical pacing. +
S3.	Group is responsible for allocation of tasks.		S4.	Line or circular type work organization. Each individual doing a whole job. Targets set by group. Feedback to group.
3. T4.	Mechanically paced line with workers able to alter the speed of line. +			
S2.	Line-type organization. Each worker does number of operations.		**8.** T5.	Individual workstations with no mechanical pacing. +
4. T4.	Mechanically paced line with workers able to alter speed of line. +		S5.	Circular work organization. Each individual doing a whole job. Group responsible for ancilliary tasks.
S3.	Group is responsible for allocation of tasks.		**9.** T1.	Line as it is now. +
5. T5.	Individual workstations with no mechanical pacing. +		S2.	Each worker assigned a number of operations.
S2.	Line-type work organization with each worker doing a number of operations.			

T = technical; S = social
Source: Adapted from Mumford and Weir, 1979, p. 116.

Work Teams

Work groups are teams in which operators share responsibilities for loading, monitoring, unloading, and tool setting. Work groups have been recommended by several observers of flexible automation (for example, Gerwin, 1982; Butera, 1984). AMT work teams vary in their precise composition, with some including only fellow operators and others including technical support staff as well. AMT work teams also vary in their degree of discretion; teams with less discretion are called semiautonomous, while others are called autonomous work teams. Specific duties of work teams can include any of the following: purchasing new equipment or parts; liaison duties with production control, quality control, materials managers, maintenance engineers, or payroll; housekeeping chores; safety functions; training; selection of members; time and record keeping; quality control; determining work assignments within and between shifts; diagnosis of equipment failures; minor machine repairs; and preventive care of the equipment.

Typically in establishing a work team job design, certain design decisions are specified in advance and certain decisions are left up to the team to decide (Davis and Wacker, 1987). Decisions specified in advance include measurable input specifications, measurable output specifications (such as quality or quantity), equipment and resources, work station layout, compensation, and information flows outside the team. Decisions typically left for the team include task assignment, scheduling, work methods, work pace, work hours, discipline, information flows within the team, selection of team leaders, and team membership.

Examples of work teams abound. At a Delco-Remy General Motors (GM) battery plant, a team-based organizational structure was developed in which plant management was considered a support team, technical staff such as maintenance and engineering were considered technical service teams, and the operators were grouped into the core plant operating teams (Cherry, 1982). At Digital Equipment Corporation's (DEC's) electronic plant in Enfield, Connecticut, a team approach replaced the standard production assembly line (Harris, 1985). Each team member is trained to perform twenty different job functions involved in producing circuit board modules. At Volvo's Kalmar auto assembly plant, the plant has been designed for group work, with each group having its own individual rest and meeting areas (Gyllenhammar, 1977). The work is organized so that each group is responsible for a particular, identifiable portion of the car—electrical systems, interiors, doors, and so on.

With all this publicity and emphasis on teams, the key question in many managers' minds is whether teams are as effective as they are purported to be. In one experiment by Fisher (1981), productivity measures were taken for four years before and after an assembly-line optical production operation was transformed to five teams of production workers. Each team received complete information about those aspects of the business for which it was responsible. A training program was also established, and employees were assured that advancement would not be by favoritism. The results indicated that overall productivity improved at a 15 percent annual rate after the teams were introduced. Research by Kemp, Wall, Chris, and Cordery (1983), Trist, Susman, and Brown (1977), Pearce and Ravlin (forthcoming), and Aguren and Edgren (1980) has shown similarly positive outcomes for teams.

Clearly, then, work teams seem to be effective. But are they always appropriate? Research on work teams suggest that they are not. Teams are most appropriate when: (1) work is not entirely unskilled; (2) the group can be defined as a meaningful unit of the organization, inputs and outputs are definite and clearly iden- tifiable, and the teams can be separated by stable buffer areas; (3) turnover in the team can be kept to a minimum; (4) there are definite criteria for performance evaluation of the group and group members; (5) timely feedback is possible; (6) the team has resources for measuring and controlling its own critical variances in the work flow; (7) tasks are highly interdependent, making it necessary for group members to work together; (8) cross-training is desired by management; and (9) jobs can be structured to balance group and individual tasks (Davis and Wacker, 1987). Apparent from this list are the many conditions that must be in place for work teams to operate successfully; thus work teams are not always appropriate.

Assuming that the work team is an appropriate job design option for AMT operators, research on group process offers several suggestions for ensuring that the team will function effectively (Pearce and Ravlin, forthcoming). Since one of the advantages of having people work in groups is to benefit from the variety of responses group members provide, team effectiveness can be encouraged by fostering this variety through open communication within the group, member selection that ensures heterogeneity, a group structure that discourages status differences, and training to improve job and decision skills of group members.

Another way to increase the effectiveness of work teams is to enhance the ability of team members to coordinate with each other. Effective strategies for encouraging coordination within the group include decentralizing the power structure in the group, using less formal mechanisms to coordinate (that is, not using memos), and encouraging "just-in-time" decision making (that is, providing the type of authority and information to group members that will allow decisions to be made as near as possible to the point at which an uncertainty occurs).

Another source of work team effectiveness is the commitment of the team members to group goals. Commitment can be encouraged in several ways: allowing the group to have autonomy over decisions that increase commitment (such as selection), designing the group task to be responsible for meaningful whole products, and having a reward and appraisal system that encourages both group and individual responsibilities.

Team effectiveness can also be enhanced by not expecting teams to do too much too soon (Hirschhorn, 1984; Cherry, 1982). Teams should be given new responsibilities only as they can handle them. This progression can begin at start-up with responsibilities for housekeeping duties and relief and break schedules. By maturity, the team can preplan changes and prepare budgets. This progression, used at the Delco-Remy battery plant, gave management a "safety valve" in case the teams didn't work. Similar to the problem of having teams do too much too soon is the response of management when teams initially don't work. Typically, when problems arise, management will either reduce team autonomy or abdicate management responsibility for the team. The first approach will lead to resentment, and the second will deprive teams of the technical support they need. Thus, when teams flounder, the best strategy is not to reduce their autonomy but to increase their technical support (through the use of training or group facilitators).

In sum, work teams seem to be a viable option for flexible manufacturing systems. The teams can optimize the coordination needs of the system, utilize the timely feedback provided by the system, act on the identifiable inputs and outputs that the system demands, facilitate the cross-training needed with the system, compensate for the monotony inherent in monitoring activities, and provide a balance of both the group and individual tasks that are needed with flexible automation. However, the team approach may not always be effective, especially when stable buffer areas cannot be distinguished, when the team cannot be provided the discretion or resources to control critical variation in its work flow, and when the team cannot be structured as a meaningful but separate unit of the organization. Moreover, the team approach will not work unless closely managed to enhance member variety, coordination, commitment, and evolution.

Ergonomics

The ergonomics approach refers to the traditional human factors orientation in which human-machine interfaces are effectively designed to reduce health hazards and increase information-processing ability. Ergonomics of the computerized workstation design, with its video display terminals, keyboards, and input devices, are classic areas of focus (Majchrzak, Chang, Barfield, Eberts, and Salvendy, 1987). For example, human factors specialists have found that information displays can cause problems in information selection and processing due to improper illumination, glare on the screen, improper contrasts in luminance, and flicker. Moreover, these specialists have also demonstrated that an operator's mental model for performing a task must conform to the computer's model if the operator is to effectively process the information output. Thus, in constructing a manufacturing cell, the location and display of information, as well as the commands the operator is expected to learn in order to interact with the equipment, become particularly important if the cell is to operate effectively. For example, in one ergonomic approach to operator job design, the human-machine interface was optimized by recommendations for changing the technical software system—not the operator's job (Turner and Karasek, 1984). Changes to the technical software included self-documentation, locally defined command sequences, abbreviations and synonyms, explanations of decisions or recommendations made by the system, and skill acquisition features for inexperienced users to become experienced in a short period of time.

Research on the effectiveness of the ergonomic approach to job design clearly indicates that it increases user/operator comfort and efficiency (Campion and Thayer, 1985; Salvendy, 1987). Thus, under the proper circumstances, such an approach is quite useful. However, with this approach, the focus is on the individual (not the group) and how to enhance utilization of the individual (rather than the system). As such, the ergonomic approach may not be appropriate under all circumstances.

Task Allocation

Traditional task allocation refers to the approach to job design whereby the production tasks needing to be performed are identified, then the best capabilities of humans and new technology are identified separately (using, for example, the well-known Fitt's list), and finally the production tasks are assigned to the most capable agent for that task. This approach has been used by the Department of Defense for more than thirty years to allocate tasks between humans and robots (Ghosh and Helander, 1986). The end result of a traditional task allocation approach is that, as technology is made more sophisticated, all tasks will be allocated to the computer.

Examples of the traditional task allocation approach abound. From Fitt's list to more modern versions, the human's capabilities are contrasted to the capabilities of the machine. For example, a general capability in which humans are regarded as superior to machines concerns cognitive tasks such as formulating generalizations, unstructured problem solving, and evaluation; computers are credited with being more efficient at such calculations as data transformation, model simulation, and display tasks (Turner and Karasek, 1984).

While there is nothing theoretically wrong with this approach to job design, the manner in which it is traditionally operationalized creates a bias in the analysis process; that bias is the allocation of human and robot tasks primarily based on the robot's rather than the human's capabilities (see a study by Edwards described in Chao and Kozlowski, 1986). Those tasks that are best performed by robots are allocated to them, and the remaining tasks are allocated to humans. Thus, humans get the leftover, or what has been referred to as "tasks performed by default" (Sharit, Chang, and Salvendy, 1987). For example, Kamali, Moodie, and Salvendy (1982) present a case study of how the tasks of an assembly operation could be allocated to humans or robots. They choose one task to illustrate their point: the verification of the size of a differential bearing shim for a transaxle. Their logic for allocation was as follows: "Verification of the shim size could be done by human or robot. The reason why automation is not a good choice . . . Therefore, a human should verify the shim size" (p. 446). Here, then again, humans are getting the leftover.

There are additional problems with the traditional task allocation approach. These include the fact that most task allocations assume that the allocation of the tasks must be static, failing to recognize that some tasks can be performed by both humans and computers and thus could be performed in an interchangeable fashion over time (Turner and Karasek, 1984). Moreover, complaints have been lodged about the lack of specificity of the approach for manufacturing strategies (Ghosh and Helander, 1986).

In response to these criticisms, a concept of the supervisory controller has been recently developed by Salvendy and his colleagues (Salvendy, 1983; Sharit, Chang, and Salvendy, 1987). The supervisory controller refers to the human and machine operating as a single system to control its own operations. As typically applied to the task allocation approach, the human is assigned responsibility for monitoring, planning, intervening, and operator training; the machine is left to perform the remaining tasks. Note that this approach is in direct contrast to other job design approaches such as one that emphasizes work as a cooperative team in conjunction with other technical support staff. Despite its differences from other approaches, this contemporary task allocation strategy is an improvement over the more traditional version because it enables the user to account for possible dynamic changes in task allocations over time as well as design a job that more explicitly considers operator control and discretion.

Fault Detection

The fault detection approach to the design of operators' jobs focuses on system errors, how to ensure that such errors don't occur, and when they do occur, how to ensure that human operators quickly diagnose and resolve the errors. There are two assumptions underlying this approach: (1) technical systems are imperfect, and (2) technical errors are actually faulty intersections of the technical and the human system.

With regard to the first assumption, error is inevitable in automatic systems because of the complicated interconnection of hydraulic, pneumatic, electrical, and mechanical subsystems that are exposed to a range of chemical and/or mechanical stresses. Hirschhorn (1984) describes one of the reasons for this inevitable failure:

> Control engineers, who tend to think in functional terms, often forget that the most complex of designs are realized in humble joints, welds, pipes, seams, and circuits, which may decay and fail. . . . Steam turbine failures [for example] have been traced to subtle degradation of materials. In one accident in which two men were killed, nine were injured, and a turbine and generators destroyed, small black particles of iron oxide had unexpectedly formed in the oil used in the pumping system. Investigation revealed that while the system was shut down for maintenance, a minuscule amount of saline solution had been accidentally introduced into the oil pipes. When the pipes were drained of oil, the solution, exposed to the air, formed black iron oxide [p. 77].

Three Mile Island and Chernobyl are also unfortunate examples.

The second assumption recognizes the additional complexity introduced by the human. To illustrate the second assumption, a mandatory inspection program of brakes on planes was found to actually increase the number of accidents due to brake failure (Hirschhorn, 1984). Upon review, it was discovered that the mechanics were breaking or weakening parts of the brake while inspecting it. Thus, the technical error could not be attributed solely to human or technology but to the intersection of the two.

In the design of today's manufacturing jobs and technology, there appears to be an unfortunate disregard for the fault detection approach. For example, in a survey of the fault detection devices among aircraft manufacturers, the following problems were identified: too many warnings requiring immediate attention, too many false alarms on warnings, few administered standards for using warnings, and generally poor lighting intensity and contrast (Thompson, 1981). In another example, Sheridan (1981) describes the results of a human factors review of nuclear power plant control room designs. The review identified the following design flaws that would decrease an operator's ability to detect faults: The left-hand side of a pair of displays was driven by the right-hand side of a pair of controls; panel meters could not be read from more than several feet away but controls for these panel meters were located thirty feet away; critical displays were located on the back side of a panel while nonimportant displays occupied centralized front panel space; two identical scales were side by side, yet one was actually a factor of ten different from the other although it was not so marked; controls jutted out so the operators could inadvertently activate them with their bodies if they walked too close; labels were ambiguous; and nomenclature on alarm annunciators differed from the supposedly corresponding nomenclature in the procedures manual.

Resolving the problem of improper attention to fault detection in job designs requires two strategies: (1) training operators to diagnose faults and (2) redesigning the job to maximize fault detection. In terms of the first strategy, recent training programs have been developed around research on human limitations in fault diagnosis (see research by Rouse, 1981). Humans are apparently unable to distinguish comfortably between information about symptoms that cause and do not cause a problem. Thus, humans often are unable to disregard unimportant information, making it extremely difficult to solve the type of large-scale, complex, multistage causal chain problems that are encountered with CIM technology. In fault detection training, then, operators are taught how to make the necessary distinctions in a graduated step-down fashion.

The second strategy to increase attention to fault detection is to design jobs for optimal fault diagnosis behavior. Such jobs are ones that are conceived with learning as well as peformance in mind (Hirschhorn, 1984). For example, operators should be able to choose when and how to engage in different diagnostic behaviors and thus learn what behaviors yield quicker and more precise fault diagnosis. Premature standardization of procedures will only hinder learning. In addition, jobs should be designed so that the operator has some knowledge of the broader picture and planning horizon. This information will help the operator exercise some control over unpredictable errors and variations in input materials. Olivetti, for example, designed machinists' jobs so that a worker planned and executed the production of a specific mechanical part and then inspected its quality. This allowed the machinist to schedule for variation and to learn from technical and human errors.

In sum, a fault detection approach to job design suggests that technology as well as the job be designed to enhance the human's ability to detect and diagnose faults in the technical system. The more integrated the technology, the more useful such a design strategy seems to be.

Synergism

Recently in the *Los Angeles Times,* a film producer was quoted as saying, "After Three Mile Island, the Challenger accident, and now the meltdown at Chernobyl, it's becoming increasingly clear that as far as high technology is concerned, nobody's really in charge, nobody has all the answers. The lesson is—always has been—don't trust the experts" (Taylor, 1986, p. C1). These accidents, as well as the increased complexity of the new technology, have led many to reconsider how operators are used in jobs (see, for example, Perrow, 1984; and Whitney, 1986). Rather than allocate tasks based on which entity—human or machine—is more capable, or focus solely on the detection of technical faults, an alternative approach to job design has been called for that characterizes the operator-technology relationships as a system with different tasks to perform. The objective with such an approach is to identify not who should do the tasks but how they should be done, so that the operator and the equipment are working in coordination rather than as appendages or tools. Thus, the technology may change in this design approach as much as the operator's job. Such an approach is referred to here as the synergistic approach to AMT operator job design.

To apply the synergistic approach, different job tasks are identified that must be part of the entire operation, whether human or machine. These tasks might include surveillance, intervention, maintenance, backup, input, output, supervision, and inspection, as suggested by Parsons and Kearsley (1982). Having identified the tasks, the human and machine are then analyzed as a system to determine how, together, they can accomplish the necessary tasks.

Common to applications of the synergistic approach is that job designs are not technologically driven; rather they are driven by the purposes and constraints of the entire human-machine system. As such, the design may not necessarily be one that is the most technologically sophisticated. For example, in one application, a robot was paced by the operator, in contrast to the more traditional approach to AMT job design wherein the operator is paced by the machine (Parsons and Kearsley, 1982). The operator directly controlled the robot and part positioner through a control console, and manually drilled missed holes in the sheet metal panel. In another example, a new paper mill was constructed in which the job designers rejected the typical arrangement of building railroad spurs and loading docks for both receiving and shipping in one physical location (Davis and Wacker, 1987). It was discovered that the typical arrangement would not have permitted employees responsible for receiving to control their own input. Thus, the plant was built to have separate sets of spurs and docks for shipping and receiving. "The extra cost was more than repaid by high performance of work teams whose job designs focused on workers' responsibility to control productivity and quality" (p. 15).

The effort to design jobs within a system that is structured for optimal joint performance by human and machine may require that the humans be provided with more technologically advanced equipment, such as computer-controlled data bases. In such applications, the advanced technology is not introduced to replace the worker or replace particular tasks; rather the technology is introduced to optimize the operator's performance in relation to the system. For example, in a foundry with substantial variations in its work flow of light and heavy castings, technology could have been introduced to smooth out such variations in the work flow and simply have operators monitor the technology, intervening only when problems arose. Instead, using a synergistic approach, the company purchased a minicomputer controlled by the operator. With the computer, the operator can now input deviations in the work flow to the computer and let the computer make the mathematical calculations of the effects of the deviations on the mix of castings. The enhanced technology of the minicomputer helps relieve the operator of the stress induced by work flow variations, and also ensures that both the human and the technology are more effectively utilized (Aguren and Edgren, 1980).

With the synergistic appoach, certain system changes seem to receive more attention than others. One of these system changes concerns the buffering of the system from unpredictabilities and domino effects of errors. Charles Perrow (1983) suggests that sequences be constructed in such a way that they can be undone, reversed, or delayed. Thus, operator procedure manuals as well as production schedules and the programming of machine operations must be constructed to yield optimal flexibility—flexibility over which the operator has control. Another simpler strategy for achieving some of the same objectives is to build in buffer areas so the operator can interrupt the production line. Or the scheduler can revise production schedules so that instead of considering them as a linear set of sequential steps, they can be planned as a set of self-contained subroutines (for example, having an operator team build an entire engine rather than parts of the engine). Subroutines decrease the linear dependence between production operations so that when one subroutine fails other operations are not put into jeopardy.

Another system focus of the synergistic approach is on control panels. Given the systems orientation of the synergistic approach, control should be exerted over the premises of operators' jobs, not over their decisions or behavior:

> Take something as simple, yet as complicated, as deciding whether to place a meter on a particular machine. To make this decision, the designer must answer questions concerning the information or feedback that the meter would give the machine operator. Does the operator really require the information? How important is ease of physical availability? What about the timeliness of the information? If the information is not to be obtained from the machine directly, then from what other source in the social system organization? If the meter is not available to give the operator direct feedback, what are the consequences for the kinds of decisions the operator can make or is prevented from making? Who else might have to apply them if the operator doesn't? In what ways would the operator then become dependent upon supervisors or others who, because they had the information, could make appropriate decisions at the workplace? What are the social consequences of this dependence? How would these social consequences affect economic consequences for the organization? As these questions illustrate, the choice goes deeply into the structure of the organization and a consideration of the ways which people will be required to work in it, how they will be supervised, and whether, in fact, much supervision will be necessary if they themselves accomplish the required activities [Fadem, 1984, p. 685-686].

Albert Macek (1982) offers practical suggestions for creating control panels that provide varying degrees of operator decision latitude. In Macek's view, there are four types of decision latitude:

1. Human has a forced choice, guided by the computer.
2. Human has free response, guided by the computer.

3. Human has forced choice, guided by humans.
4. Human has free response, guided by humans.

The first type is best for routine tasks; the second is best when information must be gathered in an unstructured manner. The third type is best when the human knows what information to request and how to select desirable system alternatives; the fourth type is the most flexible and thus most effective when used by experienced operators. For example, the foundry in which a minicomputer was installed to facilitate human decision making illustrates the third type of control panel design. Thus, control panels are structured not only with the ergonomics or fault detection strategy in mind but also in terms of who has free choice under what circumstances.

Another important concept with the synergistic approach is equifinality, or the notion that in every open system, there is more than one way to accomplish a goal. This is particularly apparent among operators since each operator seems to have his or her own procedures that deviate from standard procedures (Perrow, 1983). Rather than attempt to ignore these deviations or force conformity, the synergistic approach encourages the recognition that these deviations provide for skill development, system comprehension, and relief from tedium. Thus, designing jobs that allow for these deviations in both the human and technical performance will enhance long-term goal achievement. For example, designing operators' jobs so that they can determine when preventive maintenance should be performed would yield far greater long-term learning than predefining specifications for a preventive maintenance schedule.

In sum, the synergistic approach presents a more systems-oriented view toward job design than other approaches previously discussed. This approach perhaps comes closest to the sociotechnical systems approach as theoretically conceived, particularly if potential jobholders are included in the system and job design. However, the STS approach rarely achieves a synergistic design in which both technical and social changes are made. Thus, only a few examples exist of a human-machine system designed as part of a truly synergistic relationship.

Open Systems Match

In view of the many approaches to designing machine operators' jobs, it must be remembered that an open systems model specifies that any job design must match with the technical operations, individual, and organizational structure if it is to effectively achieve the desired outcomes of the system and organization. Thus, the job design must be matched to the five equipment parameters described in Chapter Two. A less reliable system, for example, will need to be accompanied by a job design in which maintenance and operators work closely together and/or fault detection has been designed in.

The job design must also match the needs of the work force. For example, in a review of the research on a range of human infrastructure elements, Lawler (1974) found that there were significant individual differences in persons' responses to organizational actions. Thus, the concept of individualization of human resource action was coined. The needs of the work force can be identified through such surveys as those developed by Dawes and Lofquist (1984) and Robey (1978).

Finally, the job design should be matched to the organization's existing or proposed structure. For example, studies have shown that people do not perform well in enriched jobs when they are in organizations with rigid reporting hierarchies and centralized control of decision making (Pierce, Dunham, and Blackburn, 1979; Kohler and Schultz-Wild, 1983). Nor will a job design with interdependent work teams perform well in an organization that strictly limits open sharing of information (Perrow, 1983). Finally, an organization with a climate that prioritizes efficiency at all costs probably would not be able to effectively use a synergistic job design approach.

In conclusion, this chapter has reminded us of the need to consider the job design within the technological, individual, and structural context of the organizations. Larry Hirschhorn (1984) succinctly summarizes the point:

> The new technologies do not constrain social
> life and reduce everything to a formula. On the

contrary, they demand that we develop a culture of learning, an appreciation of emergent phenomena, an understanding of tacit knowledge, a feeling for interpersonal processes, and an appreciation of our organizational design choices. It is paradoxical but true that even as we are developing more advanced, mathematical, and abstract technologies, we must depend increasingly on informal models of learning, design, and communication [p. 169].

How Technical and Administrative Support Jobs Are Affected

In this chapter the effects of AMT on five categories of technical support jobs are discussed, and job redesigns are suggested where appropriate. For the first category, skilled trades, most attention is devoted to maintenance jobs. Research results indicate that maintenance jobs will require more time and technical knowledge for problem diagnosis, prevention, and coordination with others. Personnel in the second category, quality and production control, will gain power in the organization and shift much of their attention to supporting the inspection activities of the machine operators through training, follow-up checking, quality problem diagnosis, and general coordination activities. The tasks of production control personnel will shift to master scheduling and planning as shopfloor personnel take on the tasks of control and daily scheduling. The third category of technical support jobs is programming. A frequent dispute between operators and programmers concerns who controls changes in parts programs; job designs that help alleviate this problem are described. Engineering jobs, particularly R&D designers and manufacturing engineers, constitute the fourth category of technical support jobs. For both engineering types, flexible factory automation will require increased coordination—with each other, with marketing staff for designers, and with shopfloor operators for manufacturing engineers. Designers will need to shift their focus from design solely for innovation to design for innovation and manufacturability; manufacturing engineers, however, will have many of their tasks relegated to the operator, leaving them the opportunity to focus on the challenges posed by AMT. Finally, flexible AMT requires that accountants become pathfinders rather than simply data compilers. Their jobs will need to provide time for them to develop new cost-justification formulas and new measures of performance. Marketing, too, will be affected; however, documented evidence of these effects are scarce. Marketing staff are likely to become increasingly involved in equipment purchases to ensure that market niches can be found and maintained to utilize the increased production versatility of the flexible automated factory.

Research evidence to date suggests that the implementation of flexible automation has substantial effects on technical support personnel, that is, the indirect labor force. For example, in a study by Blumberg and Gerwin (1985) of five firms adopting CIM systems, the most frequent implementation problems were found to occur in the "indirect" areas of quality control, accounting, and maintenance. As long ago as 1970, for example, the U.S. Department of Labor's Bureau of Labor Statistics surveyed twelve continuous process plants implementing computerized production control equipment and found that sixty-eight new jobs were required to operate the process computer systems in the survey plants. Systems analysis, programming, and related occupations made up about two-thirds of the new jobs; the other third consisted of supervision, computer console operation, and instrument development. More recently, Dickson (1981) studied the implementation of a mechanized materials handling system and a computer control system in a food processing plant and found that the systems increased the number of support personnel needed.

In this chapter, five categories of technical support jobs are discussed: (1) skilled trades, (2) quality and production control, (3) programming, (4) engineering, and (5) accounting and marketing. For each category, the documented effects of the introduction of flexible automation are described. Effects are discussed in terms of the same four job dimensions as those described for machine operators' jobs. In addition, suggested job designs for each are presented. This discussion is intentionally devoid of a description of the new skills needed with flexible automation, reserving a discussion of the skills until Chapter Six.

Skilled Trades

Included in the category of skilled trades are such jobs as carpenter, electrician, plumber, and tool-and-die makers. They encompass much of the skilled, hourly work force in most manufacturing facilities.

One of the most popular questions concerning the effect of flexible automation on these support jobs is how the automation will affect numbers—for example, the number of skilled laborers needed in the plant. For the most part, studies of the effects of flexible automation on maintenance jobs have found an increased need for such skilled trades as maintenance staff and technicians (Office of Technology Assessment, 1984; Lipstreu and Reed, 1965; U.S. Department of Labor, 1982; Dickson, 1981; Blumberg and Gerwin, 1985). This increase is necessary for a variety of reasons: heavy demand on the equipment caused by smaller lot sizes, unproven and in some circumstances unreliable track records of the machines, a need for high machine utilization rates to pay back on the huge capital investment, and the technological sophistication of CAM equipment that necessitates substantial tending and knowledge for it to function properly.

In addition to the effect of flexible automation on the numbers of maintenance and technicians, AMT changes the types of jobs done by the skilled work force. Among these changes is the increased importance attributed to problem diagnosis. For example, a review by Thompson and Scalpone (1983) found that FMS equipment is generally so complicated that 60 to 70 percent of the time of a maintenance worker is spent in problem diagnosis. That time must be spent determining if breakdowns are attributable to the human operator, the central computer program that provides instructions for initiating system operations, the computer program that runs the specific technical operations, the electronic logic, the electrical relays, the mechanical movements of the machine itself, and/or the signals to the central computer to terminate operations upon completion. Since each of these separate components of an FMS is a complex technical system, the maintenance worker must often apply multidisciplinary knowledge of mechanics, hydraulics, electrical circuits, electronics, and so on or learn to work with experts in these areas. In either case, skilled trades with flexible automation often find themselves spending more time in diagnosis.

In addition to changes to problem diagnosis activities, administrative activities such as maintaining proper records on maintenance and parts inventories change. With CIM, detailed records of downtime, parts failures, maintenance schedules, machine utilization, and characteristics of machine operation are critical if machine problems are to be solved quickly and prevented from occurring again. With conventional equipment, Hayes and Clark (1985) have found that machine problems are not as complex and require less need to maintain reliable records.

A final change to maintenance workers' jobs is an increased importance given to extensive communication with production floor personnel (Shaiken, 1983). Machine operators can report to the maintenance worker the circumstances leading up to a particular breakdown and thereby substantially narrow the possible causes of the problem to a manageably few alternatives. Without this coordination, maintenance workers must either start their diagnosis with guesswork or rely on their own knowledge accrued from previous dealings with the machines—both inefficient strategies.

Maintenance workers are not the only skilled labor trades to need increased coordination to carry out their work. Tool-and-die makers, pattern makers, and workers in other skilled trades involved in the development of prototypes need to work much more closely with engineering, including designers and process planners. Prototypes need to be developed within the constraints posed by tight schedules, families of group technology parts, and the needs of an integrated process plan. No single person can work alone and do justice to these concerns. While recognized as necessary, workers in many skilled trades react adversely to the increased need to coordinate with both those who are less skilled and those who are more skilled. Many are more familiar with "being their own boss," which makes the transition especially difficult. Substantial education and encouragement may be necessary to help these workers adjust to the change.

Flexible automation also affects skilled trades in the area of preventive maintenance. The popular press has discussed at length the need for more preventive maintenance with new technology.

Yet, in one study by Majchrzak and Paris (1986), there were no differences between high- and low-performing firms in the amount of time either maintenance workers or equipment operators spent doing preventive maintenance. Similarly, in the Ford Dearborn engine plant, maintenance staff bitterly complained about the lack of preventive maintenance. While there apparently was a professed management directive to schedule preventive maintenance at Ford, the repairers claimed they were spending all their time "fighting fires" (Chen and others, 1984). The less-than-overwhelming emphasis on preventive maintenance may be attributable to the relatively recent installation of the flexible automation. Moreover, preventive maintenance tends not to affect short-term performance measures. The lack of emphasis on preventive maintenance at this stage, however, may be short sighted at best.

A final change skilled trades have been found to experience in some organizations is an increased accountability for productivity. For example, a former General Electric (GE) employee was recently quoted in *Manufacturing Technology/86* as describing GE's change to maintenance: "The prime measurement of the performance of our maintenance group . . . is the number of lost starts. . . . We have equipment capable of producing a certain number of picture tubes per hour. That number's our base. Any loss or deviation from that number is considered a lost start and we view it as a hole going through the production line. [We calculate] the number of lost starts per shift . . . and the shop people—maintenance and control engineering—are held accountable for any lost starts that occur." Previously, maintenance and control personnel were not held accountable for lost starts.

In assessing the effects of flexible automation on skilled trades, the open systems model reminds us that these effects will not occur under all circumstances. For example, the effects on maintenance and pattern makers will be determined in part by whether maintenance or prototype development is subcontracted. In one survey of implementing firms by Abbott (1981), it was found that when firms subcontracted out the maintenance of the new equipment, the jobs of maintenance were actually deskilled as well as reduced. Plants may choose to subcontract for several reasons, not the least of which is the freedom from dependence on, and training of, the plant's own work force. While such a strategy may be profitable in the short run, delays in building up in-house experience are encumbered. Moreover, poor labor relations can result.

Finally, although not a skilled trade in some organizations, job setters are greatly affected by AMT. It is generally recognized that the number of job setters will decrease dramatically in CIM plants as the machine (and possibly the operator) take on more of these workers' responsibilities. For example, in the area studied at Ford's Dearborn engine plant, the number of job setters dropped from seventeen to two.

The new flexible automation seems to result in needs for problem diagnosis, prevention, and coordination, especially for maintenance jobs. These needs can be met by several alternative strategies for designing skilled trade jobs in the automated factory. Since there is more research on maintenance jobs, such jobs will be the focus here. One strategy for managing these new needs is to create specialists in different functional areas. For example, an electrician may be added to a maintenance department that initially only had mechanical repairers. Such a strategy is effective only for some of the simpler CAM equipment, however; the more complex equipment requires maintenance workers to be knowledgeable about more than one functional area. Thus, simply adding new function-oriented jobs will not meet the need for complex problem-solving skills.

An alternative option might be the reorganization of the maintenance department into repair (or corrective) maintenance and planned (or preventive) maintenance. This option was used in a continuous process facility described by Dickson (1981). This approach may be appropriate in some organizations since, with CIM, prevention demands a substantially different set of skills than corrective diagnosis. Preventive maintenance of CIM is more than a matter of simply changing the oil every 3,000 miles; it demands not only a working knowledge of the system but also a knowledge of and intuitive feel for what *could* go wrong. With CIM there is precious little experience for understanding what could go wrong with this equipment, and thus preventive maintenance workers are explorers on the forefront of the technology, even more so than the

repairers responsible for quickly getting the equipment up and
running when a breakdown occurs.

In many organizations, this option of separating maintenance jobs by prevention and correction is not feasible since there
is neither sufficient attention nor enough equipment to warrant
having workers devoted exclusively to preventive maintenance. In
such organizations, the job classification "general mechanic" is
recommended for maintenance workers who are responsible for
multiple tasks. When the equipment is too complex for one person
to have the knowledge to do all the tasks, multiskilled teams of
mechanics have been used. At one plant assembling printed wire
boards using an automated line, the maintenance team, collectively,
is expected to know how the software controls the machines, how
to use the software as a diagnostic tool, how the computers work,
how bus-driven devices work, and how freestanding testers work. In
addition, each new piece of equipment has a lead maintenance
technician assigned to it to debug it, become its first operator, and
train other maintenance personnel and operators to use it (Nieva,
Gaertner, Argoff, and Newman, 1986). Occasionally, generically
trained maintenance workers cannot know all the machines well
enough to repair them. Thus, for example, General Electric's
cathode-ray tube operations in Syracuse, New York, created
decentralized maintenance crews, each serving a different sector of
the plant. "Our objective is to have them do nothing all day long
. . . like the lonely Maytag repairman," says the former GE manager
of advanced manufacturing engineering.

Regardless of whether the maintenance worker is part of a
team or working alone, there has been some debate as to what
should be the focus of the maintenance worker's job. Commensu-
rate with a recent resurgence of industry interest in job enrichment,
there has been some discussion that the maintenance worker does
not identify enough with the final product or sufficiently understand the constraints under which others must work. To rectify
these problems, some organizations have broadened the scope of
activities of the maintenance staff—for example, by having the
repairer make schedules and order parts. The utility of such a job-
broadening approach was examined in a survey of high- and low-

performing CAM and CIM plants queried about the proportion of time maintenance workers spend doing various tasks during their workweek (Majchrzak and Paris, 1986). The tasks included ordering parts, scheduling work, and informally teaching others, in addition to repair work. Proportions of time spent on each task were compared for low- and high-performing organizations. The results, shown in Figure 4-1, indicate that, contrary to this job-broadening strategy, maintenance workers in plants with CAM or CIM should do primarily repair and troubleshooting; other tangential tasks, such as ordering parts or scheduling maintenance work, should be discouraged, since they are related to poorer organizational performance. Having maintenance workers informally teach others apparently does not harm performance, since they can undertake such an activity in the process of doing their repairs.

While the job-broadening approach to maintenance jobs with CAM may not foster high organizational performance, job simplification is not called for either. As with many jobs, too much formalization and prespecification of maintenance jobs can be harmful, particularly since maintenance workers do not use only one or two strategies to troubleshoot and diagnose faults. In fact, research has identified a variety of strategies preferred by maintenance workers in solving a repair problem. These strategies include a primary focus on sensory checks, a preference for the use of maintenance records, a "least effort" approach where the easiest checks are made first, and "reliability" strategy where the most likely failures are checked first. Moreover, substantial research on the effectiveness of these strategies indicates that none seems to be more effective at problem solving than others (Christensen and Howard, 1981). Thus, formalizing a job so that maintenance workers are forced to use a less preferred strategy may be counterproductive, especially since the specific strategy used does not seem to make a substantial difference in performance. Therefore, while the maintenance job may not need to be broadened by adding other tasks, the evidence clearly indicates that the job design should allow repairers to determine how to solve the problem themselves.

A final option to consider in designing maintenance jobs for CAM is to assign maintenance workers less responsibility for some tasks (for example, minor maintenance) and more responsibility for

Figure 4-1. AMT Maintenance Job Tasks in Successful
and Unsuccessful Plants.

Success as Reductions in WIP:

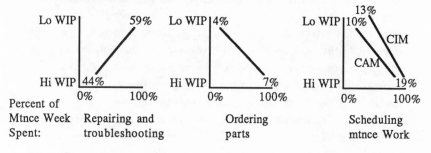

Lo WIP · · · · · 59%	Lo WIP ·4%	Lo WIP ·10% 13%
Hi WIP 44%	Hi WIP ·······7%	CIM
0% 100%	0% 100%	CAM Hi WIP 19%
Percent of		0% 100%
Mtnce Week Repairing and	Ordering	Scheduling
Spent: troubleshooting	parts	mtnce Work

Success as High Machine Uptime:

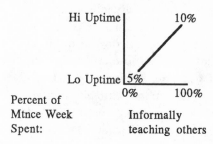

Hi Uptime ·····10%

Lo Uptime 5%
                0%   100%
Percent of
Mtnce Week   Informally
Spent: teaching others

Source: Adapted from Majchrzak and Paris, 1986.

others (for example, prevention). This option is only possible, of course, if some of the responsibilities of maintenance personnel are transferred to operators. At a Ford Motor Company transmission plant in Livonia, Michigan, for example, a "manufacturing technician" does minor maintenance and light construction, programs machines, and keeps maintenance statistics on operations. This leaves only major maintenance tasks and prevention to the maintenance job (Buss, 1985). The transfer of maintenance tasks to semiskilled technicians or operators can be a touchy issue for the skilled labor force; however, if it is managed well, this transfer of routine maintenance tasks need not cause resistance. In one company, for example:

> the attitudes of the various maintenance groups to the new technology appeared quite distinct: while the mechanical fitters exhibited general indifference (their side of the technology not being radically affected), the electrical fitters were particularly interested, for they perceived the introduction of electronics and of the automation technology as an opportunity for extending their role, and thus securing their future with the company. This perception of increased status is reflected in the lack of resistance to the transfer of simple, routine maintenance activities from themselves to the new line operators, an event which previously would have encountered strong resistance, no matter how insignificant the encroachment [Dickson, 1981, pp. 182–183].

Quality Control and Production Planning

Flexible automation poses a "unique challenge" to maintaining quality, as Thompson and Scalpone (1983), among others, have found. With the new equipment, quality is affected by a complex series of events attributed to the way pieces are loaded into fixtures, the way fixtures load on material-handling devices, the way fixtures load into the machine, the tooling, the machining center, the relationships between operations performed on different machines, and so on. In addition, with equipment that is integrated, natural breakpoints in the production process where human inspections can be performed are no longer possible. Finally, with AMT, many firms are striving for zero defects to compete with foreign importers. Zero defects necessitates a 100 percent inspection rate rather than the traditional statistical sampling of parts. In sum, flexible automation creates an increased dependence on quality control.

How these challenges and dependencies are translated into effects on quality control jobs varies tremendously from one company to another. In some firms, the quality control function becomes an integral part of the operator's job (Manufacturing Studies Board, 1986). For some of these firms, this means that the number of inspectors has decreased. At one plant, fifty inspectors were dropped from the payroll when operators' responsibilities for quality were increased. At the Canadian General Electric Bromont compressor airfoil plant, there are no quality control inspectors (Farnum, 1986). The quality control department trains management and operators in quality control techniques and priorities, and helps to ferret out sources of quality control problems.

The increased responsibility of operators for inspection need not translate into fewer inspector jobs, however. At Caterpillar Tractor's Scottish factory, a computer coordinate measuring machine was installed in the inspection department, yet no inspection jobs were lost. "This was because only a proportion of an inspector's time is spent on physical inspection. Other significant activities include receiving materials, examining drawings, interpreting inspection results, and discussing the results with machine shop management and operators" (Boddy and Buchanan, 1986, p. 209).

Not only may the number of inspectors stay the same, but in some organizations a greater dependence on quality control may yield a need for more quality control staff. At a GM assembly plant in Detroit, a new job was created: electrical technician (Buss, 1985). The electrical technician is part of a team that uses a computer to test interior electrical and electronic hookups, such as those in the instrument panels of the front-wheel-drive luxury cars built at the plant.

Challenges to quality control with flexible automation may not only affect the numbers of quality control personnel and their job titles; they may also affect their job responsibilities. Rather than actually perform inspections, for example, many inspectors monitor computer-controlled inspection equipment that carries out the work. Before such equipment was available, inspectors had substantial discretion in determining whether parts were candidates for scrap and rework, and which worker or machine was responsible for the defects. With computer-controlled inspection, some of this discretion may be removed. At Volvo's Kalmar plant, each team is responsible for its own inspection. However, "after a car passes about three work group stations, it passes through a special inspection station where people with special training test each car. A computer-based system takes quality information reports from these stations and, if there are any persistent or recurring problems, flashes the results to the proper group station, telling them also how they solved similar problems the last time. The computer also informs the teams when their work has been particularly problem-free" (Gyllenhammar, 1977, p. 106). All the inspector does is monitor the inspection process.

Volvo's Kalmar plant illustrates another effect of flexible automation on quality control: shifts in power. While in the past quality personnel could identify poor worker performance to the supervisor, the sanctions associated with high defect rates were small compared to the sanctions associated with low output rates. Thus, the operators had less to be concerned with when they were identified as producing poor quality. As product quality becomes more and more important, consequences of poor-quality work increase. Quality personnel who monitor the operators' statistical process control (SPC) results will then have much greater impact on the performance evaluations than before.

The production planning and control function will also be affected by flexible AMT. Since many companies with AMT move to a just-in-time pull-type system of inventory control, much of the parts chasing, leveling, changing orders, and unanticipated rescheduling are job tasks no longer needing to be performed. Moreover, detailed and multilevel bills of materials and work plans are also often not needed. Finally, daily scheduling and job assignments cannot be handled by the shopfloor since parts are produced on a signal resupply basis (Sepheri, 1986). Although many of the production planning and control tasks are removed, such jobs will probably not be eliminated. There is still a need for materials planning and master scheduling—a need that becomes even more acute than before as lot sizes decrease, the frequency of orders increases, and the number of different parts produced and needed increases. Moreover, in many ways the production process is not sufficiently stable to be left to a computer. Managers lose track of materials, tools to do a job are misplaced, customers make special requests to run certain jobs ahead of others, supplies fail to arrive on time, and critical machines in a production process break down. As long as this instability in the production system continues, process planners are probably here to stay (Wilkinson, 1983).

Programming

Surveys, reviews, and industry estimates have concluded that the implementation of flexible automation will create an increased need for programmers on the shopfloor (U.S. Department of Labor, 1982). Perhaps most illustrative of this new breed of computer programmer is the NC part programmer. In order to prepare a part program for NC programming, the NC programmer must determine the manufacturing segments, tool and cutting data, and manufacturing sequences. Other programmer job classifications created by AMT include technical analyst, programmer analyst, systems analyst, engineering assistant, and programming technician.

Several alternative job designs have been used with programming staff. Key to these alternatives is the issue of who controls the program. In one organization, the manager of a programming department conceived of the control problem in these words: "CNC gives management more control as to what goes on in the machine. . . . Once programming is done there should be no way anyone could mess around with it. . . . CNC was designed in the first place because semiskilled labor is cheaper. . . . Management should decide exactly what the operators' tasks are, and give us full authority for the programs" (Wilkinson, 1983, p. 63). Since operators did not agree with the program manager, there was a clash between programmers and the CNC operators on the shopfloor over whose task it was to edit the programs produced in the office and prove them at the machine tool. "This conflict was symbolized by a key on the control cabinet of each CNC machine, which locked and unlocked the type editing facility. The programmers wanted to take this key away after having proved their own computer programs, and to keep full control over use of the machine's control panel. So far, operators have managed to keep the keys on the shopfloor" (p. 61). One alternative job design for programmers is to give complete programming control and skills to nonprogramming workers, such as the machine operator, planner, or engineer, and leave the programmer to serve only as a technical consultant. In practice, this is rarely done.

A different alternative design, used in several organizations, is to rotate workers among planning, CNC operations, and initial programming tasks. Such a rotation allows operators firsthand experience programming flexible machines; programmers gain experience in machine nuances and the realities of the shopfloor; and planners gain knowledge of how programs are written to accommodate exceptions and variations in planning programs. Such a rotation scheme, then, might provide the workers with a sense of control as well as appreciation of the work of others. As with all job rotation schemes, however, such a job design would be inefficient in the short run, since CNC operators and planners have not been properly trained in programming techniques and most programmers know surprisingly little about manufacturing operations.

Yet another job design has programmers write what are referred to as "macro" programs that serve only as general algorithms for actual parts machining or production schedules. This software provides the means for the shopfloor staff to "fill in the blanks" to make the program appropriate for the particular task at hand. Such a job design necessitates some duplication of effort across programming and shopfloor departments in terms of skills training and programming time. Moreover, programmers who write macros that are so effective that they can be used for most situations risk writing themselves out of their jobs! However, since the variability on the production floor of most manufacturing facilities is such that new macros will probably always be needed, this job design may help to provide the different workers with control and ownership over a defined part of the programming task.

A final job design, used in at least one plant, is one that attempts to directly confront the control issue. In this design, the programmers have complete control over programming tasks (of all sorts). In exchange, the machine operators have control over other aspects of their jobs—for example, pace of the work, determination of defects, task assignments, determination of whether or not a part should be reworked or scrapped, or how a part should be reworked (Wilkinson, 1983). Thus operators and programmers each have control, the tasks they control purposely nonoverlapping.

Regardless of the specific job design used for programmers, the key issue for the programmer support function is control. The sooner management can resolve this control issue, the sooner the business of writing the programs can proceed.

Engineers

Engineering is a classification that could include employees with substantially varying educations and responsibilities. Two categories—R&D and manufacturing engineers—are discussed here. For R&D engineers, the implementation of flexible automation is often accompanied with the charge, "Design for manufacturability." This charge translates into an increased need to coordinate with manufacturing and marketing functions. To keep disturbances in a computer-planned work flow at a minimum, engineering change requests must also be reduced. For example, Hayes and Clark (1985) found the frequency of engineering change requests to be directly and negatively related to a measure of total plant productivity. "Getting it right in the first place," then, takes on added significance with flexible automation. To meet these demands posed by AMT, engineering design teams are often created (for example, see Shaiken, 1983). The teams typically consist of designers, drafters, and manufacturing and marketing representatives. In addition, when coupled with group technology, designers are expected to assign codes of part families to their drawings and use members of these families in their designs. For many designers, the need to use codes makes little difference in their jobs. For other designers, however, the need to use codes has caused such a dramatic change to their jobs that they have become fearful that their creativity will be limited (Hyer, 1984; Houtzeel and Brown, 1982). Particular care before, during, and after implementation is needed to avoid this sort of anxiety, resistance, and the motivational problem that may ensue. Finally, with the implementation of CAD systems, further changes occur, particularly to the designer-drafter interface. (These changes are discussed in detail in Majchrzak and others, 1987, and thus need not be repeated here.)

In addition to R&D engineers, the jobs of manufacturing engineers are also likely to change with AMT (Office of Technology Assessment, 1984). Traditionally responsible for preparing bids for customer orders, manufacturing engineers may find that much of the bidding estimation is now done by the computer (Curley and Pyburn, 1982). While manufacturing engineers have traditionally been responsible for process improvements, successful firms with CIM have recently been found to train their operators to make many process improvements themselves (Majchrzak and Paris, 1986). And the traditional responsibility of manufacturing engineers for upgrading equipment (purchasing new technology, for example) may no longer be theirs alone, but may be shared by a joint union-management committee, of which the manufacturing engineer is only one member; other members might include financial, quality control, maintenance, human resource, and R&D staff.

These trends suggest that the manufacturing engineering job will be very different in the future. Precisely what this job will entail is still unclear. In one firm the onerous task of preparing customer bids was relegated to a clerk using a manufacturing resource planning (MRP) system. The manufacturing engineers' tasks were not replaced with meaningful work, which created substantial free time and discontent (Curley and Pyburn, 1982). Judging from many currently existing firms, the likelihood that manufacturing engineers will have time to spare seems remote. Most are overwhelmed by the demands of learning, implementing, and restructuring the shopfloor for new technology. They have had to learn to prepare capital investment justifications, teach upper management about new technologies, separate the hype from the truth in vendors' sales pitches, work closely and as equals with maintenance, prototype makers, and future machine operators, and think in a systems orientation. Perhaps the notion of what manufacturing engineers will do in the future is answered here. Perhaps their role will shift from that of small process adjustors or customer-bidding estimators to that of the company's technological superstars, jumping from one successful automation project to another. Provided that they have adequate organizational support and preparation, such a role would provide invaluable service to the company.

Despite the uncertainty about manufacturing engineers' future jobs, it seems clear that one major change in their current jobs includes an increased need to coordinate with others. In one case study of a manufacturer of printed wire boards, this need to coordinate involved manufacturing engineers moving away from sole responsibility for the manufacturing end of the process to accepting a facilitating role as liaison between manufacturing and design (Houtzeel and Brown, 1982). Other organizations, such as the future Saturn facility for GM, will have teams of design and manufacturing engineers who together design parts and are responsible for both creativity and manufacturability. Finally, manufacturing engineers will also need to coordinate with nonengineers on the shopfloor. Where operators form teams responsible for a particular set of machines or cells, manufacturing engineers may be members of the teams or serve as technical support consultants to the teams. In such circumstances, the performance of manufacturing engineers will be judged by their ability to help rather than direct machine operators.

Accounting and Marketing

Robert Kaplan (1984, 1985, 1986) has written about the impact of flexible automation on the work of accountants. From his analysis, he finds that the cost accounting models used in manufacturing firms today are based on assumptions of the mass production of a mature product with known characteristics and a stable technology. These models attempt to optimize accounting or cost justification decisions by assuming the production setting is fixed rather than changeable or uncertain. Kaplan and others (for example, Gold, 1982) feel strongly that these assumptions of the cost accounting models are invalid for the modern flexible factory and thus cause accountants to generate data that often lead to incorrect decisions. For example, a factory with flexible automation may be incorrectly reported as performing less efficiently than a traditional factory, since, with the current accounting models, the reduced direct labor time will be translated into higher apparent overhead costs. Thus, stockholders or corporate executives may sanction the factory for its poor performance, drastically depleting the morale of the hardworking shopfloor personnel.

As cost accounting models become obsolete, Kaplan recommends that accounting departments rethink both the financial and nonfinancial measures of performance used by the company. With flexible automation, variable labor costs are less important, thus accountants will need to identify new ways to measure product costs and profitability. At an agricultural equipment manufacturing plant, the implementation of an FMS meant that the standard cost of machining a part could no longer be expressed in terms of direct labor hours, since this quantity did not vary with the part being processed (Gerwin and Tarondeau, 1982). Thus, new cost standards, expressed in terms of machining hours, were developed. At Hewlett-Packard, the direct labor category was eliminated from the cost accounting system, since only 3 to 5 percent of the total product cost was attributable to direct labor (Groebner and Merz, 1985). Moreover, manufacturing overhead, including end-of-month work in process inventory (WIP) and finished goods inventory, was treated as an expense charged directly to cost of goods sold. These are only two of many options available for modifying traditional cost accounting models. Most important is the recognition that when flexible automation is installed, the accountant will need to be retrained and provided the opportunity to work with management to develop new financial measures of performance.

Implementation of flexible automation will also create an increased need to measure performance in nonfinancial ways. Kaplan suggests that five categories of nonfinancial measures become particularly important in a flexible automation factory, with each necessitating measures that accountants have not traditionally used. The five categories include quality, inventory, productivity, innovation, and worker commitment. Accountants must begin to include in their balance sheets such data on quality as the percentage of defects, frequency of breakdowns, percentage of finished goods completed without any rework required, and the incidence and frequency of defects discovered by customers. For inventory, accountants need to consider data on average batch sizes, work-in-process inventory, and inventory of purchased items.

Productivity measures must no longer rely on value-added per employee or output per direct labor hour because such measures overlook gains from the more efficient use of capital, energy, and managerial efforts. Innovation must be measured, since cost minimization measures are inappropriate for evaluating costs of production for parts that are so early in their product life cycles that they still need development. Such measures as the rate of introduction of new products, the speed with which product characteristics can be varied to meet customer demand, and the delivery of new products on predictable schedules may be useful measures of innovation. Finally, as the production process becomes increasingly dependent on the motivation of workers to monitor and intervene in that process as necessary, accountants must determine ways to incorporate measures of worker commitment into their estimates of nonfinancial performance. Often, the level of worker commitment is a far better barometer of the future viability of the company than traditional productivity measures.

The implication of Kaplan's work is that accountants in manufacturing firms with CAM will need to become more innovative in their accounting strategies and must generate reports that are more multifaceted, if not more complicated. It should be noted that not all observers of AMT agree with this implication. At Hewlett-Packard, the reporting of direct labor costs was indeed eliminated; in addition, however, since scrap and rework of defective units are discovered and corrected almost immediately on the production floor, accounting for scrap and rework was also reduced. As a result, the accountant's job and reports have become much simpler, focusing in large part on manufacturing overhead rates (Groebner and Merz, 1985). The Hewlett-Packard example is not to imply that Kaplan is wrong in suggesting a more multifaceted approach to accounting in the factory of the future; however, the example does suggest that the priorities of management will determine, to some extent, the anticipated effect of flexible automation on accounting.

Regardless of whether accountants accept a more multifaceted role in collecting data, it seems clear that their cost justification strategies, such as return-on-investment formulas, will need to change. New cost justification models acceptable to multiple organizations are under development (Kaplan, 1986). Modifications include assessing costs for what happens if the firm chooses not to automate, costing out increased flexibility with the new equipment, and building into the formulas expenditures for training and equipment unreliability, as well as benefits of increased worker preparedness for future technological change. Few firms use these more encompassing cost justification methodologies; yet it is only a matter of time before accountants will need to accept (and convince management) that more reality-based cost justification methods need to be applied as the firm continues to automate.

The impending pressure on accountants to develop and apply new accounting methods to performance measures, internal cost structures, and cost justifications is undeniable, but the degree of pressure will obviously vary among organizations. Some companies will be more content to accept the limitations of traditional methods rather than experiment with untried new methods. Regardless of the extent of pressure, however, this need for new methods probably means that the most dramatic change in accountants' jobs will be the allowance of time for developmental work. Unless time and effort are expended on the modification of old procedures, the benefits of the new equipment cannot be accurately measured.

The effect of AMT on the marketing professional's job has been much less well documented than the effect on accountants' jobs. As flexible automation is installed, the firm's capability increases to produce different products in smaller batch sizes and to respond quickly to changes in consumer tastes. Thus, in theory, marketing and sales departments should be affected by an increased need to be closer to the customer, an increased need to identify new products, and an increased need to understand the technical production process to be able to identify the potentially infinite product variations that could be manufactured by the firm. These needs should result in marketing and sales staff receiving an overwhelming amount of information about the organization's new abilities to produce new products. In addition, the staff should experience overwhelming pressure to identify new markets, and an overwhelming need to either learn the production process better or work more closely with those who have the production knowledge and are able and encouraged to share it with them.

There is currently only anecdotal evidence to support these expectations. In one organization, for example, the implementation of CIM resulted in a new organizational structure (Roitman, Liker, and Roskies, 1987). Previously, engineering and marketing were separate departments, each reporting to the chief executive officer (CEO). With CIM, the engineering department was subordinated to the marketing department, signifying the increased role of marketing to ensure the customer base for the new production capability. In another manufacturing facility, management undertook an exercise that simulated the impacts on the organization when their new facilities plan, which included substantial new investment in flexible automation, was implemented (Roitman, personal communication, 1986). Management reported that a major outcome of this simulation was the recognition of the need to include members of the marketing department as plans were solidified. Previous to the simulation, the marketing department had actually preferred exclusion, since they had perceived the new technology as another case of upgrading for efficiency, rather than versatility. A third organization failed to include marketing throughout the production planning process and suffered the consequences (Majchrzak, 1985b). The flexible automation was originally purchased with the thought that there would be no layoffs because the sales people would identify new products and markets. However, the sales staff had never been included in the original purchase decision and did not understand the various ramifications of the new equipment for new product possibilities. The new equipment was never fully utilized, resulting in the feared massive layoffs.

The lack of systematic documentation of effects on marketing prevents statements that marketing jobs will definitely be affected by the implementation of flexible automation. However, one implication of an open systems approach to technological change is that if new products and markets are to be identified for the new equipment, marketing and sales jobs cannot go unaffected. Education and closer working relationships with production staff will be needed; perhaps job rotation or special liaisons should be created (possibly equivalent to the product champion or expediter of R&D departments). Moreover, if marketing is not included when equipment is being selected, a product or market niche may unfortunately be overlooked.

Conclusion

The open systems approach implies that, while specific effects may be predicted, the likelihood of particular effects occurring can be determined only within the broader context of the organization. Programmers' jobs will change only within the boundaries established for operators' jobs. Maintenance can turn to preventive tasks only if operators handle some of the corrective tasks. Freeing manufacturing engineers from certain responsibilities (for example, customer bids) is hardly worthwhile unless the tasks are replaced with other equally important responsibilities.

Moreover, changes in technical support jobs will not necessarily yield positive benefits for the equipment and the organization unless the changes are matched by concomitant changes in the human infrastructure. If increased cooperation is needed between accounting and production, between marketing and production, between design and manufacturing engineering, and between operators and planners, not only must jobs be designed to facilitate the cooperation but reward systems and organizational structure must also change. Simply placing the technology in the workplace will not be sufficient. For example, in a study of CAD's effects on coordination efforts between design engineering, drafting, and manufacturing engineering, Mosher and Majchrzak (1986) found that the CAD system created barriers to coordination where they didn't exist before, since the human infrastructure was not changed to encourage coordination. Decreased coordination was attributable to supervisors being confronted with the difficulty of managing a staff with CAD but no longer having the time to encourage or identify ways to more effectively coordinate with colleagues in other departments. Thus, AMT's effects on technical support jobs will be successful only if implementation is thought through and carefully managed.

5

The Changing Role
of Supervisors and Managers

Thus far, the effects of AMT on the job functions of machine operators and technical and administrative support personnel have been considered. In this chapter, the effects of AMT on the job functions of supervisors and managers are described. The research to date indicates that in some organizations the jobs of first-line supervisors will be eliminated as other workers in the organization take on supervisory responsibilities; however, in most organizations, supervisors will remain in their jobs, although their jobs will change dramatically. Some of these changes include a decreased need to monitor and direct subordinates' work, increased time for coordinating with other personnel, more time spent investigating complex production problems, and a decreased ability to use traditional methods to motivate and judge worker performance. Since most of a supervisor's time with conventional equipment is involved in monitoring and directing activities, the changes resulting from the implementation of AMT will give supervisors more time for other activities. This time can be used in many constructive ways, including planning, coordination, group facilitation, and change initiation and implementation. To carry out these new functions, supervisors need to learn more about the new technology, how it fits into the production systems, and how it will affect human relations and organizational change.

Changes in managers' job functions will not be as dramatic as those affecting supervisors; however, new performance demands will be made. These demands will include the ability to manage a complex, integrated business system with multiple goals. Thus, training in systems thinking as well as in the basics of the technology is essential if managers are to be prepared for the flexible automated factory.

The chapter closes with a discussion of managerial resistance to change—often more destructive than resistance on the shopfloor. Methods to counter this resistance include education, involvement, information sharing, and clarification of the future roles of the managerial work force in a flexible automated factory.

Supervisors' Job Functions and Flexible Automation

To begin our examination of the effects of flexible automation on the functions of supervisors' jobs, it is important to determine if supervisors will have jobs with flexible automation. Otherwise it makes little sense to discuss how new technology affects their job functions.

The evidence to date about the displacement of supervisors indicates quite conclusively that a few organizations implementing flexible automation do eliminate supervisors' jobs (Butera, 1984). In some organizations, the supervisor's functions are reallocated among the operators, engineers, and programmers (Manufacturing Studies Board, 1986). In other cases, self-managing work teams have eliminated the need for first-level supervisors (Roitman, in personal communication, describes such a situation for a manufacturer of floppy disks). However, the elimination of all supervisors' jobs is a rare occurrence (Manufacturing Studies Board, 1986).

The fact that only a relatively few firms actually eliminate supervisors' jobs indicates that, in spite of fears of job loss, supervisors will experience little job displacement with the implementation of flexible automation. Moreover, when the involvement of supervisors is not actively sought and utilized during the implementation of new technology, substantial problems have ensued. Supervisors have been found to be needed for their knowledge of the production process, knowledge of the work force, and capabilities of monitoring employee and equipment performance (Walton and Schlesinger, 1979). Therefore, an examination of how flexible automation affects supervisors' job functions is warranted since (1) most supervisors will remain in their jobs and (2) supervisors play an important role in ensuring efficient production with flexible automation.

Before proceeding, a set of functions needs to be defined that are typically associated with supervisors' jobs in nonautomated factories. For our purposes, I will use six functions that are applicable to most first-line supervisors' jobs. These six were originally identified in a classic study in which 452 supervisors and managers were interviewed about how they spent their workdays (Mahoney, Jerdee, and Carroll, 1965). The six functions are as follows:

1. *Supervising* the production process and people refers to the gamut of activities that supervisors do to monitor and facilitate both the technical production process as well as the behavior of subordinate staff. This supervisory function was identified in the classic study as taking, on the average, 51 percent of first-line supervisors' time.

2. *Investigating* refers to the time that supervisors spend solving problems in the production process. With conventional equipment, this activity usually entails ferreting out causes of machine breakdowns or production backlogs and taking action.

3. *Coordinating* involves the time that supervisors spend on actually working as a team member with other employees to solve problems or identify future opportunities. Thus, the coordinating activities may be with subordinates, other supervisors, managers, or support staff.

4. *Planning and scheduling* refer to the supervisory activity of scheduling materials, people, and machines to meet customer orders and overcome bottlenecks, in addition to planning ahead to avoid potential bottlenecks and identifying ways to smooth the work flow. Most supervisors spend substantially more time on the scheduling function than the planning one.

5. *Staffing and training* refer to the functions of recruiting and terminating subordinates as well as providing training (usually informal, on-the-job training) and selecting people for training.

6. *Evaluating* is the supervisory function of appraising the performance of subordinate employees and ensuring that employees are feeling adequately compensated for their efforts.

For each of these six functions of supervisors in plants with conventional manufacturing equipment, the effects of introducing flexible automation are described. Then implications of these effects for the job design, selection, and training of first-line supervisors are discussed.

Changes in the Supervision of Production Process and People

This first supervisory function can be divided between supervising the technical production process (for example, machines) and supervising the people who work for the supervisor.

Supervising the Technical Process. Flexible automation makes it possible for equipment to regulate and adjust itself to variations in the production process. Just as this self-regulating capability of machines means that operators do not need to be as closely involved in the activities of each machine, the same applies to supervisors. Therefore, many plants implementing flexible automation find that a first change to technical supervisory functions is that the supervisors can be given responsibility for more machines and a greater proportion of the production run (Shaiken, 1983).

Installing the new equipment brings about another change to technical supervisory responsibilities. The increased expenditure of the equipment and the increased severity of consequences associated with downtime necessitate that supervisors devote greater percentages of their technical supervisory time to system maintenance (Butera, 1984). Thus, rather than supervise only the production process per se, the supervisor with flexible automation must become more involved in an effective maintenance program.

As the equipment is integrated using computer-based linkages, the interdependence of the machines increases, often necessitating an increase in the interdependence of functional areas working with the equipment. In many organizations, this increased interdependence has meant that supervisors have been made responsible for a greater number of functional areas. The National Academy of Sciences study (Manufacturing Studies Board, 1986) provides several examples of this broader responsibility of supervisors:

- An electronics equipment plant assigned individuals from information services, quality control, and packaging to the first-level supervisor.
- An engine plant assigned part of support services, such as tooling and material stores, to first-level supervisors.
- An engine plant dedicated some support personnel (for example, a numerical control programmer and a tool engineer) to its flexible manufacturing system to report to the supervisor.

A final change to the technical supervisory function with flexible automation concerns supervisors' autonomy. Since the details of the production process are more visible to higher-level managers with flexible automation, some case studies have found that supervisors' traditional autonomous control over the production process has been substantially eroded (Shaiken, 1983; Rothwell, 1985). Thus, with flexible automation, supervisors often no longer have the discretion to wait to run a part until a more experienced operator is available. Nor can they choose to allow a machine to break down frequently rather than take the time to identify the problem and fix it. For some supervisors, this decreased freedom may be constraining, particularly if not compensated by increased freedom in other areas.

Supervising People. The self-regulation capability of flexible automation equipment means that operators become more machine tenders than individuals actually performing sequential steps in the production process. In an attending capacity, the operators' specific actions are not as regulated by the machine as they might have been with conventional equipment. Thus, AMT operators must exert some self-direction over how, when, and to what they attend. Moreover, if their jobs involve a broad array of responsibilities, they will become self-directive in deciding when they need parts, how to schedule runs, and when and how to perform. They will also undertake minor repairs. This change to operators' jobs directly affects the way in which they must be supervised.

One way that operators' self-direction affects their supervision is that not as much close, continuous task guidance is needed. Supervisors, however, have a difficult time not closely supervising their staff, since this function formerly occupied so much of their time. Thus, a common complaint of workers with the implementation of flexible automation is that they are too closely supervised (Lipstreu and Reed, 1965; Shaiken, 1983). Operators' self-direction also removes some of the supervisor's control and knowledge of the day-to-day "nuts and bolts" of the production process. This loss of control is contrasted with the supervisor's responsibility for a larger part of the production process. Thus, supervisors with flexible automation become more dependent on subordinate staff (Roitman, Liker, and Roskies, 1987). This dependence is manifested by supervisors now having to expect subordinates to make the right decisions, without the supervisor's input, as well as keep the supervisor informed of events that may affect other parts of the process for which the supervisor is responsible. A supervisor with flexible automation then must spend more time encouraging upward communication. Additionally, the supervisor must build up the competence of the staff to make correct decisions about their own tasks as well as about what information needs to be conveyed to others.

Given operators' self-direction, they cannot have their performance judged in the same way as with conventional equipment, and this change also affects supervision of their work. Traditionally, supervisors have measured operator performance by the extent and way they physically intervene in the production process. With flexible automation, however, operator performance depends on a different set of activities. Operators need to know when to take breaks from observations, and when to informally speak with fellow workers, engineers, or maintenance workers. A supervisor who fails to understand the need for these activities may inadvertently force workers to intervene inappropriately and counterproductively in the production process. In fact, this was a complaint lodged by many workers when an agricultural equipment manufacturer first implemented some flexible automation equipment (Shaiken, 1983). Thus, instead of obedience and physical activity, AMT supervisors need to reward workers for innovation, reliability, proper judgment, knowledge, quality, cooperation, and initiative.

Another way that operators' self-direction affects supervisory activities is that old nonfinancial ways of motivating workers are no longer appropriate. Offering certain workers more discretion than others, a tactic often used to motivate workers, may no longer be feasible since all workers may have similar discretionary responsibilities. Rewarding workers with certain production runs or shifts may be prevented as well by centralized computer scheduling. Instead of offering additional discretion, overtime, time off, special attention in scheduling, or special assignments, then, the supervisor will need to use new nonfinancial motivators. These may include employee development and training—"carrots" that supervisors have not traditionally used.

A final change in the way people are supervised is that with flexible automation, fewer people are needed to operate any one piece of equipment. Thus, for production supervisors, while the span of control over the production process increases, the number of workers involved in the process may decrease. For example, Dickson (1981) describes a food processing plant that implemented automated materials-handling equipment with the result that the supervisor-staff ratio dropped from 1:25 to 1:10.

Changes in the Investigation and Solving of Problems

The second job function of supervisors is investigation. All supervisors are confronted daily with hundreds of problems that must be solved. Some of these problems the supervisor can react to without much attention. Other problems demand more supervisory attention, for information must be obtained before some action can be determined. This activity of gathering information is referred to as the investigating function of the supervisor. Often with conventional equipment, when supervisors are confronted with the need to investigate a problem, they can gather the information and determine a course of action with minimal help from others. They can search for the lost wrench, or track down the parts that haven't shown up in their right place, or go find the maintenance worker who fixed the machine the last time, or look at a scrapped part and offer some advice to the machinist about the underlying problem that might have caused the scrappage.

With flexible automation, supervisors are no longer responsible for a single type of machine or an independently functioning area. Instead, they supervise events in the midst of an open system that is both technically and organizationally complex. Scrappage, for example, is unlikely to be explained from a single piece of information that a supervisor working alone is able to obtain. Rather, the supervisor needs to work with the maintenance and engineering crews and/or the operator to determine—with them— whether the scrap problem was attributable to the particular machine (for example, bad programming, bad mechanics, bad electronics), the raw material, or a machine earlier in the process. As another example, if parts are missing from the input queue, the supervisor can no longer simply find the part and order it brought to its proper place. Even if the supervisor could find the missing part, physically putting the part into its proper place could create serious problems for the complete production planning system. Because of the complexity of the integrated AMT system, the supervisor needs to review all of the circumstances surrounding the missing part to understand how a computer-integrated materials-handling system could have routed the part incorrectly (Thompson and Scalpone, 1983). Thus, with AMT, investigating activities must be done from a systems perspective.

Supervisors will also need to adopt a more proactive stance toward problem solving with flexible automation than with conventional equipment. Using the missing part as an example again, with conventional equipment, the supervisor could simply find the part, correct the entry in the planning system, and not spend time figuring out whether the missing part signified a problem with the human or machine system. With flexible automation, however, failing to search for underlying causes runs the risk of a major malfunction occurring later because of the same problem. Thus, with flexible automation, supervisors need to do more than simply solve the apparent problem at hand; they need to delve into it to determine if some problem of greater long-term significance lurks close behind.

Finally, integrated systems involve an increased amount of information that the supervisor needs to assimilate and integrate in any investigation (Butera, 1984). With more information available there is greater likelihood of obtaining more discrepant types of information. An engineer may blame a scrappage rate on faulty machine design and call in the machine vendor. The maintenance worker, however, may insist that the scrappage problem is the result of unpredictable electronic surges that occur when airplanes fly over. Finally, an experienced operator may insist that the raw material input to the machine is of a slightly different density than the supplier normally provides and as a result is out of specification for the machine. Thus, supervisors responsible for flexible automation will find themselves spending more time figuring out how to integrate information, testing conflicting inputs, and checking decisions against multiple sources—in short, acting like information brokers rather than hands-on bosses.

Changes in the Coordination of Activities

The theoretical literature has predicted that the implementation of flexible automation will create an increased need for supervisors to coordinate with others, for example, support staff (Kerr, Hill, and Broedling, 1986). These predictions are thus far borne out by case examples. In at least two series of case studies (Thompson and Scalpone, 1983, and Shaiken, 1983), supervisors responsible for flexible automation spent more time in discussions with engineers, systems people, maintenance workers, and operators after AMT was installed. In another set of case studies (Manufacturing Studies Board, 1986), supervisors spent more time managing interactions between operators and support staff than before AMT. In an organization that switched from an old mill-type baking plant to an automated facility, interdependence between supervisors of different departments increased (Lipstreu and Reed, 1965). Thus, the case examples do support the fact that with flexible automation the coordination function of the supervisor will involve more time and take on more importance. Why is this so?

Some of the reasons increased coordination is necessary have already been discussed: chiefly, the supervisor is generally responsible for a large part of the production process, which makes the involvement of people with different types of expertise essential to achieving proper operation and solving problems. While the supervisor's varied staff may be quite self-directing, they still need to be able to coordinate with others. Yet they frequently lack the skills, time, perspective, and authority to manage the coordination process. Thus, the supervisor needs to facilitate coordination between groups. Supervisors can identify the people who need to be consulted, can cross the language barriers between functions, have the perspective to know what the systems implications of an issue might be, and have the authority to encourage cooperation. Finally, since the staff members' job activities require less scrutiny by the supervisor, the supervisor has the time to take responsibility for effective coordination. This role may include preparing for meetings, building and maintaining a support network of people inside and outside the organization who can be contacted for various types of problems, planning strategies for ensuring that various peoples' agendas are met for different coordination activities, maintaining knowledge and perspective on the system at large, and taking a step back now and then to figure out how to do something differently or why something went wrong. These coordination activities are essential in an integrated factory; if the supervisor doesn't do them, who will?

Changes in Duties Related to Planning and Scheduling

Planning and scheduling refers to preparing and meeting the requirements of production schedules, maintenance schedules, and training schedules. *Scheduling* refers to organizing the production process to meet immediate requirements, while *planning* means establishing longer-term future schedules. Supervisory time spent in scheduling is valuable time spent away from important other functions, such as identifying innovative changes to the organization (Farris, 1973). Therefore, increasing scheduling efficiency to allow more time for planning would seem to be an optimal change. Such a change seems to be achievable with flexible automation. In one case of a small-batch component producer, the CNC machines it implemented had the capability to provide supervisors considerable information about such production aspects as up-to-date, detailed reports on the status of orders and batches of components. The company purchased video-display terminals and software so that the information could be easily accessible to the supervisors on the floor. As a result, the supervisors became more efficient at handling their production scheduling responsibilities (Abbott, 1981). At an agricultural equipment manufacturer, an interactive computer-based labor-reporting system provided supervisors with clearer indications of where the materials were, what people were doing, and what bottlenecks were occurring (Shaiken, 1983). As a result, the system was used to help supervisors predict where bottlenecks were likely to occur and to schedule efficiently to avert them.

Because of this increased efficiency in scheduling, supervisors responsible for flexible automation have often taken on more responsibility for planning (Manufacturing Studies Board, 1986). This was found for the small-batch component case just described (Abbott, 1981). In another case, freight operations at British Rail were computerized, allowing supervisors to spend less time closely supervising the activities of subordinates and more time in the strategic planning for effective freight operations (Dawson and McLoughlin, 1986).

Changes in Staffing and Training Responsibilities

In addition to other responsibilities, supervisors are often responsible for the selection, training, and termination of their staff. There seems to be no general statement that can be made about how the selection function will change with flexible automation. For some companies, supervisors are included in the selection of workers to receive training on the new equipment. In other organizations, supervisors relinquish any responsibility for selection to the work team itself. Thus, the effect on the selection function seems to result primarily from a preference of management and not the new technology. The same conclusion appears appropriate for the supervisor's ability to terminate employees. In unionized plants, this function has traditionally been largely contractual and thus the supervisor's discretion is minimal anyway.

In nonunionized organizations, the supervisor may exert somewhat more control; however, any change to that discretion is unlikely to result from implementing new technology per se.

In contrast to the selection and termination functions, training and development of staff is a supervisory function that undergoes substantial change with flexible automation (Manufacturing Studies Board, 1986). As will be discussed in more detail in Chapter Seven, training of production workers increases in importance with flexible automation. Moreover, training and development become important motivators with flexible automation, since other more traditional motivators are eliminated. Thus, the implementation of flexible automation will increase the supervisor's concern for training.

Supervisors may manifest that increased concern simply by being more cognizant of the benefits of training, and may not complain so much or put roadblocks up every time a worker is sent off for training. Supervisors may be consulted about the content of a training program before it is delivered to the workers, or they may be asked to help prepare the documentation and user manuals for the new equipment. Finally, supervisors may actually provide the training, as was found by Argoff (1983–84). Thus, training clearly increases in importance for the supervisor in an automated factory, and the supervisor's involvement with training can vary dramatically from organization to organization.

Changes in Performance Evaluation

First-line supervisors are responsible for the evaluation of subordinates. Carrying out this function typically involves performance appraisals of subordinates and reminders to subordinates of jobs well done.

As already discussed, the basis for judging performance will change. In addition, however, the time allocated to appraisals may change. The National Academy of Sciences (Manufacturing Studies Board, 1986) reports that a change to supervisory functions observed in several of its cases was an increased involvement of the supervisor in appraising performance of the subordinates. This increased involvement was possible because the supervisor had more time to do it. While the results of only one study are not necessarily indicative of a general trend, it may be safe to say that, in many organizations, the close supervisory direction traditionally provided by supervisors may be replaced by more time spent in performance appraisals.

Summary of Effects of Flexible Automation on Supervisors' Job Functions

The implementation of flexible automation is likely to affect the functions of supervisors in the following ways:

1. The need to monitor and direct precise activities of subordinates is decreased.
2. The sphere of responsibility increases to encompass a greater part of the business.
3. New ways need to be found to motivate and judge worker performance.
4. Complex systems demand investigations that cannot be solely reactive and that cannot be completed by the supervisor alone.
5. The time needed for coordinating efforts among support personnel and other supervisors, as well as integrating information from multiple sources, is increased.
6. Computerized information systems decrease the amount of time needed for scheduling, leaving more time for planning.
7. Training of subordinates is an area of increased concern and involvement.
8. Involvement in performance appraisals is increased for some supervisors.

With these conclusions in mind, it is time to examine how these effects on supervisors' functions alter the job designs, selection, and training needs of supervisors.

Implications for Supervisor's Job Design. The supervisor's job is increasingly dependent on operators, support personnel, and other supervisors. Thus, to effectively coordinate with others, supervisors' jobs need to be structured so that they can initiate and maintain horizontal linkages with others. Formal mechanisms for encouraging these linkages, especially with peers, will need to be developed. These may include monthly meetings of supervisors, after-hours get-togethers, or special-interest brown-bag lunch meetings to discuss production process problems.

An additional change to the supervisor's job with AMT is that many of the traditional tasks, from scheduling to supervision, are performed either by computers, machines, or subordinates. Yet, as indicated at the outset of this chapter, the supervisor's job is an essential one. Thus, the challenge is to replace the traditional tasks with new tasks more directly focused on the organization's needs. When this adjustment is not made, supervisors often feel that their traditional responsibilities have been eroded and frequently express confusion about where their jobs begin and end (Kerr, Hill, and Broedling, 1986; Manz and Sims, 1984; Liker and Thomas, 1987). Moreover, with no guidance on what new tasks to perform, supervisors may engage in activities with which they are familiar, such as directing the production activities of their people. As we have seen, however, such involvement is likely to lead to accusations that supervisors are watching operators too closely. Or the supervisor may not know how to fill in the time and be accused of being useless: "In the words of one manufacturing technician at Ford's transmission plant in Livonia, Michigan, 'The supervisor is just dead weight, a pencil pusher, in my department'" (Buss, 1985).

Thus, keys to redesigning the supervisor's job with flexible automation are (1) identify new tasks that better match the supervisor's abilities and position to organizational needs, (2) clarify supervisors' new role responsibilities, and (3) communicate these responsibilities to the supervisors, their immediate superiors, and their immediate subordinates.

We have already discussed numerous types of new tasks that supervisors could, and should, perform, such as planning instead of fighting scheduling fires. Another is cross-department coordination—establishing and maintaining linkages, running meetings, and essentially serving as the center spoke in the "open systems wheel" of the automation cell.

A third task the supervisor can do is spend more time in employee development and training, possibly even delivering the training themselves. Another, appropriate if cell operators have been structured into teams, is group facilitation, that is, encouraging team problem solving, providing technical support when needed, and helping the team to mature as a viable business group. Team members themselves would find it difficult to be sufficiently objective about the team experience to serve in this capacity; since supervisors know the members, the production process, and the problems they are working on, supervisors may be in the best position to serve in such a role.

Finally, supervisors need to fill the role of catalyst and implementor of change. In a flexible automation factory, the likelihood of technological obsolescence is so great that upgrading of equipment will be an almost continuous process, along with concomitant changes in the human infrastructure. Labor reporting systems may change; pay schedules may switch from all salary to skill-based salary to salary-plus-gainsharing; new training programs will be instituted; teams may be tried out for awhile; experiments with different job rotation schemes may be undertaken; job descriptions may be rewritten; and so on. In the midst of almost continous change, workers need to have a symbol of stability from which they can obtain a sense of security and reliable information. Supervisors have been known to be an important source of information for workers, particularly during periods of job changes (Majchrzak and Cotton, 1986; Leonard-Barton, 1986b; Argote and Goodman, 1986). Thus, having supervisors manage change for their departments and coordinate changes with other departments is a strategy likely to help the change process substantially and also provide workers with the ideal central person to turn to for information and stability.

For supervisors to serve effectively in the capacity of central contact point and catalyst for change, they must become sufficiently involved in change efforts to understand the reasons for them. Moreover, their involvement must help them to accept the rationale for the change option selected, even if they feel that it is not what they might have preferred. Only if supervisors are convinced of the need for the change can they convince subordinates. Involving supervisors in planning for the change effort, preparing the work force for that change, and then implementing the change will yield productive use of the supervisor's time that is no longer needed for other activities.

Several organizations with flexible automation use supervisors in organizational change activities. At a computerized sawmill, supervisors were extensively involved in the change to computerization; they received the vendor training themselves and wrote the training manuals and lesson plans for each of the work stations (Saari, 1985). At Westinghouse's Defense and Electronics Systems Center, supervisors were involved in both the development and delivery of the flexible automation training (Argoff, 1983-84). Westinghouse felt that the involvement of supervisors was so effective that the supervisors will continue to be used in future organizational change efforts. To facilitate their effectiveness, supervisors were trained not only on the technology and training methods but also on the management of change, exploring opportunities for change, overcoming resistance to change, and introducing change. The management of change training teaches supervisors how to plan for both self-initiated change and change imposed by upper management. The training includes defining goals, identifying approaches, considering alternatives, communicating the fact of change and the reasons for it to employees, consulting employees on the best way to accommodate the change, planning for training that may be required, and evaluating the impact of the change once it has occurred.

Implications of Effects for Supervisor Selection and Training. One of the major controversies in the selection and training of supervisors for flexible automation is over the relative importance of technical skills versus human relations skills. Several studies have addressed this point. John Ettlie (1986b), Manz and Sims (1984), and Rothwell, (1985) conducted empirical studies of supervisors and found that social, human relations, and communication skills were the most critical factors common to new supervisory roles with AMT. In contrast, Saari (1985), Blumberg and Gerwin (1985), and Chen and others (1984) have found that technical skills are as important as ever. Finally, Argoff (1983-84) describes Westinghouse's needs analysis for supervisors' jobs with flexible automation. The results of the needs analysis indicated that four basic areas of competence—equally important for all supervisors—were technical, administrative, interpersonal, and approach to job.

It is apparent that the results of these studies are contradictory and thus fail to clearly lead to a conclusion about the relative importance of technical versus human relations skills. The likely "truth" is that neither technical nor human relations skills can be ignored in the selection and training of supervisors with flexible automation. For example, in one study of supervisors, two plants are described, each of which selected supervisors based on different criteria; yet both plants suffered substantial delays in the change effort (Walton and Schlesinger, 1979). The first plant selected supervisors with little experience with the complex technology; the result was that the supervisors were relegated to "go-for" roles since they had little to offer their work groups. In the second plant, supervisors were hired who were technically experienced but with limited human relations skills to help work groups perform on their own; the result was substantial conflict between teams and supervisors which took valuable time away from more productive activity. Thus, a balance of both skills is essential.

To ensure adequate technical and human relations skills, what should AMT supervisors be taught? Supervisors should receive as much technical training about the new technology as their workers. This training should include such skill as fault finding and repairing, inputting data, adjusting computer programs, correcting errors, and problem solving (Rothwell, 1985). By gaining this knowledge, supervisors are likely to know at least as much as the workers do. Moreover, if, in addition to this basic technical training, supervisors receive an overall introduction to other systems being installed (including, for example, the basic functions the equipment serves and how the machines interrelate), supervisors will know a great deal more than their workers; they will know what questions to ask of whom about the system when machinery breaks down. Thus, Cincinnati-Milacron, for example, has discussed offering special training to supervisors that goes beyond operator skills to provide an overview of planning, programming, and maintenance (Argoff, 1983–84).

In addition to technical training, supervisors must be taught a range of human relations skills, from motivating workers so that they remain attentive to machine operations, to coordinating meetings. The following list summarizes many of the human relations skills that supervisors appear to need in flexible factories:

- giving recognition
- motivating for poor performance
- team building
- resolving conflict
- problem solving for self and for groups
- running meetings
- facilitating groups
- spanning boundaries between functions and departments
- communicating effectively, both orally and in writing

In order to learn these skills, however, supervisors must be motivated; unfortunately, resistance to change may hamper such motivation. At the end of this chapter, resistance to change of supervisors and options for dealing with it are discussed.

Managers and Flexible Automation

Managers' job functions obviously differ from those of supervisors. In companies with conventional equipment, managers spend much of their time setting objectives, allocating resources, performing liaison activites, and being entrepreneurs (Mintzberg, 1973). Some observers have claimed that because managers' job functions do not directly involve production technologies, changes in production technologies are not likely to affect their jobs (see, for example, Abbott, 1981). The evidence to date, however, suggests that the implementation of flexible automation does seem to affect higher-level managers. As one example: "The machine breakdowns [created by the new AMT] are taking a toll on human beings, too. Early this year Hamtramck's plant manager, Earl Harper, took what GM terms an indefinite 'medical leave' for ailments that were 'aggravated' by the pressure of the job. Mr. Harper, 60, says he had expected the plant to reach normal production much faster than it has, and now he wants to 'get away and relax.' He says he is retiring" (Nag, 1986, p. 27).

It appears that the implementation of flexible automation will not only cause stress to higher-level managers but it will cost some of them their jobs. At one company, the implementation of flexible automation created a new modular structure of $10 million minibusinesses for which first-line supervisors were now responsible (Manufacturing Studies Board, 1986). "These supervisors significantly displace the responsibility and authority of the next level of management, which becomes precariously redundant unless augmented with higher responsibilities" (p. 32). Thus, despite the predictions of some observers, flexible automation does appear to affect the roles of higher-level management.

Effects of Flexible Automation on Managerial Functions. Assuming, for the moment at least, that most organizations will not eliminate higher-level managers simply because flexible automation has been installed, it becomes important to understand the ways that flexible automation can change the job functions of managers.

If the flexible automation is linked with an information system, as most are, the new technology will help to free the manager from routine, programmable decisions such as production scheduling, inventory and shipment scheduling, and capital budgeting (found in studies reviewed by Anshen, 1962, and Tomeski and Lazarus, 1975). This freed-up time could then be more productively used in finding problems, assigning priorities to these problems, selecting targets for performance achievement, and encouraging innovation. Managers could also spend this time looking at the operation and introducing efficiency changes, solving personnel problems, or identifying ways to enhance the interrelationships with other parts of the business.

Another change to managers' jobs is that the manner in which they established objectives before will no longer be appropriate. Traditionally, managers focus departmental objectives on the cost-efficiency of the production system (Skinner, 1974, 1986). With AMT, cost-efficiency is no longer the sole or best criterion on which to judge performance. Instead, objectives must focus on such other aspects of the business as customer response time, product quality, product change flexibility, volume change flexibility, and so on. For managers to establish realistic objectives about these aspects of the business, they will need to understand how parts of the process affect these objectives. Thus, managers will need to spend more time learning about production and business problems, understanding how the process works, and monitoring progress of the business toward multiple goals. In so doing, managers of flexible factories will probably find themselves spending more time working with other functions in the company. Otherwise, realistic objectives may not be met.

Finally, since there is increased importance of supervisory training, as discussed in the previous section, managers will need to spend more time distinguishing training needs of supervisors from motivational or organizational problems (Rothwell, 1985). This need will translate into managers striving to better understand their supervisors. For example, if a supervisor seems to be exhibiting substantial hostility toward a new piece of equipment, the source of the hostility needs to be identified. Is the problem attributable to an organizational source—for example, did no one ask his opinion on the new equipment? Is it due to a motivational problem—for example, is he afraid that the new equipment will further erode his authority over the production process? Or is it a training problem—for example, is he afraid that the technology is so complex that he won't be able to understand it? At Westinghouse's Defense and Electronics Center, a problem developed when a supervisor was asked to train his workers in the new AMT (Argoff, 1983-84). The supervisor was overly domineering in the classroom and thus failed to be an effective teacher. At first the problem was thought to be motivational, that is, the supervisor did not want to be doing the training. However, after some discussion, it turned out that the problem was one of inadequate training: The supervisor felt incapable of leading a class discussion. After the problem was identified, the supervisor was sent to obtain more training about how to lead classroom discussions and became an effective teacher and ardent supporter of AMT.

In conclusion, the ways managers' functions change as a result of implementing flexible automation indicate that although higher-level managers will be affected by the new technology, their jobs will not change as much as the jobs of supervisors. Nevertheless, some changes will occur. These changes involve the need to manage a complex integrated business system with multiple goals, an increased importance at skillfully managing supervisors, and time freed from routine decision making.

Implications for Managers' Job Design, Selection, and Skills. The changes in the design of managers' jobs as a result of the implementation of flexible automation are less dramatic than the changes in supervisors' job designs. The managers continue to be responsible for objective setting, allocating resources, being entrepreneurs, and performing liaison activities. While there is some shifting of priorities among these activities (for example, more time is available for entrepreneurship as routine decisions are made elsewhere), all the functions are as important as before. Changes are primarily in the ways the different activities are accomplished, and this fact affects selection and training more than it does job design.

For managers to work effectively in flexible factories, three types of new knowledge are needed: technical system knowledge, ability to anticipate rather than simply react, and knowledge of managing in an open system. The need for managers to have technical system knowledge tends to be surprisingly overlooked in organizations (Love and Walker, 1986). Apparently, many automation project teams assume that managers want to know as little as possible about the technology, and thus they are informed of only necessary details (such as what products it can produce, how quickly it can be made to operate, and which competitors already have the equipment). And executives do not tend to ask for more information about the technology itself: "Most executives are somewhat bashful about saying they don't understand technology," says Lewis Campbell, the manufacturing manager at the Chevrolet Pontiac-Canada Group of GM. "So when the engineer out on the floor says 'well, this is a PL3,' you say, 'uh-huh' without really understanding what the engineer is talking about" (Buss, 1985, p. 1). This lack of knowledge may yield poor management commitment to the project, inadequate support needed for interdepartmental coordination and information sharing, and incorrect decisions about strategic use of the equipment (Hyer, 1984). Thus, a primary training need for managers in flexible factories is education about the technology: its technical capabilities and how it works. Obviously managers do not need to learn the same things that the operator learns, but giving managers training similar to that of the supervisors (for example, teaching them how the systems interrelate) will go a long way toward providing them more information than they now have.

In addition to technical knowledge of the system, managers in flexible factories need to be educated about how to adopt an anticipatory style of management. In Dickson's (1981) study of a food processing plant, the implementation of advanced technology made it necessary for managers to receive training in the kind of long-term planning thought to be best associated with automated technology. Thus, courses on long-range planning, such as forecasting, action planning, testing assumptions, and implementation, were developed.

Finally, managers in flexible factories need to learn how to manage in a system that is much more integrated than before. This means that managers must be more cognizant of the impact of their decisions on other functional areas, as well as able to observe events and predict the long-range impact on their area. For this type of management, skills are needed in synthesizing information from multiple and conflicting sources; keeping substantial amounts of information at the forefront of their attention; resolving conflict; addressing and leading meetings; knowing who to go to for various types of information; managing teams rather than managing independent individuals; and maintaining communication among peers and staff so that managers are kept aware of interdependencies in the system (Skinner, 1978).

How does one train for a systems approach to management? Clearly it is not easy. Managers find it difficult enough to fight fires in their own departments, let alone anticipate and monitor interactions between others' departments and their own. Moreover, expecting managers to also be able to predict how current difficulties will affect future objectives of the department and to ensure that other departments' objectives are not in conflict represents another level of complexity. Most managers are not familiar with thinking in such complex terms and thus lack the experience to know when their instincts are correct about information, sources, events, and predictions.

How to teach a systems approach is not a primary focus of this book; however, one method that has been effectively used to train managers in systems thinking is worth brief mention. This is the use of systems-oriented simulations (Lansley, 1982). In these simulations the managers, usually in their daily roles as members of the company's management team, play a management game. The game will usually be realistic for the company and involve some organizational change. As the game is played out, with the managers in the roles they normally occupy, reverberations of their actions throughout the company become painfully clear. After several rounds of the game and time to discuss and acknowledge the consequences of failing to think in a systems context, the game can be played again to give the participants the opportunity to practice their newfound knowledge. An example of such a simulation specifically created for manufacturing plants implementing flexible automation is described in more detail in Exhibit 5-1. This simulation has been used successfully in organizations because, in the words of one company president who played the game, "it establishes convincingly that implementing new technology requires active participation and communication across organizational and functional boundaries."

Managerial and Supervisory Resistance to Change

Harley-Davidson's strategy to maintain economic viability combined Japanese robotics and participative management with a "macho" American style. In introducing these changes, a spokesman for the company reported that the problem with the implementation was not the shopfloor but management acceptance. Barbara Fossum (1985), in a study of twelve companies implementing CIM, asked managers from each company to list nontechnical barriers to CIM. She found that the barriers most commonly mentioned were manifestations of managerial resistance to change: production managers' attitudes ("if it's not broke, don't fix it"), fear of the unknown, managerial caution, and a managerial preference for traditional rather than systems thinking. Managers at an agricultur-

Exhibit 5-1. The Advanced Manufacturing Technology Implementation Game (ADVANTIG).

How is ADVANTIG played?

While playing ADVANTIG, a team from a manufacturing firm attempts to take F.L.I. Casting, Inc. through a complete manufacturing transformation from a low-technology profile to a high-technology profile. Decisions regarding F.L.I. strategy, technology it will employ, and implementation tactics it will use are the heart of the exercise.

Key management personnel from different departments of a company adopt roles such as CEO; Production Manager; Machine Operator; and Heads of Engineering, Marketing, and Finance for F.L.I. Casting, Inc. Their challenge is to select AMT and use it profitably while meeting customer obligations and securing new business.

The simulation is conducted around four main areas or departments—production, management, engineering systems, and AMT systems vendor. Management staff set F.L.I. strategy, bid on contracts, and track F.L.I. progress by keeping records such as contract forms, balance sheets, and material and equipment requisitions. Engineering staff investigate, purchase and deploy new technology with assistance from the AMT systems vendor. On the production floor, new technology is implemented and debugged while machine operators produce parts to meet customer contracts.

ADVANTIG is very realistic. It is not a computer game and it encourages a high level of participation on the part of all players. The simulation uses specially designed machines, work stations, and procedures to simulate a real production circuit.

Following the simulation there is a debriefing that lasts several hours. Each debriefing is tailored by the Industrial Technology Institute to address the participating company's needs and goals.

ADVANTIG requires only one large room to run and from 8-21 participants. Some prior knowledge of CAD, CNC, robotics, various assembly technologies, and MRP is assumed. The duration of the simulation game is 4-5 hours, and the debriefing sessions last 2-4 hours.

Who developed ADVANTIG?

ADVANTIG was developed by the Industrial Technology Institute, a not-for-profit R&D and consulting organization headquartered in Ann Arbor, Michigan. The Institute's primary mission is to foster the development, dissemination and implementation of advanced manufacturing technologies.

Source: Industrial Technology Institute brochure on AMT, 1986.

al equipment manufacturing plant were asked to identify what they thought were the important constraints that have affected the introduction and deployment of technology at the company (Shaiken, 1983). One of the constraints identified was managerial resistance to change. Other cases similarly reporting managerial resistance abound (Boddy and Buchanan, 1985; Foulkes and Hirsch, 1984). Clearly, not all managers accept this new technology with open arms; there is some resistance.

What are the sources of this resistance? One, already mentioned, is the lack of role clarity for supervisors that tends to accompany the implementation of new technology. Management fails to think through supervisors' roles clearly enough; this ambiguity leaves the supervisors wondering whether they will have jobs once the technology is in place and, if so, what those jobs will be like. This role ambiguity also leads to the fear that their status will be eroded as production workers accept some of the supervisors' responsibilities. Along with these concerns is the need to learn new technical and nontechnical skills. Abbott (1981) describes the impact of these concerns on supervisors' adjustment when a plant that manufactured forklift trucks implemented flexible automation: "The major problem of adjustment to the change had been among production supervisors. The difficulties for these people during the change period had apparently been considerable. In general, they had worked for many years with the old mechanical system, and considerable education and effort was required to equip them with the skills to supervise work on the new system. In addition, the desire of supervisors to differentiate themselves from the shopfloor and to identify with staff in status terms had presented them with problems of adjustment" (p. 53).

A third source of resistance stems from the possible loss of power. Managers do not like to lose power that they have fought hard to gain. Many managers measure their power by their authority to make decisions. If subordinates are allowed to make decisions or if a computer makes them, the manager experiences a loss of power. "At Boeing Aerospace (Seattle), for example, installation of a flexible manufacturing system to make parts for air-launched cruise missiles was fought by 'middle managers afraid of relinquishing authority' recalls principal research engineer Richard Martell" (Brody, 1985, p. 41).

Managers and supervisors also display resistance because it is so difficult to remain current with the new technology, and they often find themselves less knowledgeable than those around them. Dickson (1981) coined the term *hierarchical estrangement* for this phenomenon. The managers and supervisors who worked their way up from the shopfloor must increasingly deal with complex technology and with knowledgeable yet younger superiors. In the push for new technology, resistance is created, since the skills that the more experienced managers and supervisors bring to bear on the problem often tend to be ignored.

This problem of managerial resistance is serious. Unless managers at all levels in the organization are willing to critically assess new technology and work together to implement it, the new technology will fail completely, create many more problems than necessary, or never be utilized to its complete capacity.

Overcoming Management Resistance. What can be done about management resistance? Four actions need to be taken: education, involvement, information sharing, and role clarification.

Education is a counterforce to managerial resistance. In the example provided earlier of the GM corporate manufacturing manager confiding that most executives know little about new technology, the manager went on to say: "And then when the project comes forward to be approved, the tendency is not to approve it, more out of a lack of understanding than a disagreement with the project concept" (Buss, 1985). Moreover, people fear the unknown; the more managers know, the more likely they are not only to become enthusiastic about the project but to offer advice on how they can help. Thus, informal and formal efforts to educate managers and supervisors about the technology are needed.

The dictum that people accept change when they can participate in the change applies to managers as well. This involvement can take a variety of different forms. Involving supervisors in training development, as the Westinghouse Defense and Electronics Center has done, is one approach. Another approach is to teach higher-level managers enough about alternative projects so they are able to identify project priorities rather than simply make "go–no go" decisions. A third approach is to involve managers and supervisors in the implementation process of communicating the purpose of the change to the workers. Ken Knight (1985) of Westinghouse's Manufacturing Systems and Technology Center describes a case where, prior to implementation of a robot, he solicited the aid of the supervisors to help him develop a presentation for the workers. Supervisors prepared a list of questions that workers might ask of them. The questions included: Why a robot for our business? What labor grade will operate the system? How was the labor grade determined? Who will write programs for operation? How will we maintain configuration control? Who will perform system maintenance? How will the process be supported? When will we begin operation? What will the robot be expected to produce? What is the integration plan? Then, in conjunction with the supervisors, a sound-and-slide presentation covering these questions was developed. The slide presentation was then actually delivered by the manufacturing manager to the workers with supervisors present. Thus, both supervisors and managers became involved in the process and had the opportunity to work through their concerns about the system before facing the workers.

A third way to reduce managerial resistance is through information sharing. Plans for new technology change almost daily as analysis continues and thinking crystallizes. Keeping managers informed of this process gives them some appreciation of the many options that were considered in making any one decision and why alternatives were rejected. A weekly memo that summarizes the week's deliberations might be one method for sharing information.

Finally, as discussed earlier, managers, particularly at the supervisory level, resist the implementation of new technology because it is unclear how it will affect their jobs. Management needs to respond to this kind of resistance and anxiety by defining future roles. Either this can be done for the supervisors, or the supervisors can become involved in the process of redefining their own roles. In any case, the action needs to be taken early, before the lack of clarity creates an ingrained resistance that is difficult to change.

In conclusion, the resistance that many managers and supervisors demonstrate toward the implementation of new technology usually stems from sources that can be addressed: fear of the unknown, fear of technological obsolescence, loss of power, need to learn new skills, and so on. However, it should be remembered that not all resistance is necessarily negative. Managers may resist because they are convinced that bringing in new technology is a wrong decision for the company. If these managers cannot be convinced otherwise and they articulate a viable argument, it may be time to sit down and listen to them.

6

Specifying
New Job Skills
and Selection Criteria

This chapter focuses on both the new skills needed by nonsupervisory AMT personnel and the changes to the selection process created by AMT. Skill changes are discussed for the job classifications identified in Chapters Three and Four. For AMT operators, minimal changes in skill levels include decreased need for manual dexterity, increased perceptual and conceptual abilities, increased problem diagnosis skills, and increased human relations skills; these skill changes are even necessary for the "deskilled" machine tender. AMT maintenance personnel will need to further develop an interdisciplinary knowledge of technical systems and specific equipment as well as an ability to communicate. Since most companies cannot upgrade the abilities of the maintenance staff quickly enough to meet these basic skill requirements, plants have utilized a number of methods to compensate for skill inadequacies, which are described in this chapter. Engineering professionals will need to acquire a greater breadth of information about manufacturing system design, problem solving, and communication. For NC parts programmers, machining knowledge, math, three-dimensional visualization, and communication are needed skills. For the other job classifications (for example, quality control personnel), skills needed vary so much with the job design that minimal skill requirements cannot be specified.

In the selection of AMT workers who have these skills, three questions are often asked. In response to the first question—How many AMT workers are needed—management is admonished not to use direct labor replacement ratios; other factors such as production capability should have greater impact on the numbers decision. The second

130

question—Where do the applicants come from?—is addressed with a discussion on effectively defining the recruiting pool. Encouraging the entire existing work force to be potential applicants for AMT jobs is highly recommended. The final question—What criteria should be used for selection—is addressed by first criticizing the use of seniority and creaming to select AMT personnel. Alternatives successfully used today in flexible automated factories are described.

Skill Changes with Flexible Automation

There are many ways to categorize skill requirements of jobs. Dawes and Lofquist (1984) describe skill requirements as consisting of three content areas and three process areas. Their three content areas are *symbolic* (for example, verbal fluency, spatial reasoning), *interpersonal* (for example, group dynamics, communicating), and *sensorimotor* (for example, sensory judgment, mechanical reasoning) skills. The three process areas are the ability to perceive inputs, process those inputs, and achieve outputs according to specifications. Kenneth Spenner (1983) suggests a far simpler categorization: skill as autonomy-control (for example, responsibility, decision making) and skill as substantive complexity (for example, physical effort, mental effort, manipulative dexterity, variety of tasks). The *Dictionary of Occupational Titles* (U.S. Department of Labor, 1977) describes skill categories by the job's relationship to data, people, and things. Bright (1958) describes twelve job skills including physical effort, education, general skill experience, mental effort, and responsibility. Hazlehurst, Bradbury, and Corlett (1969) distinguished four job skills—motor, perceptual, conceptual, and discretionary skills—that could change with the installation of CNC machines. One could choose any of these skill classifications to summarize the data on skill changes with flexible automation. However, given the extent of the data thus far, a complex skill classification scheme, like Dawes and Lofquist's or the *Dictionary's* does not appear warranted; instead a version of Hazlehurst's is used here.

Adapting Hazlehurst's system yields five types of skills which are most likely to be affected by AMT: perceptual, conceptual, manual dexterity, discretionary, and human relations. Perceptual skills include vigilance, concentration, attention, and judging abilities. Conceptual skills include interpretation, abstraction, comprehension of complexity, and inference as well as knowledge of the subject matter. Manual dexterity refers to motor abilities used in material handling, picking, and placing. Discretionary skills include autonomy and individual problem-solving abilities. Finally, human relations skills include communication, team problem solving, and coordination abilities. Using these five categories, in the sections that follow I review the research on how AMT affects skills required for the positions of operator, maintenance worker, engineer, systems analyst, and programmer.

Operators. Chapter Three described different job designs that can be considered for AMT operators. The designs ranged from a job rotation strategy, in which operators responsible only for attending machines rotate among different machines, to general technical jobs, in which self-managed work groups have complete responsibility for production. Clearly, the particular job design selected will determine the skills needed. Nevertheless, there is a common core of basic skills that appears to be needed for AMT operators' jobs. In addition to the obvious technical machine operator skills, these basic skills are in the areas of perceptual and conceptual skills, problem diagnosis, and human relations.

One of the best-documented skill shifts with AMT is a reduced need for manual dexterity skills and an increased need for *perceptual and conceptual skills* (Riche, 1982; U.S. Department of Labor, 1982). This shift is attributed to the reduced need to have operators directly intervene in the machine process and, instead, carefully watch the process to identify actual and potential problems. Perceptual and conceptual skills that have been documented in AMT studies include vigilance, machine monitoring, mental alertness, interpretation of symbolic information from drawings, planning instructions, performing calculations, and interpreting electrical/electronic measuring devices (Hazlehurst, Bradbury, and Corlett, 1969; Chen and others, 1984; Majchrzak and Cotton, 1985; Hull and Lovett, 1985).

The second common core of basic skills needed by operators of AMT is *problem diagnostic skills*. As described in Chapter Three, operators need to be effective diagnosticians if the complex AMT equipment is to be quickly repaired so that downtime can be avoided. Even when operators are designated as "deskilled" machine tenders, their relevant knowledge of the peculiarities of the machine and production process may make the difference between a maintenance man fixing an AMT efficiently or floundering for days. Additionally, operators will need diagnostic skills in order to know what parts of their knowledge are relevant to the repairer (Thompson and Scalpone, 1983).

Given the importance of diagnostic skills for any operator of AMT—no matter what the job design—an understanding of what those skills involve is necessary. Hirschhorn (1984) has studied the diagnostic skill needs of operators of highly integrated production systems and concludes that effective diagnosis demands three types of knowledge: (1) a sufficient feel for the production process to be aware of anomalies that might otherwise go unnoticed, (2) heuristic knowledge, which is knowledge of how the equipment is supposed to operate and react, and (3) theoretical knowledge, which is knowledge of the theory of the production process so the operator can interpret information that is incongruent with the heuristic knowledge. Hirschhorn believes that an operator's ability to diagnose is dependent on the ability to integrate these three types of knowledge and apply them to every possible circumstance encountered. Having only one type of knowledge or applying the knowledge to only certain circumstances will lead to the type of fault misdiagnosis found at Three Mile Island. For example, having a sufficient feel for the prodution process alone, the first type of knowledge, may make the operator aware of certain inputs but won't give him or her the skills to know how to interpret the information. Having heuristic knowledge alone would inhibit diagnosis in unexpected situations. Finally, theoretical knowledge alone will be useless, since machine peculiarities suggest that few machines operate according to theory all the time. Thus, as flexible automation is implemented, diagnostic skills of operators become more complex and interactive.

The third common core of basic skills needed by operators of AMT is *human relations skills*. For example, in a survey of skills needed with AMT, the installation of a robot was most closely related to skills in human relations (Majchrzak, 1986a). One such human relations skill is an increased ability to communicate with others about possible equipment problems (Thompson and Scalpone, 1983). An effective communicator must be able to not only enunciate clearly but also conceptualize abstract notions in a way that others can understand. Also, an effective communicator must be able to confront conflict when it arises if problems associated with defensiveness and self-esteem are to be overcome in the information exchange. In addition to effective communication skills, flexible automation operators must be able to feel comfortable working with others. As noted in Chapter Three, flexible automation demands increased coordination of all parties involved. To be an effective "team player," the individual must be able to subordinate personal goals to group goals and adjust personal problem solving styles to those of others. For example, an operator explaining events preceding an equipment breakdown to a maintenance person may find that different maintenance people prefer to be told the operator's information in different ways. One person may prefer to be told everything at once. Another person may prefer to have the operator only respond to questions as the repairer needs the answers. To coordinate with others the operator needs to be able to adjust to both styles, even if neither one is the operator's preferred style.

In addition to the common core of basic skills, additional skills may be needed as the tasks of operators broaden. For example, the Center for Occupational Research and Development has examined the skill requirements of general technicians—workers who are responsible not only for equipment operation but for installing, setting up, troubleshooting, repairing and replacing parts, modifying, and testing of AMT (Hull and Lovett, 1985). Based on their review, the center determined that such technicians need to have the skills to handle more than one functional aspect of the new AMT systems—for example, electrical, hydraulic, and pneumatic operations. "In addition, they need to be familiar with programming, computers, microprocessors, programmable controllers, grippers, vision systems, and many more. A technician must know how sensors, solenoids, relays, power supplies, dc motors, servosystems, pumps, valves, and safety devices operate individually and, when assembled, how they contribute to system operation" (p. 42). Thus, the broadened job of a technician of flexible automation systems necessitates skills in an array of disciplines: electrical, mechanical, hydraulics, thermal, optical, and microcomputers.

In addition to knowledge of different disciplines, other skills necessary for AMT technician jobs include knowledge of basic math, physics, and machine shop practices, as well as a mechanical inclination and an aptitude for concentration and precision (U.S. Department of Labor, 1980). For the AMT operator with a job defined much more broadly than simply machine tending, then, many skills are needed above and beyond the core of basic skills. This range of skills is summarized in Table 6-1.

Maintenance Personnel. Flexible automation poses major problems to the maintenance worker. Equipment that is complex to understand and fix, that is very expensive, and that is highly integrated with other equipment makes the maintenance job a challenge in flexible automated factories. These challenges create the need for a common core of basic skills for AMT maintenance workers ("Why Technical Training . . . ," 1982; Saari, 1985; Bright, 1958; Chauvin, 1981; Thompson and Scalpone, 1983). These skills include both technical and human relations skills. Technical skills include the ability to rapidly learn technical features of new equipment; problem solving and logical thinking; knowledge of mechanical, electronic, electrical, and hydraulic systems; and basic math and science. Human relations skills include the ability to communicate well, in addition to a willingness to take risks with new equipment, as well as an ability to know when to take them. This last human relations skill is necessary because a maintenance worker is constantly required to make judgment calls on whether some repair will or will not work and what the consequences might be. Skill in knowing when and how to make these calls and the ability to effectively communicate the reasons for them to others are essential.

Although these skills are the basic skills needed for AMT maintenance workers, the existing single-circuitry skills of our maintenance work force today and the rapidly changing nature of the technology mean that these basic skills cannot often be achieved

Table 6-1. New Skills for Flexible Automation Operators.

Area	Skills
Applied math and science	Algebra/trigonometry Analytic geometry
Communications	Technical communications Computer basics
Socioeconomic	Economics Industrial relations
Technical core	Electricity/electronics Graphics Properties of materials Mechanical devices Manufacturing processes Electronic devices Heating and cooling Fluid power Instrumentation and control Computer applications Industrial electrical power and equipment
Specialty	Manufacturing tools, fixtures, and measurements CAD/CAM system hardware and functions CNC programming Fundamentals of robotics Automated integrated manufacturing systems

Source: Hull and Lovett, 1985, p. 50.

in factories. A maintenance worker expert in mechanical systems is often unable to quickly gain the experience in electronics necessary to adequately service a new AMT. If the new AMT was built by a vendor with which the maintenance worker has no experience, the worker is at an additional disadvantage because of the lack of design compatibility among vendors.

In recognizing the infeasibility of having each maintenance worker achieve these basic skills, many plants have scaled back on the skill demands of individual workers as long as all the basic skills are covered by the maintenance work force as a whole. Arrangements to allow this to happen may include allowing maintenance workers to specialize by equipment or vendors, corrective versus preventive maintenance, or start-up versus operational maintenance problems. Maintenance personnel specializing by equipment would be responsible for only certain types of AMTs and thus only machine-specific skills. For example, the NC repairer needs to have skills in blueprint reading, mechanical components, computer programming, and drafting, in addition to basic math, science, hydraulics and pneumatics, repair and problem solving. For repairers of robots, on the other hand, drafting would be less necessary. For repairers of machining cells using group technology, an understanding of the parts families and their relationships to product and part design would be a necessary additional skill.

For maintenance personnel specializing in corrective maintenance, skills in effectively diagnosing causes of existing symptoms and knowledge of heuristics are needed; for a preventive specialty, skills are needed in inventing potential symptoms and generating creative conceptions of how different equipment features may interact to produce problems in the future. Finally, for maintenance personnel to specialize in start-up problems, knowledge of the entire technical system being installed and experience with starting up other automated systems is needed; for specialists of operational problems only, less broad knowledge and experience will suffice.

In conclusion, while certain basic skills for AMT maintenance workers can be identified, having each worker achieve those skills appears to be difficult. Thus, ways to scale back the skill needs of individual maintenance personnel have been instituted in many plants today. However, while this reduced set of skills will alleviate the problem in the short run, it is doubtful that a flexible automated factory can remain viable without a fully functional, cross-disciplinary team of maintenance personnel.

Engineering Professionals. One of the major skill changes engineers will experience with flexible automation is the need for a greater breadth of knowledge in the design of information and manufacturing systems (Clayton, 1982). This knowledge will be required as they work with computer-integrated systems, since such systems demand an understanding not only of a particular piece of equipment but how the equipment fits into the entire production and information system as well. For this, they need to understand control theory, information theory, and concepts basic to CIM, such as interfacing and software development. Moreover, in order to have their knowledge remain current in a technologically dynamic area, they must be able to have the skills to quickly learn new technical developments and integrate the latest ideas with current applications.

In addition to specific systems-oriented knowledge, engineers in factories of the future will be coordinating with a greater number of people—from the machine operator to the manager of the automation cells. Thus, such professionals will need exceptional human relations skills, such as communicating and coordinating. Additionally, as they work in teams to solve more and more complex problems, the professionals will need to have learned how to engage in effective problem solving as a member of a group rather than as solo individuals. Problem solving in groups is a very different skill than solving problems alone. The need for these "nontechnical" skills cannot be overemphasized. Graham and Rosenthal (1985) found, for example, that a common problem with project teams in FMS factories was that the internal skill base of the team was too closely tied to the hardware of the manufacturing technology rather than the human relations or software skills needed.

Programming. Of all the programming occupations, NC programming will register the greatest skill changes. It is the programming occupation closest to manufacturing and so varies the most with updates in CNC machine tools.

An effective NC part programmer must have some knowledge of cutting and tooling principles. Without this knowledge, the programmer is likely to write programs that fail to optimize the machine tool or the parts being machined. In addition, some observers have recommended that cutting and tooling knowledge is not sufficient for effective part programming; the programmer also needs to have a "machine sense." Such a sense would help the programmer to write programs that reflect the realities of the shopfloor as opposed to the theoretical schedules and tolerances that are supposed to exist.

In addition to machining skills, NC part programming demands skills in mathematics, visualizing in three dimensions, and reading engineering drawings (Belitsky, 1978; U.S. Department of Labor, 1982). While mathematics and blueprint reading are skills found in most good machinists who might be selected for NC part programming jobs, even machinists (let alone traditionally trained computer programmers) often do not need to visualize three dimensions, since they can work directly with the machine in three dimensions. NC part programmers, on the other hand, must have the visualization capability, since they write two-dimensional documents that essentially do three-dimensional work.

NC part programmers also need such human relations skills as coordination and communication because of the extent to which they must depend on operators to run and often prove the programs. Thus, the programs of someone who engenders substantial hostility among operators may not be adequately proved during the initial production runs. Such programs may lead to shorter tool lives, poor-quality cuts, and serious machine damage over time— outcomes that fall far short of program optimization. Therefore, the programmer needs to have the skills to appreciate the involvement of operators and to communicate with them.

Other Occupations. Four other occupations were discussed in Chapter Four as likely to be affected by flexible automation: quality control, production control, accounting, and marketing. The research to date has been inconclusive as to the types of changes AMT is likely to effect on job designs for these four occupations. For quality inspection, job effects ranged from complete elimination to increased job responsibilities. For accounting, an increased awareness of alternative financial and nonfinancial accounting methods was indicated, although few companies had used their accountants to develop new methods. For marketing, major changes in the type of products sold, the way they are sold, and the involvement of marketing in manufacturing decisions were predicted; however, few actual changes in marketing jobs could be documented. Production control is another area in which needed changes can be described but few have as yet been manifested in the workplace.

Given the substantial variety of effects AMT can have on job designs for these occupations, it is understandably difficult to formulate conclusions about skill changes likely to occur. For example, Ayres and Miller (1983) suggest that, since the inspector in an automated factory must inspect for higher standards than in conventional factories, inspection will involve an increased perceptual ability to verify dimensions as well as a greater reasoning ability. However, the job of inspector may not exist at all in an automated factory, and if there is such an occupation, the inspector may be greatly assisted by electronic devices. An inspector in such a job may not need increased perceptual and reasoning abilities, but rather a knowledge of electronics. This is the case in a GM-Detroit assembly plant where inspectors, called electrical technicians, use a computer to test interior electrical and electronic hookups, such as those in the instrument panels of front-wheel-drive luxury cars. The technician position involves skill requirements in electronics including a knowledge of trigonometry and solid-state circuitry.

Changes to skills in accounting may vary as greatly as those in inspection. If company accountants are expected to derive new accounting formulas to take advantage of the flexible factory, the kinds of new skills they will need will include an ability to communicate with others to obtain input in developing the formulas, creativity as new solutions are suggested for the many problems attributed to the old formulas, knowledge of the manufacturing process so that suggested formulas will have utility on the shopfloor as well as in the executive suite, and current knowledge of model development and optimization, including recent software packages that may be helpful. However, if organizations do not desire to develop new accounting formulas, the skills of accountants will not change with the implementation of new technology.

As with accounting, changes to marketing skills will vary. In an organization that integrates marketing and manufacturing, the skill changes to marketing will be quite substantial. These changes will include the acquisition of a general knowledge of the manufacturing process, as well as specific knowledge of the capabilities of specific flexible automation equipment. In addition, as marketing personnel work more closely with technically oriented engineers and shopfloor operators, the human relations skills of communication, coordination, and team problem solving increase in importance. Rather than integrate marketing into AMT implementation efforts, many firms have treated flexible automation as primarily a shopfloor phenomenon. In these cases, marketing skills are hardly affected, if at all.

Conclusion of Skill Changes

Table 6-2 presents a summary of the skill changes likely to occur with flexible automation for each of the major occupations discussed in this book. This table suggests that while some of the changes will depend on the particular job designs adopted with flexible automation, there are certain changes that can be expected, regardless of the job designs chosen. For machine operators' jobs, skill requirements will increase in perceptual, conceptual, and human relations areas and decrease in manual dexterity. For maintenance jobs, requirements will increase for conceptual, discretionary, and human relations skills. Technical professional staff will experience demands for increased conceptual and human relations skills. And NC parts programmer jobs will require increased perceptual, conceptual, and human relations skills. Thus flexible automation will have an effect on many skills required for shopfloor occupations involved with the new equipment; some of these changes will occur regardless of the specific job design selected.

In addition to occupation-specific changes brought about by the implementation of flexible automation, general statements can be made about the types of skills likely to be needed by all shopfloor and technical staff involved in flexible automation. A survey of 150 plants with flexible automation identified certain skills that were needed to help the plant work force in general adapt to the new technology (Majchrzak, 1986b). The results, listed in Table 6-3, indicate that the skills perceived as most likely to be helpful were new safety knowledge, knowledge of the specific machine, and general knowledge of technological advances. In addition though, over two-thirds of the plants indicated that other skills were required. These included maintenance and troubleshooting, and computer programming. Finally, *all* of the skills queried were thought to be important by a sizable proportion of the survey respondents; even the least popular skill, basic physical science (a

Table 6-2. Summary of Skill Changes with Flexible Automation for Different Occupations.

Occupations	Skills				
	Perceptual	*Conceptual*	*Manual Dexterity*	*Discretionary*	*Human Relations*
Operator	Increased need for observation skills and concentration Blueprint reading	Increased need for diagnostic skills	Decreased need	Depends on responsibilities	Increased need for communication and coordination
Maintenance	Depends on responsibilities	Increased need for knowledge about mechanical, electrical, and electronic systems Increased need for diagnostic skills	Decreased need	Increased need for risk-taking Learning ability	Increased need for communication and coordination
Engineering and Systems Analysts	Stays the same	Increased need for knowledge about information and manufacturing system design	Stays the same	Depends on responsibilities	Increased need for group problem solving Increased need for communication and coordination
NC Parts Programmer	Reading engineering drawings	Cutting and tooling knowledge Math ability Ability to visualize objects in three dimensions	Stays the same	Depends on responsibilities	Increased need for coordination with machine operators

Table 6-3. Skills Taught by In-House Training Programs of Plants
with Flexible Automation.

Skill	Percentage of Plants Needing
General knowledge of safety procedures	95%
Specific machine operation	89%
General knowledge of technological advances in manufacturing	82%
Computer programming	74%
Maintenance and troubleshooting	74%
Developing sufficient knowledge of the entire manufacturing process in order to work with others in different departments and at different levels	69%
Problem solving (for example, making use of objective data for decision making)	69%
Human relations (for example, dealing with worker morale)	53%
Knowledge of basic engineering concepts	52%
Basic reading, writing, and arithmetic	44%
Basic physical science	34%

Source: Majchrzak, 1986b, p. 200. Copyright © 1986, IEEE. Used by permission.

skill that managers were likely to feel should be taught in public educational institutions), was important in 34 percent of the plants.

The results of the survey and the research reported in this chapter lead to the conclusion that it is shortsighted to expect only a few skill changes or only changes directly affecting the operation of specific equipment for a select few. Instead, a broad range of skills for a broad range of workers is needed with flexible automation. These skills include human relations skills, such as coordination and team problem solving; knowledge of the manufacturing system to understand interrelationships among systems and equipment; and basic skills in reading, writing, and arithmetic to do the rudimentary blueprint reading, calculations for machining and scheduling, and computer program development needed by most occupations with flexible automation.

Finally, from a systems perspective, skill needs can be expected to vary not only according to the specific equipment employed and by job design but also by the organizational context. Perhaps one of the more conclusive studies on this issue was done by Hazlehurst, Bradbury, and Corlett (1969), who compared job skills of machinists on NC and conventional machines. These researchers found that while some skill changes seemed to be necessary for all machinist-operators on the NC machines, other factors exerted as much influence over the skill changes as the machines. These factors included company policies on minimal uptime, precision, batch sizes, and inspection systems; the technical ability of the programmer; and the perceived important features of the job (unit cost figures versus inspection standards). Thus, skill changes do not occur as a sole function of the occupation or equipment. Personnel policies, organizational structure, and such constraints as management's human resource philosophy are important influences as well.

Selection

Having identified the skill requirements needed for AMT jobs, careful selection of workers for the AMT jobs is essential. The adequate selection of AMT workers revolves around effectively answering three questions:

1. How many AMT workers are needed?
2. Where do they come from? (that is, how is the recruiting pool defined?)
3. What criteria should be used for selection?

How Many?

The decision about how many direct and indirect workers are needed to operate an AMT system should depend on four assumptions management makes about the new system: expected replacement ratio, new production rate with equipment, speed of equipment installation, and job designs.

Expected Replacement Ratio. In determining numbers of workers needed, the direct labor replacement factor provided by vendors is often used as the sole basis for estimating the number of AMT operators needed and the number of conventional equipment operators no longer needed. Estimates of from 1.7 to 6 employees per shift for robots have been used to determine the number of fewer operators/assemblers/craftworkers needed to run the same operations (Foulkes and Hirsch, 1984; Davis, 1985b). This strategy of using expected replacement ratios as the sole basis for determining the number of AMT workers needed is riddled with problems.

A first problem is that extrapolating from the number of direct labor to the number of indirect labor needed with AMT is difficult at best. While new needs are created by AMT in programming, engineering, maintenance, scheduling, and coordination, to what extent the new needs can be handled by the existing staff varies from machine to machine and from organization to organization. Replacement ratios fail to provide guidance in this regard.

Second, even estimating the number of direct labor with AMT is difficult. In 1970 a survey of process production facilities implementing computerized process control found that "although the computer assumed some of the manual tasks of the operators, the crew size was generally maintained at its previous level to cope with emergencies that might arise or possible computer failure" (U.S. Department of Labor, 1970). In another example, a mill-type plant was converted into a highly automated, continuous process facility (Lipstreu and Reed, 1965). The company expected decreased staffing needs, yet found that when they reduced numbers of people, "all hell broke loose. One year after the change, the mixing department had virtually the same staffing pattern initially visualized only necessary during the debugging process" (pp. 29–30). Thus, the number of direct labor needed may also be inaccurately estimated.

In sum, while the expected replacement ratio is often used as the basis of cost justification figures for the new equipment, the vendor-supplied ratios may not be accurate for the particular organization. Instead, other factors such as those described next should be used in determining the number of workers needed.

New Production Rate with AMT. When planning for the flexible factory is done inadequately, the new equipment will not be able to be used at full capacity, either in scope or in scale (Goldhar and Jelinek, 1983). This may be because of poor inventory planning, marketing failures, or equipment unreliability. Whatever the reason, AMT equipment that runs at less than full capacity needs fewer workers. On the other hand, planning for high capacity will ensure full use of workers. At Rockwell International's Collins Defense Communications facility in Cedar Rapids, Iowa, for example, the new facility replaced a 1940 plant and represented an $11 million CIM investment. Says Herm Reininga, vice-president for operations, "We've been able to create an automated factory without creating a new loss in jobs by increasing production. We had 600 employees involved in manufacturing prior to our automation program; and we're holding at that 600 figure now in two production shifts" (Teresko, 1986, p. 76).

Speed of Equipment Installation. When AMT is installed in a planned, graduated fashion over time, the number of workers needed often stays surprisingly constant. This is because the organization as a system has enough time to absorb additional workers into other production environments, create market niches, and control for seasonal flux in inventories. A company that replaces all of its equipment all at once, however, will often need to lay off some workers because of machine downtime, to recruit new workers with special technical skills, and to eventually recall some of those laid off as production rates increase.

Job Designs. A final factor affecting the number of workers needed is the job design decisions made about direct and indirect AMT jobs. Job designs that are very rigid and narrowly defined, such as those in certain traditionally organized and unionized shops, may require more people than flexible job designs that allow workers to share job tasks.

Conclusions on Numbers of Workers. There is no pre-established number of workers needed to operate flexible equipment. Replacement ratios are often misleading and their importance should be downplayed in estimating numbers of needed workers. Instead, other factors such as production capacity, speed of equipment installation, and job designs should be considered in answering the question, How many?

How Is the Recruiting Pool Defined?

In addition to how many workers, selection involves identifying a pool of workers from which AMT jobs will be filled. Just as the question of how many depended on a set of assumptions, so does the answer to the question of where they come from. Some of these assumptions, or factors, include problems associated with layoffs and top management's philosophy about retraining.

Problems Associated with Layoffs. In many plants, management may not (or cannot) define the recruiting pool to include new hires off the street. The effect on worker motivation may be seriously impaired with a "fire the old skills, hire new skills" strategy. Moreover, union contracts may prevent a policy of hiring new workers off the street. Therefore, for many plants, the recruiting pool for AMT jobs may be limited to the existing work force. Moreover, depending on how job descriptions are written, the recruiting pool may be further delimited to the pool of displaced machinists or skilled trades. Thus, the recruiting pool may be predefined to some extent.

Top Management's Philosophy About Retraining. A second factor to consider in identifying the recruiting pool is the management's attitudes about retraining. In one company implementing robots, for example, "one of the biggest questions was what to do with the displaced workers. The [company] spokesman suspects a layoff along with an addition of skilled maintenance people. For the skilled positions, they would probably have to hire from outside the plant because he feels it would be too difficult to retrain the present workers, as a training program could take up to four years" (Ayres and Miller, 1983, p. 112). However, in a different company also described by Ayres and Miller, a computer-automated circular conveyor belt with robots was installed, causing the rearrangement of workers into teams around workstations along the conveyor belt. While the teams involved a fewer number of total workers than were needed on the old assembly line, the displaced workers were retrained for inspection and technician jobs. Through retraining and attrition, no one was laid off. Thus, the recruiting pool will be defined in part by the extent to which retraining is an alternative considered by management.

Conclusions on Recruiting Pool. The recruiting pool may best be defined as including all those workers in the existing plant (and not applicants from outside). A strategy that considers the existing work force as the pool of potential AMT workers is, in the long term, the most effective strategy. Directing worker attention toward acceptance of the fact that eventually they will all produce more because they will all work with AMT is a far more productive strategy than one that encourages job security fears and turf protection battles.

While the strategy that considers the recruiting pool as the entire work force is more effective in the long term, it need not lead to lesser-qualified workers in the short term. In one unionized automobile components plant, which treated its entire existing work force as the recruiting pool, a rigorous selection process was instituted to ensure that only highly qualified workers became AMT operators: "Applicants for skilled jobs had to complete an eight-hour assessment of their technical and interpersonal skills, which was conducted by a local community college. They then took a four- to six-hour skill-level inventory. Finally, the applicants attended a family night with spouses to discuss the program. The 45 applicants remaining from an initial 100 were then ranked by seniority. Some of these 45 workers declined the new jobs, and 16 were eventually placed." (Manufacturing Studies Board, 1986, p. 52).

What Criteria Should Be Used to Select AMT Workers?

In establishing a selection procedure for AMT, it is necessary to determine the selection criteria. Two systems are used in many manufacturing plants today. In the first, seniority is the essential factor. In many unionized plants, the most senior workers are selected for a posted, defined job. An alternative system used in many plants has been called creaming off (Kohler and Schultz-Wild, 1983). Creaming off involves recruiting the "best and the brightest" personnel. In this system, selection criteria include breadth of experience and skills, and demonstrated initiative to handle any problems that might arise. In addition, creaming off involves picking workers management personally knows and trusts.

There are several problems with the use of either system. If seniority is the primary selection criterion, everything but that one factor is likely to be overlooked. An applicant's ability to acquire new skills in such areas as human relations, programming, or an interdisciplinary knowledge of circuitry are all but ignored in a seniority-based selection approach. The use of seniority also ignores the fact that older workers may retire from the organization sooner than younger workers, perhaps before they have acquired enough useful knowledge of the particular machine to be able to pass information along to the next generation of workers. Finally, selection based on seniority has not been shown by research to be related to organizational performance. In a survey about human resource factors related to organizational performance with flexible automation, survey respondents were asked to indicate how important different criteria, including seniority, were in the selection of workers for operator and maintenance jobs with flexible automation (Majchrzak and Paris, 1986). The results indicated that organizations that select workers based on seniority are likely to perform less well on scrap and rework rate than are organizations that do not use seniority as a criterion. This finding was true for both union and nonunion plants. Apparently, when seniority is used as a selection criterion, other important factors are overlooked—such as those to be described here.

The other traditional approach to selection—creaming off the best and the brightest—presents problems as well. While it keeps training costs down, it results in a disproportionate dependency on a few select workers. For example, in a GM plant implementing computer-automated stamping presses, management attempted to select favorite employees and train them in everything. When they more carefully considered the implications of this strategy, they lamented that the hand-selected individuals would be spread too thin. With this increased dependency also comes concerns that when the "best" leave for better wages or better working conditions, what is the organization left with? Thus, while in the short term the creaming off strategy may effectively keep training costs down, eventually more typical workers will need to be recruited for AMT jobs. By not including more typical workers until the pool of the "best" workers has been used up, a significant amount of worker mistrust about management's intentions and attitudes toward the work force may have been built up; this second round of workers then may be far less motivated than the first.

There are several alternative selection systems that can be used instead of seniority or creaming. Four approaches that have been used in plants with flexible automation are work force choice, machine skills and experience, human relations skills, and individual interest. These are not necessarily mutually exclusive; however, each represents a slightly different approach to using criteria for selecting AMT operators and maintenance staff. Moreover, as will become apparent from their descriptions, the best selection strategy for a firm is one that combines several of these approaches.

Work Force Choice. Workers responsible for operating and supporting flexible automation equipment are often selected by management. However, managers may not always have the needs of the AMT system foremost in their minds. For example, at an automotive engine plant, a supervisor was asked to recommend an hourly person to be trained to operate the new line. "A man was suggested and trained and lasted only three weeks on the project. Follow-up with the supervisor who made the recommendation revealed that the man selected had been a difficult employee with an attendance problem. Because the system was to be located in another department, the foreman saw an opportunity to transfer this employee out of his supervisory area" (Ettlie, 1986b, p. 4).

An alternative strategy is to involve worker representatives, such as the union. This approach may well overcome problems related to management selection, and the more the work force can feel that the selection criteria have been applied fairly and equitably to all job applicants, the more likely that rejected as well as accepted workers will be motivated to perform well.

If union or worker representatives are involved in selection, one option is to have them choose the job applicants. This strategy was used at a GM stamping plant, since the union insisted that any other strategy provided management with too much control. Thus, the union committee was able to pick the team of operators responsible for operating the first CIM press machine to arrive. Interestingly enough, the highest-seniority workers were not selected; rather, technical qualifications and an ability to work with others became the selection criteria. An obvious problem with this approach to worker involvement is that the unions may pick workers who need extensive training before they can be productive, or in a hostile climate, those least likely to succeed may be picked. Despite these problems, if the union is sufficiently suspicious of management control, this may be the only feasible strategy.

Another option for worker involvement in selection is to have the workers picked by lottery. This option was considered by a major appliance manufacturer implementing robots and CNC machines (Nulty, 1982). Management preferred the lottery system because it avoided selection by seniority, which the union originally proposed. After substantial discussion, the management-union bargaining team decided against a lottery and agreed instead to have the union select the workers in any way it preferred, as long as selection was not based on seniority.

A final option for involving workers is to create a worker-management committee to define selection criteria before the process starts. This committee could establish its own criteria or use some of those to be suggested here. By involving the workers in this fashion, management may still be able to maintain some control yet allow the workers the voice they feel they need.

Machine Skills and Experience. The earlier discussion in this chapter on skill changes indicated that knowledge of the equipment, system elements (such as control circuitry), and the production process are essential skill requirements for many of the occupations affected by flexible automation. Therefore, machine skills and experience should be important selection criteria.

Many case studies have documented the use of machine knowledge as a selection criterion. NC parts programmers have been selected from pools of former machinists (Shaiken, 1983), automation equipment operators have been selected based on their "machine sense" (Chen and others, 1984), and FMS attendants have been selected based on their previous start-up experience (Graham and Rosenthal, 1985).

Machine skills can be used as a selection criterion in a number of different ways without the process falling into a creaming-off strategy. First, machine skills can be used as part of a job applicant's experience base with that experience matched to the type of equipment to be installed. Or machine skills can be incorporated into a set of skill-based tests that the successful applicant is expected to pass. Finally, machine skills may be considered as a potentially trainable aptitude; however, such an aptitude is only trainable if the applicant meets minimal reading, writing, and arithmetic requirements (such as at the sixth- to eighth-grade level). An applicant without these basic skills is unlikely to accurately understand documentation, maintenance flowcharts, engineering blueprints, and statistical process control outputs. Remedial education may be necessary if no applicants can be identified who meet the minimal basic skill requirements.

Human Relations Skills. A third set of selection criteria that are used to select AMT personnel are minimal human relations skills. The importance of using human relations skills was documented in Majchrzak and Paris's (1986) survey of high- and low-performing flexible automated factories. The results from this survey indicated that managers of plants with better scrap rates and met delivery schedules assigned greater importance to human relations skills as selection criteria than did managers of poor-performing plants.

Human relations skills used as selection criteria have included an ability to work with others, leadership, creativity, communication, conflict resolution style, and group problem-solving experience. At two firms implementing FMSs, FMS attendants were selected on the basis of their team-building skills (Graham and Rosenthal, 1985). At a Kimberly-Clark plant, applicants for machine operator jobs are put through "leadership-simulation" exercises. "In one session, the job candidate is asked to play the role of a supervisor directing a seasoned subordinate to switch to a more demanding job. The worker's role is played by a trained supervisor. Says Mr. Goehring [manager of human resources development]: 'We're looking for people who can assume workgroup leadership, even if they wouldn't have that responsibility initially'" (Reibstein, 1986, p. 25). A Midwest food-products company selected blue-collar technicians and maintenance personnel based on their abilities to work in groups. They use team exercises, with applicants simulating running a plant that produces circuit boards.

Individual Interest. The concept of individualization was introduced in Chapter Three, referring to the need to match various human resource options to the specific needs of each individual. Carrying this notion into the realm of selection criteria implies that people should be selected based on their level of interest in the job. There is experimental support for the positive outcomes of using interest in this way. Morse (1975) conducted an experiment that compared individuals' reactions to their jobs when either they were placed on jobs that were matched to both their skills and professed needs (that is, interest) or they were placed on jobs according to their skills only. After eight months on their jobs, the eighty-five people who were in jobs matched to their skills and needs were found to be more satisfied and felt more competent than did the fifty persons who were in jobs matched to their skills alone. In the Majchrzak and Paris (1986) survey of high- and low-performing flexible automated factories, plant managers were asked about the importance of applicant interest as a selection criterion. The results indicated that managers of plants performing well on met delivery schedules assigned more importance to interest than did managers of plants performing less well. While hardly conclusive, these results suggest that selection based on individual interest may help with some measures of performance and not with others. Regardless, the notion of including individual interest, particularly in combination with some minimal skill competency, seems warranted.

Conclusions on Selection Criteria. This discussion of selection suggests that the traditional methods of seniority and creaming are inappropriate for flexible automation. Continued use of these systems seems to be particularly unfortunate in light of the existence of effective alternative criteria. These alternative criteria have been found to be effective because they promote the selection of personnel who are likely to be matched to the specific demands of the production process, are motivated to learn, and are capable of working with others as a team to keep the equipment operational. But such personnel can only be selected if multiple selection criteria are used: interest, machine skills, and human relations skills are all necessary criteria for selecting flexible automation personnel.

Developing Training Programs That Match New Job Needs

In plants implementing AMT, management consistently underestimates the training needs created by the new technology. Training budgets are often allocated only 1 percent of the total cost of a new system, despite the fact that managers report that 5 to 10 percent is necessary (Thompson and Scalpone, 1983). Companies generally rely on vendor training even though vendors tend to present information that is too general for the specific needs of the plant's production environment and even though failing to build in-house training experience is more costly in the long run. Unstructured on-the-job-training is used with amazing tenacity, despite the deficiencies of such an approach.

In this chapter, research evidence is presented to document the need for structured in-house training programs when AMT is implemented. The elements of such a training program, specifically suited to the introduction of AMT, include (1) a multiple purpose approach, (2) off-the-job classroom training followed by structured and supervised on-the-job experience, (3) individualized training in modules, (4) repeated offerings of initial training courses to accommodate personnel turnover, (5) coupling of initial training with follow-on skill development training, (6) utilization of alternative types of trainers such as supervisors and manufacturing engineers, (7) active learning methods, such as simulations, (8) completion of most of the training before the equipment arrives, (9) a curriculum that includes both generic and job-specific courses, and (10) evaluation of the training programs. In addition to these suggested elements, sets of curricula offered by flexible automated factories with in-house training programs are presented. The message of this chapter, then, is unambiguous and conclusive: Develop and initiate

*an in-house training program for AMT before the equipment is installed
and have workers go through the program before they begin to work on
the new technology.*

Status and Structure of Flexible Automation Training

For the purposes of clarity, training is defined in this chapter as encompassing most of the activities that constitute either education or training. According to the Conference Board's definition, education concerns information, concepts, and intellectual abilities, while training concerns skills acquisition through repetition in performance (Lusterman, 1977). Since both are needed with flexible automation, this chapter is concerned with programs that deal with both education and training, although only the word *training* is used.

Historical Priority of Training Among Manufacturing Industries. Compared to other industries, manufacturing plants have historically been some of the worst providers of structured training to the nonexempt employee. For example, a 1974 U.S. Department of Labor survey of 2,829 manufacturing establishments found only 15 percent providing structured training to manual workers. In 1977, the Conference Board surveyed 610 companies in a variety of different industries and found that manufacturing plants annually spent only eleven dollars per employee for training, compared to thirty-six dollars for transportation companies and fifty-six dollars for financial institutions (Lusterman, 1977). Moreover, breaking down the number of workers receiving training according to different occupational groups indicated that nonexempt hourly workers, constituting a majority of the manufacturing work force, receive a disproportionately smaller amount of training of any kind (see Table 7-1). A resurvey of many of the same firms in 1985 found that the situation has changed little over the last decade for the nonexempt employee (Lusterman, 1985). Thus, compared to other industries, the manufacturing industry has not historically given a high priority to the education and training of shopfloor workers.

Table 7-1. Education and Training Provided to Occupational Groups
in Manufacturing Relative to Distribution in Work Force.

Occupation	Percentage in Manufacturing Work Force	Percentage Work Force Enrolled in	
		"People" Courses	Functional/ Technical Courses
Managerial	11	53	33
Professional and Technical	12	29	20
Sales and Marketing	8	27	28
Other Non-exempt Hourly	69	7	18

Source: Adapted from Lusterman, 1977, p. 16.

Training Provided for Firms with Flexible Automation. Has
the introduction of AMT changed the amount of training provided
to nonexempt manufacturing workers? Surprisingly enough,
evidence from surveys indicates that the provision of structured
training to nonexempt employees is not dramatically different in
firms with and without AMT. For example, in a survey of 133
manufacturing plants with flexible automation equipment, only 45
percent offered a structured training program to prepare the work
force for the new equipment (Majchrzak, 1986b). Other studies
similarly indicate that structured training has not dramatically
increased in AMT plants (Pullen, 1976; Clutterbuck and Hill, 1981).

Given the skill changes necessary with AMT as reviewed in
Chapter Five, the relatively small number of plants finding a need
to offer structured training is puzzling. If structured training is not
being provided, how are the new skills being acquired? Surveys to
date suggest that the most popular means for imparting the new
AMT skills is through unstructured on-the-job training (OJT). For
example, in a 1985 survey of 202 Michigan auto suppliers implementing CAD or CNC, three-quarters of the firms performed
training through informal OJT (Jacobs, 1985). Other surveys
attesting to the predominance of ad hoc and unstructured training
have been reported by the National Center for Productivity and
Quality of Working Life (1977) and by Love and Walker (1986).

Case for Structured AMT Training. Is there anything wrong with unstructured OJT as the primary mode of AMT training? While OJT provides the trainee with inexpensive, hands-on experience invaluable for learning job duties, the use of unstructured OJT as the primary means to impart AMT skills has many problems. First, unstructured OJT disrupts production. In the words of one Eastman Kodak training executive, "The traditional way of training people to become spoolers is to turn them over to instructors at the job site. While they observe and listen to all that is being said, they tend to interrupt the work of machine operators" (Lusterman, 1977, p. 8). The Conference Board has recommended that, considering the costs of mistakes and lowered efficiency that OJT can create in some situations, plus the increased complexity of work skills with new technology, alternatives to OJT should be explored by firms today. A second problem is that, by focusing exclusively on the particular tasks at hand, unstructured OJT fails to educate workers to accommodate fully to technological change (National Center for Productivity and Quality of Working Life, 1977). For example, AMT has given operators the ability to detect faults early, before irreversible damage to the production process occurs. Since many of these faults are the result of a complicated set of interdependencies between the human, the machine, and the materials, training operators with OJT alone cannot expose the operator to the full range of situations in which fault detection skills are needed. Thus, an operator trained only with OJT would be inadequately prepared. A third problem is that the trainee who learns entirely through OJT is most likely to learn only those techniques used by the OJT instructor. Argoff (1983–84) found this result in a series of in-depth case studies on training programs for automation undertaken for the Office of Technology Assessment. Thus, there is no assurance that all the appropriate information is covered by OJT.

These problems clearly indicate, then, that there is much that is wrong with using unstructured OJT as the primary source of training when flexible automation is installed. However, few firms have instituted alternatives to their unstructured OJT. Why? In one study reported by Nieva, Majchrzak, and Huneycutt (1982), firms not providing structured training programs for AMT were asked why. The most frequently mentioned reason was that the costs of not having a structured training program did not appear to outweigh the benefits of having one; thus, they didn't bother.

Unfortunately, this suggests that many AMT managers are not aware of the research evidence indicating the benefits of a structured training program. Moreover, these plant managers are apparently not listening to their workers, among whom "there is widespread concern about what they [the workers] perceive to be inadequate training for their jobs" (Shaiken, 1983, p. 59). These managers also seem to be unaware of the research that has clearly linked the provision of structured training to the successful implementation of new technology. For example, in a study by Ettlie (1973) of ten firms implementing CNC machines, a significant factor in the extent to which the machines were used was the extent of the training received by the NC operator, programmer, and supervisor. Surveys of manufacturing plants with AMT have found similar results (U.S. Department of Labor, 1970, 1982; Ettlie, 1986a). Moreover, individual firms report a link between training and technological success. For example, industry analysts say that Chrysler Corporation is the automaker that has paid the most attention to managing its new technology for the auto workers. "The key, says Richard E. Dauch, executive vice-president for manufacturing, is laying out thorough training programs to prepare workers for the new technology. We've had tremendous success, with very few factory-of-the-future headaches" ("High Tech to the Rescue," 1986, p. 104). Finally, the managers who believe the benefits of structured training are insufficient must also be unaware of the research indicating that the attitudes of workers about new technology are directly affected by training. For example, in a survey of workers about to encounter major technological change at a manufacturer of printed circuit boards, those receiving formal training were found to be more optimistic about the new technology, while those receiving unstructured OJT were more pessimistic (Nieva, Gaertner, Argoff, and Newman, 1986).

In sum, the costs of not having structured training for AMT seem to far outweigh the costs of having it. While OJT is less complex to administer, it is also insufficient to meet the needs of AMT workers. Moreover, without structured training the flexible automated factory risks worker concern about inadequate training, failed or suboptimal use of new technology, and worker resistance to change. Therefore, a firm implementing AMT should have a structured training program for the work force. Who should provide such training is discussed next.

Sources of a Structured AMT Training Program

In this section, the major sources for delivering structured training are described. As shown in Table 7-2, a survey of AMT training programs has found several alternative sources for training. The most frequently used are vendors, training consultants, industry-university cooperative programs, and in-house programs. In addition, corporate training is considered, since this is a clear option for most larger firms. After a brief description of each source, the advantages and disadvantages of using each as the primary source of structured training are discussed.

Vendors. It is apparent from Table 7-2 and other studies (for example, Jacobs, 1985) that the most popular source of structured training is the AMT vendor. Usually, the vendor trains a few workers employed at the firm purchasing the new system. For example, at the robot manufacturer Automatix the usual procedure is for customers to send the foreman or welding engineer to the training classes (Argoff, 1983–84). On the trainee's return to the plant, he or she is expected to teach the operators and maintenance crew about the machine.

An obvious advantage of using vendors as the primary source of training for new technology is that, since they developed the new system, they are most knowledgeable about how to maintain and operate it (Liker and Thomas, 1987). Thus, the firm that uses vendor training need not reinvent the wheel or rely on trial-and-error learning as the system becomes operational. The automation equipment operators at Ford's Dearborn plant, for example, reported that the most valuable training they received came from vendors with whom they worked initially when the equipment was set up and qualified (Chen and others, 1984).

Table 7-2. Sources of In-House Training Programs of Plants with Flexible Automation.

Source	Percentage of Plants Using
Vendors or manufacturers of computer-automated equipment	87%
In-house instructors	80%
Traditional educational institutions	54%
Training industry and management consultants	47%
Proprietary educational institutions (for example, ITT, Control Data)	21%
Other government-sponsored instructional programs (for example, Private Sector Initiative Program)	13%
Unions	5%

Source: Majchrzak, 1986b, p. 200. Copyright © 1986, IEEE. Used by permission.

Despite the advantages of vendor training, many concerns have been raised about manufacturing plants that allow the AMT vendors to become their primary source of training. The first concern is the level of generality of the courses provided by the vendor. Argoff (1983–84) reports that vendors admit that their standard courses are not designed to address specific customer applications; the level of generality substantially reduces the utility of some of the training. Since the specific applications may make all the difference in the world in the way the machine is used and the type of breakdowns that should be expected, a course providing only general material may mislead or misinform trainees about what to expect from the machine installed in their particular plant.

Another disadvantage of vendor training is that the courses are designed as machine-specific training. Training that ties the machines together, integrates the machines with the production process, and discusses more generic skills needed with new flexible automation is often ignored (Argoff, 1983–84). Complaints have been lodged against vendors about their courses not providing the right type of information.

Another problem with vendor courses as the primary source of training is that all vendors insist that the trainees sent by the customer have a certain knowledge base. This is obviously important to the vendor because classroom-type training is more efficient than one-on-one training. However, the prerequisites are often seen by customers as infeasible for their work force. For example, the prerequisite skills for Cincinnati-Milacron's robot training include knowledge of hydraulics, electronics, and oscilloscopes, although few firms have personnel who are knowledgeable about oscilloscopes.

A final problem with using vendors as the primary source of training is that the sale of a system usually includes only a few training slots. At Cincinnati-Milacron, for example, the usual number of training slots is four. While firms can purchase more slots if they choose, they rarely do. Limiting initial training to only four workers may create a selection problem for the manufacturing firm. In one firm implementing a computer-controlled parts fabrication machine, for example, the developmental engineers were sent to the vendor to receive the training. The choice of the engineers caused the union to file a grievance; in the workers' words, "something is wrong with a system that sends everyone involved with the equipment to school except the four people responsible to operate and maintain it eight hours a day. A grievance was filed because we began to realize that we were being deliberately kept away from the information required to do our job" (Nulty, 1982, p. 127).

In sum, vendor training as the primary source of training has certain advantages difficult to match—namely, the special expertise of the vendor with the new equipment. However, there are many problems with vendor training. These problems include the fact that vendors tend to convey information that is too standardized and thus too general, fail to provide a systems perspective on training, demand certain prerequisite skills that may not be available among those selected to receive the training, and provide only a few training slots. Any of these problems can be overcome by customizing the vendor training to the needs of the particular firm, but customization is an expensive proposition. And when the user recognizes a need to customize the training, it is not obvious that the vendor, whose skills lie with system development and not with system management or implementation, is the best contractor for this purpose.

Corporate Training. Corporate-level training departments (in those firms that have them) are responsible for providing training to company divisions and plants. An example of such a department is General Electric's Learning and Communication Center (Harris, 1985). The center is a six-million-dollar facility with fully equipped classrooms and high-technology laboratories for training in machine tool control and system applications, diesel engine maintenance, rotating electrical machinery, and locomotive maintenance.

Corporate training as the primary source of training has the obvious advantage of professional trainers. The corporate training department has the skills to provide training using the latest instructional techniques. Unfortunately, because corporate training departments serve several clients, they suffer from many of the same problems as vendors. They typically prefer to provide corporate-wide training rather than specific plant training (documented by Lusterman, 1977). When they do provide specific plant training, they often lack specific knowledge of the plant's production and management processes; they are therefore often criticized for their generality. Thus, while corporate training is clearly an option for some plants, the plant that turns to the corporate training plant to provide training for new technology may experience many of the same frustrations that it experienced with vendor training.

Training Consultants. Training consultants are used by a large group of firms implementing flexible automation, as indicated in Table 7-2. Training consultants may be specialists in training methods or in training particularly for AMT. The advantages of training consultants are in some ways similar to those of both vendors and corporate training departments. Consultants are professional trainers and, as such, are well versed in the latest teaching techniques. Training consultants specializing in advanced technology are also well versed in the technology itself and thus are able to teach machine specifics to the work force. Therefore, in one sense, the training consultant combines the best of both the corporate training department and the vendor.

Likewise, the training consultant offers some of the same disadvantages. The consultant does not know the particular production process of the plant and thus must either learn it or offer more general courses. In addition, by using a training consultant for initial training, the firm becomes dependent on continued use of the consultant as new equipment is brought in; this is a problem common to the use of all three of these sources. Such dependency may not prove to be cost-effective in the long term as the company continues to invest in new equipment.

Local Educational Institutions. Manufacturing plants often have entered into agreements with local community colleges and universities to help educate various groups of workers. The community college may help to train robot technicians, while the local university may teach a CAD course.

There are several advantages to using local educational institutions. TRW in Texas has been a consistent user of local educational facilities for years (Argoff, 1983-84). TRW managers have reported that a primary benefit to the company is that educational institutions provide an excellent pool of new talent, especially talent knowledgeable about advanced manufacturing techniques. The Manufacturing Studies Board (1986) reports that many community colleges have successfully trained workers in the new technologies for local industries. Moreover, many public institutions have helped to develop customized training programs for companies. A Westinghouse facility, for example, uses interns from a local university to help develop its training modules (Argoff, 1983-84). Using local institutions also offers substantial benefits to the small company that feels unable to invest its small resource base in consultants or an in-house program. By joining with other small companies, it is able to substantially increase its influence on the educational institution to provide training in certain skills and knowledge areas.

The use of local educational institutions as a primary source of training for new technology has its problems, however. The amount of influence exerted on local educational institutions varies greatly, depending on the dominance of the company or consortium of companies as a hiring force in the community. Caterpillar Tractor reports having tremendous leverage on the local institutions in Peoria but little leverage in Milwaukee (Lusterman, 1977).

Another disadvantage of local institutions is that often their educational programs are not well suited to the needs of industry. The Center for Occupational Research and Development (CORD) conducted a 1985 survey of fifty-six schools offering robotics/ automated systems technician training (Hull and Lovett, 1985). CORD found most of the programs to be narrowly focused on existing equipment, highly specialized, and substantially electronic in design. The programs lacked courses in math and science, and they offered little or no interdisciplinary preparation in electrical, electronic, mechanical, electromechanical, fluid, thermal, and optical devices. CORD concluded that there is a significant difference between the education and training requirements for robotics/automated system technician jobs and the content of established programs at public institutions. This is a damning statement about the use of local educational institutions as the primary source of a plant's training for new technology.

In-House Training Programs. The final source considered here is an in-house training program—that is, a program that is planned, controlled, and operated by the manufacturing plant itself. The advantages of an in-house program are many. With an in-house program, the plant is able to decrease its dependence on outside sources and can thus build up a knowledge base as experience with new technology is acquired. Also, because of the ever-present reality of personnel turnover and knowledge deterioration, in-house programs are more cost-effective for reoffering initial courses or providing refresher courses as needed (Ettlie, 1986a).

While in-house training programs appear to be essential to the ability of an organization to successfully implement new technology, they are not without their problems. In-house programs tend to be expensive and thus are typically developed only by larger firms (Majchrzak, 1986b; Lusterman, 1977). Because of the expense of preparing a curriculum and training trainers, having an in-house program only makes sense if the new technology is to be used frequently. Finally, an in-house training program focuses both blame and praise for the training solely on plant management rather than outside sources; perhaps that is the greatest risk of all.

Despite these disadvantages, many plants have found in-house training programs invaluable. A superintendent of maintenance and tooling at a General Motors plant reported that the sophistication of the new machinery and the high costs incurred when the machines are not well maintained and quickly repaired "make in-plant training a must" (Argoff, 1983–84). Moreover, in a review of twenty-four flexible automated factories, the Manufacturing Studies Board (1986) found that "companies that have successfully implemented [flexible automation] are far more likely to have major [in-house] training programs for the production workers. . . . Those training programs start earlier, last longer, and include far more than their predecessors with traditional technology" (p. 55). Thus, the advantages appear to outweigh the disadvantages for many flexible factories.

Recommendations for Training Sources. A review of the alternative sources of training for new technology indicates that each source has advantages and disadvantages. Thus, an organization implementing new technology should probably consider a mixture of the different alternatives. For most manufacturing facilities, the best strategy will be one where the firm sends its critical personnel to receive initial vendor training but then builds in-house training expertise as the primary source of training. In addition, local educational institutions should be cultivated to improve the recruiting pool. Finally, for equipment that is used infrequently, having vendor films on hand may be sufficient. A mixed strategy was used successfully by one firm to implement its new technology: "We went to the vendors for the generalized, basic training for both instrumentation and computer concepts . . . and took advantage of applicable courses given by various technical schools . . . and subscribed to specialized courses given by computer system consultants. As we built up the internal computer experience base, we shifted more to in-house courses given by our automation group" (Fraade, 1979, p. 38). The plant implementing new technology may initially use outside sources alone or to supplement an existing in-house program. However, the base of the training for the plant needs to be in-house—if not now, at least in the near future. The remainder of this chapter discusses elements of an in-house training program for advanced manufacturing systems.

Elements of an In-House AMT Training Program

In this section, nine elements of an in-house training program are discussed as they pertain to training for flexible automation. The nine elements are (1) purpose, (2) format, (3) individualization, (4) extensiveness, (5) trainer, (6) presentation, (7) timing, (8) curriculum, and (9) evaluation.

Purpose. The starting point of any in-house training program is to determine why the training program is there. Is it to provide needed skills only? Is it to convey a new culture? Is it to provide workers with information about the future? Is it to be the kick off for the modernization effort?

Perhaps the most basic purpose is the provision of skills to those identified as needing them. Nevertheless, an in-house training program can have other purposes as well. It may be used to show the extent to which management supports the modernization program. If everyone is expected to participate and is rewarded for participation in a certain amount of training, workers see that management is serious about optimal utilization of the new equipment and serious about keeping the workers around. "Having a highly systematic training program was useful since, when word got out that this new way of life was adequately supported and prepared, interest level and enthusiasm noticeably rose," noted one case study of AMT implementation (Fraade, 1979, p. 39).

An in-house training program may also be used for career development. A plan might be drawn up outlining the courses that different groups of workers should take as the plant gradually modernizes its technology. Eventually, and at a measured pace, the workers will be able to accept the level of responsibility that management has determined is necessary for the efficient operation of a technologically sophisticated production process.

The training program may also be used for selection purposes. At a Delco-Remy battery plant in Georgia, training was considered to be a part of the selection process, and only one-tenth of the trainees were eventually hired (Cherry, 1982).

Finally, the in-house training program may be used as a means of orienting the workers to the new technology. Instead of simply imparting new skills, the training can provide workers with information about the future of the plant and their jobs.

Obviously, the purpose of the program will affect the contents of the training. An orientation-focused training program would primarily deliver information, probably in a lecture or small-discussion format. (This type of training is discussed in more detail in Chapters Ten and Eleven.). A training program intended to impart skills and promote career development would provide training that is more continuous than the typical one-shot type of training. A training program intended to show workers how much management is supporting the modernization program might be fairly extensive and involve courses other than structured OJT. A training program intended in part to help select automation workers would be staged so that extensive training is only given to those eventually selected. The manager attempting to develop an adequate in-house training program for new technology must determine first of all which of these purposes the training program is intended to serve.

The purposes of a training program may also vary for the different occupational groups of workers. For example, in a survey of training programs of manufacturers with statistical process control (SPC), SPC training was found to have different purposes for production workers and for managers (Jacobs, 1985). For production workers, the purpose of the training was to teach them the skills with which they could actually use SPC as part of their daily tasks. For managers, who didn't need to actually use SPC, the purpose of the training was to teach them an awareness of the need for quality.

Therefore, the first step for an in-house training program for flexible automation is to delineate the purposes of the training and whether the purposes will vary for different groups of workers. From here, preparation for the next elements of the training program can begin.

Format. The format of a training program refers to where the training is to occur. Traditional in-house training programs use either planned on-the-job training or off-the-job classroom teaching. Planned or structured OJT can take several forms. Manuals and job performance aids may be placed in a convenient location for the worker to use while learning the new job. Planned OJT may also take the form of an apprenticeship program. Existing apprenticeship programs often are not appropriate to advanced manufacturing because they are too general and thus fail to provide the apprentice with experience specifically focused on the new technology (Abbott, 1981). New apprenticeship programs are beginning to be developed, however. Cameron Iron Works trains electronic numerical control apprentices (Chauvin, 1981) using the program model presented in Exhibit 7-1. Finally, the workers (usually maintenance workers and operators) may be selected in advance of the arrival of the new equipment so that they can be on the floor during the debug phase of equipment installation. If the workers become actively involved at this point, they are more likely to have a greater knowledge of the new equipment than if the format of their training consists primarily of manuals or off-the-job lectures.

While planned OJT can provide many training advantages, it suffers from many of the problems of unstructured OJT. Planned OJT interrupts experienced workers on the production line. It also may convey information to trainees that is idiosyncratic to a particular instructor. Given the problems of planned OJT, an alternative format may need to be considered. Off-the-job training can be such an alternative. Off-the-job training may take many forms, the best-known of which is classes. In another form of off-the-job training, the operator and maintenance personnel leave the plant to go to the vendor site and participate in the equipment teardown. Or, as described by Saari (1985), the trainees can gain knowledge off the job by visiting other facilities that have the new equipment and observing how others are working with that equipment. On some visits, the workers have even been allowed to try out the equipment themselves.

Clearly, there are several options available for the in-house training format. The choice among the options should depend on

Exhibit 7-1. Electronic Numerical Control Apprenticeship Program Model.

On-the-Job Training Phases for Electronic Numerical Control Apprentice

1. *General* - Assist Journeyman; learn nomenclature, simple electrical circuits and temporary lighting; install low-voltage signaling devices and small motors; learn use of basic testing equipment; learn to identify parts and how to order replacement. *1,000 hrs.*
2. Conduit installation for light, power, and messenger cable; installation of switches; pulling light and power wiring through conduit (both overhead and underground). *1,000 hrs.*
3. Field trouble diagnosis; repair and maintenance of switches, controls and regulating devices, line-starters, drum controllers, static controls and magnetic amplifiers, motor trouble diagnosis; work with capacitor checker, oscilloscope, signal generator, ammeter, phase meter, tube and transistor testors, digital volt meters, and chart recorder. *1,500 hrs.*
4. Air conditioning repair work. *500 hrs.*
5. Shop repair of motors, generators, and transformers; vacuum induction furnace coil repair and insulation. *350 hrs.*
6. Electrical drafting. *500 hrs.*
7. Line work in yard; learn substation and plant power layout; transformer hook-up and pole work. *500 hrs.*
8. Numerical Control Maintenance Familiarization; basic level repair work, and preventive maintenance of numerical-controlled equipment. *1,000 hrs.*
9. Connect heavy power—welders, electrical furnaces, and so on; install and repair solid state furnace and motor controls. *1,000 hrs.*
10. Camvac (digital electronic gauges). *650 hrs.*
11. Electronic Numerical Control Maintenance. *—12 mos.*

Textbooks

1. *Basic Mathematics for Electricity and Electronics* - Bertrand Singer, McGraw-Hill.
2. *Basic Electronics* - Bernard Grob, McGraw-Hill.
3. *Plant Engineering Training Systems, Electrical Maintenance* - (10 Volumes) Technical Publishing Co., Barrington, Illinois.
4. *Digital Electronics: Logic and Systems* - John D. Kershaw, Wadsworth Publishing Co., Belmont, California.
5. *Electronics In Industry* - George and Robert Chute, McGraw-Hill.
6. *National Electrical Code Blueprint Reading* - 7th Edition - Kenneth L. Gebert, American Technical Society, Chicago, Illinois.

Source: Chauvin, 1981, p. 109.

the extensiveness of the skills to be learned, the existing skill levels of the work force to be trained, the purpose of the training, the capabilities of shopfloor workers to utilize the training effectively, and the production pressures during start-up. The more extensive the training and the greater the production pressures, the more likely that the plant will want off-the-job classes. The greater the personnel turnover at the plant, the less cost-effective worker participation in teardowns and debugging may be. Despite these contingencies, generally speaking, the most effective strategy for most plants is to combine off-the-job training with planned on-the-job training. By first receiving off-the-job classroom training, the operator (or repairer or engineer or manager) can learn the theory of the operations and what the machine or system is supposed to do. Then, in a structured, supervised period of on-the-job experience, the trainee can learn how the machine actually works. Ideally, following this period of on-the-job experience building, the trainee is brought back into the classroom to rectify learning errors and to be exposed to the next level of skills.

Individualization. Training programs can be geared to the average student or tailored to the particular needs and skills of each individual. The typical approach in most training is to develop a single lesson plan around what the average student is able to learn. This approach tends to be more cost-efficient with respect to trainers' time and involves less curriculum planning. Despite these advantages, however, the notion of an "average student" tends to have little applicability to the shopfloor, where educational backgrounds may range from a few years of elementary school to some college. Moreover, some workers are fresh out of school and others haven't seen a classroom in decades. Therefore, a trend toward individualization of training programs has recently been observed (Lusterman, 1985).

The first step toward individualizing a training program is to review the skills that are to be taught. From this review, the skills are broken down into modules, or discrete learning units. For example, in training engineers about CAD/CAM, the Twelve-College CAD/CAM Consortium identified eleven modules of instruction (Gibson and Richards, 1983). The eleven modules are computers in engineering, engineering graphics, computational geometry, transportation engineering, engineering systems, solid mechanics, linear control systems, digital systems and signals, modern digital and analog filtering, dynamic electric and magnetic fields, and fluid mechanics and aerodynamics. Each of the eleven modules includes a narrative introduction and discussion, a guide for the instructor on using the module to train students, and computer software to drive the interactive graphics part of the training. After the modules are developed, each one is made self-paced and proficiency-based. That is, the module is individualized so that the trainee can do the specific task required by the module again and again, at the trainee's own pace, until he or she gets it right. Then, and only then, does the trainee move on to the next module. Typically, individualized modules are coupled with in-class training lectures for all trainees together. The lectures give the instructor the opportunity to keep the trainees on target and give the trainees the opportunity to learn from each other in a group setting.

Westinghouse Defense and Electronics Systems Center has used individualized modules as the building block of its entire training program for implementing advanced technology (Argoff, 1983–84). Westinghouse spokespeople claim that the modules are one of the main reasons that the massive training of a wide variety of people went as smoothly and quickly as it did.

Extensiveness. When the extensiveness of a training program is being considered, three questions should be asked:

1.   How many hours of initial training are needed?
2.   Can initial training be offered once and for all?
3.   Is there a need for more than initial training?

The first question concerns how much training is needed when new technology is initially installed. The second question is concerned with the one-shot training program—if we offer the courses once, will that be enough? And the third question is concerned with continuing education—is it really necessary?

With respect to the need for initial training, GM's experience at a Detroit assembly plant can be instructive. The company has put each of its 3,000 hourly workers through between 200 and 2,000 hours of technical and human resource training to adapt them to working under one of GM's most advanced production systems and dealing with the plant's 2,000 programmable devices (Buss, 1985). If GM's experience is any indication, a lot of training is needed.

But how do you decide how much? Maybe you're not a GM with a multibillion-dollar training budget. Obviously, the amount of training to be provided depends to some extent on the assessment of skill changes. Thus, on the basis of the assessment of skill changes described in Chapter Six, maintenance staff and operators should probably receive about equal amounts of training, and each should receive more than engineers. Nonskill-related factors also determine extensiveness, however. For example, plant management may prefer that a particular occupational group know more than others (whether or not it needs to) and thus create greater training needs for engineers than for operators. Thus, the amount of skill changes needed with flexible automation may not translate directly into the amount of training to be delivered.

Because of the influence of nonskill-related factors in determining the amount of training to be offered, documented training times allocated to different occupational groups vary among organizations. At a commercial aircraft manufacturer, maintenance workers received about 160 hours of training in the new technology, far more than the CNC operators (Argoff, 1983–84). At Ford's Dearborn plant, three-quarters of the six-million-dollar training budget was allocated to maintenance and other skilled trades (Chen and others, 1984). At a GM stamping plant implementing automated stamping presses, operators receive more training than maintenance; at the latest estimate, mechanical maintenance workers receive 80 hours, electrical support staff 560 hours, and press operators 678 hours.

Thus, to answer the question about the amount of initial training, both the needed skill changes and the HR philosophy of management must be identified. If the number of estimated hours exceeds some of the higher total hours described here for some of the firms, the manager should rest assured that the organization will be providing enough training.

But is providing initial training once enough? In an examination of plants implementing FMSS, plant managers were found to have underestimated the amount of training needed by making no allowance for transfers, expansions, and in-service skill building (Thompson and Scalpone, 1983). At a GE Louisville appliance manufacturing plant, problems in implementing the flexible automation equipment required changes in the training schedule. "We made sure we had the first shift fully oriented to run the operation," says Raymond Rissler, general manager for the automation project. "But because of demand we had to add a second shift six months before we thought it would be needed. And of course that resulted in some problems. We learned that training programs for this type of plant can't be off-and-on; they must be continuous and permanent features of the overall operation" (DeYoung, 1985, p. 33). High personnel turnover also made it necessary to offer the same courses over and over again at the GM Pontiac plant and at a commercial airplane manufacturer. Had the courses not been repeated, a spokesperson of the airplane manufacturer noted, the present level of CAD/CAM use would have decreased (Argoff, 1983–84). These examples clearly suggest that a one-shot initial training effort is not enough. Rather, initial training must be made a fixture of the organization, one that can be easily reactivated as needed.

Finally, is initial training enough? Or is what some GM employees refer to as lifelong learning necessary? Kathleen Curley and Phil Pyburn (1982) studied companies implementing new technology and distinguished between successful and unsuccessful technology users. They found that the training provided by successful users promoted two types of learning patterns: (1) the typical formal training representing single-loop learning and (2) ongoing adaptive learning representing double-loop learning. The second type of learning was needed because the direction and dimensions of new technology learning often cannot be specified in advance; the learner must be able to influence significantly the decision about what must be learned. Thus, in answer to the third question, these researchers found that initial training was not enough. Instead, workers required training that provided for continued skill development in order to use the new equipment adequately.

Training that provides for continued skill development is useful in a variety of ways. First, skill development courses provide refreshers so that training isn't forgotten by the time the system breaks down. Second, skill development courses help to prepare workers for technologies that are yet to be installed. Third, continued training can help to remind workers of the goals of the new AMT system. Fourth, trainees cannot learn everything at once; thus a measured training approach where the worker gradually learns more advanced skills is better than training in all skills at once.

In sum, initial training should be offered continuously to adapt workers to a dynamic workplace. Initial training must be coupled with follow-on skill development training. The amount of initial training to be provided will depend on the job designs, skill changes, and the human resource philosophy of top management.

Selection of Trainers. A trainer can be one of three types: a professional instructor, a technical expert about the system, or a user or manager of the system. Examples of plants using each type of trainer can be found. Professional trainers were used by Ford's Dearborn plant. A commercial airplane manufacturer hired trainers on the basis of their technical qualifications and experience. GM's Pontiac plant had maintenance supervisors provide the training to maintenance workers; the maintenance supervisors were also completely responsible for curriculum development and scheduling the training.

Perhaps the most interesting approach to trainer selection and use is that of the Westinghouse Defense and Electronics Center (Argoff, 1983–84). The main trainers at Westinghouse were the first-line supervisors of each production worker; thus, workers were taught only by their immediate bosses. Supervisors were used reportedly because they created a more relaxed training atmosphere and had more intimate knowledge of the procedures in their own departments. Having supervisors as trainers, however, required that the entire training program be structured around this type of delivery. Therefore, supervisors were given well-structured lesson plans with little room for error. Self-paced, proficiency-based modules were developed that allowed the trainees to know for themselves when they were proficient. All training was task- or machine-specific; thus, supervisors did not have to teach generic skills like human relations, problem solving, general pneumatics, or basic engineering. Supervisors were trained by technically proficient systems experts. These technical experts were on hand to observe classes and offer the supervisors assistance as needed. Plant management explicitly supported these training responsibilities by requiring that everyone in the center be involved in at least eight hours of either giving or receiving training. An interesting feature of the Westinghouse approach was that the technical experts who trained the supervisors were the engineers responsible for developing the system, not the vendors. The developmental engineers taught the supervisors how to perform all of the tasks involved in operating the entire system and thus gave the supervisors an overview of where each worker's tasks fit in. Having engineers do the "master training" not only taught supervisors what they needed to know but also gave the engineers (1) the opportunity to review lesson plans to make sure that they were technically correct, (2) experience in explaining highly technical subjects to nonexperts, and (3) an opportunity for direct exchange of information with users of the system.

Each type of trainer has advantages and disadvantages. With professional trainers, the technical expertise and knowledge of the production process may be missing from the training or too difficult for the trainer to acquire. Yet the use of a professional trainer increases the chances that the information will be delivered in a manner that is seen as impartial and that it will be retained. A technical expert like a developmental engineer may be inexperienced at communicating information to laypeople, uncomfortable with teaching others, and more familiar with the equipment than the peculiarities of the particular production process. Yet technical experts are the most knowledgeable about the system and thus have the potential to impart the most information about the equipment. Having a manager or user of the system, such as a production supervisor, deliver the training creates a likelihood of partiality in information delivery and, for those workers who do not like their supervisors, an intolerable learning situation. Yet the use of supervisors as trainers has several advantages: They are most familiar with the particular process in which the equipment will be used, they will benefit from the responsibility for training delivery by gaining more knowledge of the system and credibility with subordinates, and they are likely to create the most relaxed atmosphere among those workers who like them.

In sum, none of these options for selecting trainers is without problems. The use of any one of them will depend on the organization. If engineers can talk to others and supervisors are well liked, an approach similar to that of Westinghouse may be useful. Otherwise, in the short term, the more traditional approach of using professional trainers may be preferred.

Presentation. Another element of in-house training programs to consider is how to present the material. Is the material best conveyed when the student is treated as a passive learner, or is it best conveyed when the student is an active learner? The most notable passive teaching method is the lecture. When substantial amounts of information must be conveyed in a short period of time, the lecture tends to be the preferred method. However, industry spokespeople warn us that workers learn best when they take active roles in their education (Lusterman, 1977). Thus, methods for presenting teaching material to encourage active learning have received some attention from firms implementing flexible automation.

Simulations are one method to induce active learning. Hirschhorn (1984) suggests the use of a simulator in which a computer model mimics the operation of a machine. With the simulation, not only will the worker actively be involved in learning the new job but the worker can learn fault-detection skills, such as how one decision can set off a chain of events. For example, in a batch chemical processing plant in which computer control was introduced, a graphic simulator of each process control computer system was used to train the workers (Fraade, 1979). With the simulator, the workers could see how the computer reacted to changing process conditions as well as to software that was incorrectly written and proven. General Motors' Pontiac plant has a training laboratory that has a robot to allow for simulations of variations in tasks that maintenance needs to do (Argoff, 1983–84). An unplanned side benefit of the training robot is that it provides a way for workers to try out new process improvement ideas.

Simulations certainly seem to be a good idea for inducing active learning when training for flexible automation. However, certain issues need to be considered before one selects simulations as a major training method. First, simulations create the need for dedicated training equipment. At a commercial airplane manufacturer, management refused to have dedicated training equipment because all equipment had to be used a minimum of two shifts to be cost-justifiable (Argoff, 1983–84). Second, simulations must be as similar as possible to the actual equipment so that the simulation imparts as much useful training as possible (Fraade, 1979). This is obviously expensive. Third, simulations must be constructed so that they do things that the actual equipment would not normally do. Thus, rather than having the worker learn about "standard accidents," the simulations must be configured so that bizarre, completely unexpected situations are encountered in training. If these nonstandard accidents are not encountered in the simulation, the worker will not know how to handle them when they occur on the production line (Sheridan, 1981).

Other active learning methods for off-the-job training exist. One example is computer-aided instruction, such as Rouse's (1981) FAULT software, which provides a way for a worker to learn fault detection skills. Other examples can easily be found. The point is that in many ways there is no substitute for hands-on learning. Because of both the production costs and the narrowed learning focus of doing hands-on learning out on the floor, developing some method of providing this hands-on learning in the classroom seems the best strategy for presentation.

Timing. Timing is concerned with when training should occur. Traditionally, manufacturing plants wait until the equipment has been ordered and is about to be installed before starting training. However, as reported by a commercial airplane manufacturer, such a strategy can create substantial problems (Argoff, 1983–84). The largest problem is that peak training activities end up coinciding with peak start-up activities. Because start-up is the time when production pressures are the greatest, departments at the aerospace company were understandably unwilling to give up their workers to training. Now, this company conducts the bulk of its training well before the equipment is installed. Some firms have even pushed the training cycle to start earlier. For example, AT&T's training staff participate in new product planning so that they can become aware of training needs and design training programs six to nine months before the equipment goes on-line (Davis, 1986b).

Therefore, in determining the timing of the training, there are no choices. Training plans must be under development when equipment selection is first being considered; selection and training must be almost completed before the equipment arrives. Waiting until later can create substantial start-up conflicts between training and production staff that may take years to fix.

Curriculum. There are two issues to consider in curriculum development: who develops the curriculum and what courses should be offered. Numerous options are possible concerning who develops the curriculum. The example of CAD/CAM modules for engineers (described in the section on individualization of training programs) was developed by college faculty. At Westinghouse, systems engineers developed the technical specifications that were converted into user manuals by technical writers, which were then translated into lesson plans and courses by local university education interns. A popular approach among firms is to have the curriculum developed by corporate management in conjunction with technical and training experts (Jacobs, 1985). At GE, a training advisory committee consisting of technical and management people reviews proposed courses. At a GM stamping plant, the training vendor (EDS) is developing the training curriculum for its high-tech stamping presses.

An interesting observation one can make about this sample of options is the relative infrequency with which users (including supervisors as well as maintenance staff and operators) are consulted about the curriculum. One exception is Westinghouse, which based its task modules (and thus the curriculum) on what workers actually did with the new equipment. Whether users are actually involved in the development or review of the curriculum depends on management's human resource philosophy. Nevertheless, if training is to be pertinent to the work environment and not

Exhibit 7-2. Robotics/Automated Systems Partial Task Analysis by Course Listing.

Electrical/Electronic Tasks	BASIC										TECHNICAL CORE												SPECIALTY					
	Algebra	Trigonometry	Geometry/Calculus	UTC Physics I	UTC Physics II	UTC Physics III	Technical Communications	Computer Basics	Economics in Technology	Industrial Relations	Fundamentals of Electricity & Electronics	Analog Circuits and Active Devices	Graphics	Manufacturing Processes	Properties of Materials	Mechanical Devices and Systems	Fluid Power	Instrumentation & Controls	Computer Applications	Industrial Electrical Power and Equipment	Digital Electronics	Electromechanical Devices	Fund. of Robotics and Automated Systems	Controllers for Robots and Automated Systems	Automated Systems and Support Components	Robotics/Automated Systems Interfaces	Robotics/Automated Systems at Work	Automated Work Cell Integration
1. Use manufacturers' parts list and drawings concerning replacement parts for robots/automated systems to																												
a. Identify part numbers							●						●															
b. Order replacement parts							●						●															
c. Install replacement parts							●						●															
2. Adjust, troubleshoot, repair, and/or replace:																												
a. Power supplies											●							●		●				●				
b. Servo amplifiers											●							●		●				●	●			
c. Motor control circuits												●						●		●				●				
d. Electronic sensors												●						●		●				●				
e. Transducers																		●										
3. Attach and replace connectors to wire and fiber optic cables.											●							●										
4. Install low- and high-voltage and interconnecting signal (wire and fiber optic) cables.											●							●		●								
5. Troubleshoot and repair wire and fiber optic system cable faults.											●							●										
6. Conduct routine preventive maintenance on electrical and electronic equipment in accordance with manufacturer's recommendations.											●									●								
7. Troubleshoot electronic failures to the circuit board level; replace defective circuit board.											●							●			●							

to be judged as too general and irrelevant by the trainees, some early involvement of the users should be incorporated.

Development of curriculum ideally will follow from task analysis. For example, the Center for Occupational Research and Development analyzed the tasks of a robot technician (Hull and Lovett, 1985). From the list of tasks, courses were created to ensure that multiple task skills were covered in multiple ways. Their resultant tasks-by-course matrix is presented in part in Exhibit 7-2.

From the matrix of tasks and courses, curricula will be identified for specific jobs as well as for those generic courses that need to be taught to everyone working with the new equipment. For AMT operators, the curriculum may include any of the courses described in Tables 7-3 and 7-4. The first list of courses is used by

Table 7-3. Courses for Transfer Press Operator Technician at a GM Stamping Plant.

Required Course List	Hours Required
SAFETY	2
BASIC MATH	40
STAT PROCESS CTL	16
TECH. PROBLEM SOLVING	40
FINANCIAL MGM'T	8
BLUEPRINT READING	40
MECHANISMS	120
LUBRICATION	40
HYDRAULICS	50
PNEUMATICS	30
INTRO TO PC	16
LADDER DIAGRAMS	36
GE DRIVE	32
RELIANCE DRIVE	N/A
ALLEN BRADLEY	N/A
UNICO SERVO	N/A
AUTO TECH	N/A
PLC2	40
PLC3	40
RELIANCE CONTROL	N/A
DATA HWY	40
FLUKE	8
CANBERRA INTRO	40
CANBERRA HARDWARE	40
PREREQUISITE SUB TOTALS	678

Source: Dale Romine, personal correspondence.

Table 7-4. CORD's Brief Description of Technical Core.

ELECTRICITY AND ELECTRONICS

Basic knowledge and skills in dc and ac electrical circuits to include circuit analysis, recognition and use of electrical components and electrical measurement instruments. Topics presented include voltage, resistance, current, power, Ohm's law, inductors, capacitors, series and parallel circuits, and magnetic circuits and devices.

ELECTRONIC DEVICES

Working knowledge of modern electronic devices and circuits in which they are employed. Electronic devices covered include PN diodes, Zener diodes, pnp and npn transistors, SCRs, unijunction transistors, JFETs, MOSFETs, and integrated circuits containing these devices. Devices used as digital switches, analog amplifiers, and oscillators. Input and output devices; analog and digital systems.

CIRCUIT ANALYSIS (Replaces ELECTRONIC DEVICES in Computer and Microelectronics specialty areas)

Equivalent circuits; loop and mode analysis, series/parallel circuits; resonance; filters; transients; time constants; pulse power circuits (pfn, Marks gen, etc.).

GRAPHICS

A beginning course in drawing/graphics. Includes lettering, line work, electrical symbols, mechanical symbols, blueprints, schematics, and shop drawings.

PROPERTIES OF MATERIALS

Comprehensive description of material properties under the separate classifications of physical, chemical, mechanical, thermal, electrical, magnetic, acoustical, and optical properties. Typical properties studied include density, porosity, hygroscopicity, corrosiveness, composition, tension, compression, flexure, shear, impact, fatigue, elasticity, resilience, ductility, hardness, lubricity, brittleness, conductivity, heat capacity, permeability, and acoustic/optic transmissivity, and reflectivity. Resource tables/handbooks identified and used extensively.

MECHANICAL DEVICES AND SYSTEMS

Belt drives, chain drives, gear drives, drive trains, linkages, fans, blowers, valves. Covers operational procedures, use, maintenance, troubleshooting, repair, and replacement.

HEATING AND COOLING

Radiation, convection, conduction, and refrigeration; heat exchangers and heat balancing; temperature control and analysis of heat balance requirements for typical industrial devices and systems.

Table 7-4. CORD's Brief Description of Technical Core, Cont'd.

FLUID POWER SYSTEMS

Overview of fluid power technology. Working knowledge of components in fluid power circuits. Hydraulic and pneumatic systems. Topics include fundamentals of fluid dynamics, fluid storage, conditioning and maintenance, pumps and compressors, actuators and fluid motors, fluid distribution and control devices, fluid circuits, and troubleshooting.

INSTRUMENTATION AND CONTROL

Practical knowledge and skills in specification, use, and calibration of measuring devices. Principles and applications of automatic control processes. Topics include process control, pressure/level measurements, flow measurement, temperature measurement, mechanical measurement, and pneumatic controls.

COMPUTER APPLICATIONS

Use of microprocessors and control devices for automated manufacturing, process control and data acquisition. Interfaces signals from measurement devices with computers; programs computer to analyze system condition from measured data and determined control device change required to optimize system operation; conditions output command signal from computer to automatically operated system control devices such as valves, pumps, boilers, etc.

MANUFACTURING PROCESSES

This course provides a background in manufacturing materials and manufacturing methods employed in cold working processes. Through lecture, demonstration, and practical applications the student becomes familiar with various types of machine tools, tooling, measuring, and inspection procedures. Automation and numerical control for machine tools are introduced.

INDUSTRIAL ELECTRICAL POWER AND EQUIPMENT

This course deals with the source, distribution, and use of electrical power in industrial plants. The first part of the course describes ac electrical power as it arrives at the plant substation and the electrical equipment needed to transform it to useful voltages, distribute it effectively, and protect it from overcurrent conditions. Equipment typically includes transformers, switchgear, fuses, and relays. The second part of the course deals with electromechanical equipment required to convert electrical power into useful, rotational mechanical energy. Equipment typically includes ac and dc motors, motor controllers, and synchromechanisms.

Source: Hull and Lovett, 1985, pp. 48–49.

Table 7-5. Ford Dearborn Partial Course Listing
for Maintenance Workers.

TRAINING PROGRAM SUMMARIES

Relay Logic - The relay logic program has been developed to enable participants to maintain and troubleshoot relay logic systems. The objectives of this program are to assist the participants to:

• Identify components and relate the physical object to the symbol.
• Interpret relay schematics.
• Maintain and troubleshoot relay systems such as the mills and washers on the cylinder block line.

This program will also prepare participants to accept programmable controller training on Modicon and Allen Bradley systems.

Basic Electronics - This program is primarily designed for maintenance personnel who will service equipment with solid state electronic controls. The program participants will learn the fundamentals of solid state electronics as well as develop troubleshooting skills to diagnose and correct electronic faults. The objectives of this program are to enable the participant to:

• Identify typical solid state symbols.
• Interpret solid state electronic schematic diagrams.
• Maintain and troubleshoot equipment with solid state electronic controls such as the electronic gage systems located on the cylinder block line.

Basic Hydraulics - The hydraulic program has been developed to qualify Hydraulic Repairmen to maintain and troubleshoot hydraulic systems. The objectives of this program are to enable the participants to:

• Identify typical hydraulic components.
• Interpret hydraulic circuit operations from schematic diagrams.
• Logically troubleshoot a typical hydraulic circuit and determine the component which is malfunctioning.
• Perform tests to determine operating condition of hydraulic components.

Basic Pneumatics - The pneumatics program has been developed to qualify pipefitters to maintain and troubleshoot pneumatic systems. The objectives of this program are to enable participants to:

• Identify typical pneumatic components.
• Interpret pneumatic circuit operations from schematic diagrams.
• Logically troubleshoot a typical pneumatic circuit and determine which component is malfunctioning.

Metrics - This training program provides participants with a view of why industry is beginning to use metric measurement. Presentation of the simple terms (meter, litre, gram, milli, centi, kilo, Celsius) most employees will encounter at work is highlighted. Explanation of the International System of Units (S.I.) and how it applies to employees is also provided.

**Table 7-5. Ford Dearborn Partial Course Listing
for Maintenance Workers, Cont'd.**

Fundamentals of Gasoline Engines - This program covers all of the systems of the basic piston engine, i.e., induction, compression, exhaust, valve train and camshaft, lubrication, cooling, and crankcase ventilation. Ignition and carburetion are covered only to the extent necessary to explain functioning of the total engine system. This presentation also covers typical construction and functioning of engines used for automotive applications.

Allen-Bradley 1 (Basic) - An introduction to Allen-Bradley Programmable Controller (P.L.C.) familiarizes electrical personnel with the concept of controllers and their applications as directed toward industry. All electrical personnel will complete this program prior to visiting vendor facilities during the de-bug and tryout period.

Allen-Bradley 2 (Advanced) - An in-depth program will totally familiarize electrical personnel with P.L.C.'s. The participants will learn detailed component descriptions and troubleshooting procedures. Participants will be exposed to basic programming and troubleshooting utilizing a CRT programming panel.

Source: Chen and others, 1984, pp. 44–45.

**Table 7-6. General Motors Truck and Bus "S" Plant, Pontiac, Michigan,
Partial Course Listing for Maintenance Workers.**

- Robot and PLC maintenance, operation, and programming
- Pneumatics theory and operation
- Basic hydraulics
- Weld controls
- Weld quality and technology
- Hydrostatic drive theory
- Automatic spray painting operation

Source: Adapted from Argoff, 1983–84.

General Motors; the second list was compiled during the CORD study.

For maintenance workers of flexible automation, the course listings provided in Table 7-5 for Ford and Table 7-6 for General Motors illustrate a different training emphasis from that of the AMT operators.

Finally, Table 7-7 lists courses used by several different firms to prepare their engineers for new technology.

These sets of courses indicate that there are some differences in courses offered by different firms. Moreover, there are differences in courses offered to the different job categories. Despite these differences, however, a core set of curricula appropriate to all job positions seems to be necessary.

One set of courses often included in this core provides *human relations* training. Such training includes courses in basic communication skills, interpersonal skills, problem solving, decision making, team building, and group problem solving.

A second set of courses often included in the core provides *knowledge of the manufacturing process* and how the equipment fits into that process. The Manufacturing Studies Board (1986) review of plants successfully implementing flexible automation found that companies are training employees not only for work in occupation-specific subjects but also in the way a specific machine process fits into the entire plant perspective. At a GE plant in Canada, new employees undergo a five-month training program designed to familiarize them not only with their particular jobs but with the manufacturing processes and the plant's management system as well (Farnum, 1986). At the GM stamping plant implementing multimillion-dollar automated stamping presses, a series of overview courses on the new process are offered to all employees. These cover such topics as press room organization, an introduction to preventive maintenance and productivity, press room computerization, a description of modernized press room personnel, and a brief description of the new technology. These overview topics are covered in twenty-four hours of classroom training.

A third set of courses in the core may be *basic skills* training. Many employees, regardless of their jobs, may need this training to achieve high school reading and math skills.

In sum, there is clearly no established curriculum that can be readily applied to a particular plant. What seems to be apparent with flexible automation is that occupation- or machine-specific training is not sufficient. All firms find it necessary to offer training in skills that cut across functional boundaries. These generic

Table 7-7. Courses for Engineers for Computer Automation.

Type of Company	Course Title	Course Description
Electrical equipment manufacturer	Welding Engineering	Five days. *Objective:* to help individuals who have metal-joining responsibilities in a managing or engineering function. *Method:* Course will cover the fundamentals of welding engineering; welding processes; design for welding; welding metallurgy, standards, codes; cost calculating; and welding applications.
Plastics manufacturer	Instrumentation and Process Control for Engineers	Thirty hours. *Description:* This is a practical program to introduce new engineers to process control instrumentation by combining control theory with problems taken from actual plant experience. It includes a review of process control hardware, a workshop on control problems, an introduction to control theory, a survey of methods for testing and setting controllers, and a brief look at direct digital control.
Research and development firm	Applied Statistics for Engineers	Taught one evening per week. This course will stress the uses of statistical analysis methods applied in biological, physical, and engineering sciences. Topics will include univariate and multivariate analysis methods in linear and nonlinear models framework, sampling and experimental designs considerations and parameter estimation, time series analysis, and other methods presented to establish the effectiveness of statistics as a tool for applied scientific and engineering employees. Students should have good working knowledge of matrix algebra, some appreciation of probability distribution theory, and ability to work in differential and integral calculus. If sufficient interest is expressed the course will span two semesters.

Table 7-7. Courses for Engineers for Computer Automation, Cont'd.

Type of Company	Course Title	Course Description
Engineering design	New Engineering Concepts	Ten days. *Objectives:* to expose participants to new technology and science important to the company and to acquaint participants with the corporate personnel working with this science and technology; to stimulate the participants' thinking of the effect of the energy crisis and changes in the socioeconomic environment (that is ecology and consumerism) on engineering designs; and to develop insights into tools and techniques affecting engineering design.

Source: Lusterman, 1977, pp. 88–89.

courses may be the key to integrating the factory of the future. They should be given careful consideration in planning for an in-house AMT training program.

Evaluation. A trend to more systematic evaluation of training programs has been identified by several observers (for example, Lusterman, 1977, 1985). Yet evaluations are still quite primitive, relying primarily on judgment. The Conference Board found in their survey of training that "the most common source of information for evaluation is perhaps the least objective one and certainly the most remote from on-the-job behavior: the opinions of participants" (Lusterman, 1977, p. 59). There are exceptions, of course. AT&T's training evaluation program includes comparisons of trainee performance before and after training, and computes the worth of training on the basis of estimates of increased productivity; this is certainly not a primitive evaluation methodology. But most manufacturing firms are not like AT&T. Thus, managers are left to wonder if their training programs need to be as extensive as they are and whether they are as helpful as they might be.

In evaluating an in-house training program for flexible automation, the first question to address is, Why is the evaluation being done? Is it to provide top management with a reason to maintain continuous skill development training instead of having only one-shot initial training? Is it to refine the way the courses are presented? Is it to determine if some instructors are better than others? Is it to convince first-line supervisors to approve worker time off the line for training? Is it to support an enlarged training budget? Obviously, these different purposes yield different evaluation criteria and different degrees of effort in the evaluation. Refining course presentations, for example, is a far more straightforward evaluation criterion than persuading production supervisors to send their workers to training.

Having defined the purposes of the evaluation, the type of information desired by the audience must be determined. Top management usually says that it wants to see cost figures to know if a particular program is working; yet its lack of true financial analyses with new equipment suggests that its decision-making strategy is based less on cost figures and more on tangible results. For many organizations, then, a detailed quantitative analysis of the benefits of a training program may be less necessary than a description of what the program has done. For example, the human resource department at Mead Corporation was recently asked to prove to top management that its employee involvement program (EIP) was cost-effective. Instead of playing with numbers, the department put together a videotape in which EIP workers described in their own words how EIP had helped them do their jobs. In a particularly pertinent anecdote, a worker described how he had been involved in the selection and installation of AMT equipment, and how, because of the employees' involvement, the equipment was up and running within twenty-four hours of its arrival—far sooner than anyone would have predicted. Anecdotes like these are quite convincing and may be the evaluation information that is needed. Although Mead management had initially asked for cost information, it stopped asking after seeing the videotape.

The purpose and information desired by management help to define how the evaluation will proceed. If we assume for the moment that the purpose of an evaluation is to judge the overall effectiveness of the in-house training program, three evaluation criteria are typically considered and quantified: (1) the performance of the individual and the organization, (2) the satisfaction of the trainees, and (3) the efficiency or cost-benefit. The performance of the individual and the organization should be divided into process objectives (such as proficiency and certification of course completion) and performance outcomes (such as increased uptime, increased fault detection, increased production improvements from workers, decreased accidents, and decreased scrap rates). For example, GM's Pontiac plant boasted .3 percent downtime as a result of the training program. The second evaluation criterion, trainee satisfaction, can include satisfaction with the overall content of the course as well as satisfaction with such specific elements as intructors or format. The final criterion, cost-efficiency, can include a formal cost-benefit analysis or a less formal one. Ron Zukowski (1984), for example, constructed an informal cost-benefit analysis of General Electric's in-house training program for engineers. He compared costs of retraining to costs of rehiring and found that it cost $76,000 to train twenty design engineers in digital technology (including unproductive salaries, instructor fees, and course development) and $200,000 to lay off the engineers (with severance pay and idle time) and hire replacements. A more complicated approach is described by Cascio (1982), in which a utility model of the costs and training outcomes can be quantified. Factors to be included in training costs might be trainer time, lost productivity during training, and training development costs. Factors to be included in returns on training investment might include less resistance to change, resolution of production problems, and such organizational performance measures as lowered scrap rates. Also to be included in returns on training investment is the cost to the organization if an individual is not trained (in accidents, poor production, and so on).

The problem with formal cost-benefit analyses has always been that the estimates of costs are questionable. Unless the organization is willing to undertake an experiment in which trained and nontrained workers can be compared, returns on training investment are difficult to estimate accurately. Thus, most organizations will find it more beneficial to undertake less formal cost-benefit analyses, like that done by Zukowski. Moreover, with respect to the purpose of the evaluation and what information decision makers actually want, a cost-benefit analysis may prove extraneous at best and a stall tactic at worst.

Conclusion

The *Wall Street Journal* (Nag, 1986) reported that automakers were having enormous problems both in coordinating sophisticated machinery and in training their workers to handle it. Given these problems, one might expect to see a lot of structured training in firms implementing flexible automation. Unfortunately, as discussed in the beginning of this chapter, many firms are content to rely on unstructured OJT. This may be a major reason that only half of many advanced systems today are working (Ettlie, 1986c).

The value of an in-house training program was expounded upon in this chapter. Such a program need not be expensive. Having unpaid local college interns develop the curriculum is obviously a low-cost approach. Providing training before production pressures mount (when the new equipment is installed) is cheaper than pulling people away from production just when they are most needed. Using simulations on demonstration equipment in protected classrooms is a lower-cost strategy than waiting until the equipment malfunctions on-line before the operator or maintenance worker figures out how to detect and fix the problem. Thus, a structured in-house training program need not be expensive.

When implementing AMT, a training program will work only when it is established in a fully supportive organizational context. Management must assign training the priority it needs. Westinghouse's requirement for all to take or teach eight hours of training per month illustrates the needed management commitment. Management must allow the employee enough time to complete the entire training process, and should not allow transfers in and out of classes before training is completed. Also, it is essential that equipment be dedicated to training for hands-on learning. This might mean having training on a third-shift-only basis; regardless, trainees must have the opportunity to make mistakes off-line. Bringing the work force up to a minimum skill level may be necessary before needed skills training can occur. Job designs that allow the trainee to practice the lessons learned in training are needed. A career development personnel policy should be designed to match with a skill development training program. The concept of a proper match is essential with training. Training does not solve all problems. Training does not reduce absenteeism or increase worker morale; the organizational context does that. Unless it is properly developed, training can cause more problems than it solves.

8

Adapting Personnel Policies to Facilitate Automation

In this chapter, the effects of flexible automation on personnel policies are discussed. This chapter is not a general introduction to all personnel policies; rather, only those personnel policy areas likely to be most affected by the implementation of flexible automation are discussed. Six such policy areas are identified: (1) job classifications, (2) pay, (3) career development, (4) job security, (5) shift work, and (6) union-management relations.

A review of AMT case studies to date indicates that flexible automation broadens job classifications so that fewer classifications are needed. Job descriptions with AMT tend to focus on roles rather than tasks. Moreover, as teams are increasingly used on the shopfloor, there may be a need to write job descriptions for teams rather than individuals.

AMT also affects policies by introducing new priorities and bases for pay. Options used by AMT plants to meet these new needs range from basing individual worker pay on the contribution of both the group and individual to innovation bonus plans. Each option is evaluated for its ability to meet several criteria necessary for effective pay policies in flexible automated factories. From this evaluation, it is concluded that no single option meets all the criteria; thus, a flexible automated factory needs to develop a pay policy that combines in one comprehensive pay plan aspects of several different options.

For personnel policies regarding career progression, research indicates that having specified career progression policies for production workers and technical staff is far more necessary with flexible automation than with traditional equipment. Examples of career progression plans are identified, such as crossing over the barrier between operators and engineers.

193

Job security policies that promise there will no layoffs with the new technology are critical to the successful implementation of flexible automation. Since it is important not to renege on these promises, several options are described for planning the technological implementation in such a way that job security promises can be met.

The installation of flexible automation creates an increased need for shift work. Moreover, since the installation of flexible automation changes everything from job design to training needs, existing shift work policies often need to be reexamined in the light of these changes. Reexamination is likely to lead to changes in the number of hours per shift, the task responsibilities of off-shift workers, shift assignments, and the use of technical support workers on off-shifts.

Finally, changes in union-management relationships revolve in part around how the role of the union must change in a flexible automated factory. Several suggestions are offered in an effort to preserve constructive relationships as both union and management struggle with the unpredictable future of the union, new technology, a new market, and a new factory. These suggestions include giving the union advance notice of the intent to automate, using union representatives specifically familiar with technology issues, bargaining over work rule options for coping with the effects of the technical change rather than over specific contractual work rules, making liberal use of union membership surveys, and establishing written principles to describe a shared vision of the types of work force effects to be promoted and avoided.

Job Classifications

Flexible automation affects job classifications and job descriptions. As firms move to flexible automation, they find that in order for the work force to make optimal use of the new equipment, workers must have overlapping job responsibilities, be knowledgeable about a wide variety of issues, and be flexible to redeploy on the shopfloor as needs arise. These changes to the work force tend to become reflected in much broader job descriptions (Butera, 1984). Such job descriptions often put less emphasis on a predictable sequence of actions in individual specialized jobs;

instead, they emphasize roles, mobility between tasks, membership in groups, personal reliability, decision making, and problem-solving responsibilities (Manufacturing Studies Board, 1986). The following job description for a robotics/automated systems technician indicates the breadth of talents and responsibilities that might be included.

> Technicians are technical specialists with broad-based electromechanical skills who are familiar with electrical, electronic, mechanical and hydraulic devices. They are usually specialists in one or two identifiable types of specialty equipment. In their one or two identifiable types of specialty, they can install, set up, troubleshoot, repair/replace parts, modify, test and operate the equipment. They may work either under the supervision of an enginer, as a member of a team, or as a supervisor of other technicians [Hull and Lovett, 1985, p. 42].

Not only are job descriptions broader, but as the jobs come to demand greater responsibility as well as the greater mental effort required to monitor equipment, their descriptions are often upgraded beyond those that required knowledge only of the conventional equipment (Argote, Goodman, and Schkade, 1983; Graham and Rosenthal, 1985). While the degree to which the job is upgraded depends to some extent on the job design of the operator and technical support personnel, it appears that in a fair number of plants, job descriptions need to be rewritten to reflect the types of increased skills discussed in Chapter Six. When this is done, the descriptions reflect higher-grade jobs than were adequate with conventional equipment.

Flexible automated factories that choose to design AMT jobs around teams may find the traditional approach, in which job descriptions are written for individuals, inappropriate. For example, in Davis and Wacker's (1987) food processing plant where work teams were implemented, detailed individualized job descriptions could not convey what was required of workers (that is, to respond as a team to unforeseen problems), nor could detailed job descriptions address what the workers desired from the company (that is, recognition, challenge, and a secure career path). Human resource personnel at the plant met this challenge to traditional concepts of job descriptions by writing descriptions for teams. These descriptions provided detailed delineation of such team responsibilities as operating a packaging line for a product, maintaining certain machines, and inspecting materials. The job descriptions for the individuals were very general, specifying only that the individual was to help carry out the team responsibilities, participate in team decisions, cross-train, and use his or her judgment to contribute to team productivity, quality, maintenance, and development. Thus, while the team job descriptions were quite detailed, the individual job descriptions were not.

With job descriptions that are broader than before, fewer job classifications are needed. The National Academy of Sciences study (Manufacturing Studies Board, 1986) provides several examples of companies reducing the number of job classifications when flexible automation was implemented:

- A unionized automobile components plant, with a $60 million flexible manufacturing system, planned to have three hourly job classifications, two skilled and one unskilled. In a unionized assembly plant of the same company, job classifications were reduced from 200 to 34.

- An engine plant had only two job classifications, "resources" and "technicians."

- A manufacturer of military vehicle components, with an FMS, had one job classification, system operator, which was equivalent to the highest machine operator in other departments.

- An aerospace company with 530 employees at a unionized plant eliminated 39 classifications. Another of its unionized plants with 95 employees went from 20 to 5 classifications. At its nonunion plant, the work was structured into five versatile and flexible classifications [pp. 3-7].

With fewer job classifications, management flexibility is enhanced to redeploy workers throughout the shopfloor.

Pay Policies

A second personnel policy affected by AMT is the compensation policy of the plant. Pay or compensation policies serve three purposes for a company. First, they provide compensation to individuals for their time at work and for their loyalty. Second, they help to differentiate among people with varying skills and organizational status. Third, they provide incentives and rewards for more and better effort on the job.

How does the introduction of AMT affect the manner in which each of these purposes is achieved? To achieve the first purpose of a compensation policy—paying for time at work and loyalty—workers in conventional factories have traditionally been paid according to the number of hours worked and company seniority. For flexible automated factories, however, the number of hours spent at work is less important than what the workers do while they are there. The worker with flexible automation must, at a minimum, be attentive to the production process and be sufficiently involved to recognize potential problems before they occur. To encourage this, workers must be paid according to what they do rather than the time they put in at work.

The second purpose of a pay policy—differentiating among people—has traditionally been accomplished in conventional factories by having numerous job classifications and paying salaries only to exempt workers. With flexible automation, however, job classifications are broader, yielding less differentiation in the pay system. Moreover, as teamwork and coordination increase in importance with AMT, status differences, such as those between salaried and hourly workers, will need to be deemphasized. Finally, as hourly workers take on more and more of the responsibilities traditionally given to salaried workers (for example, scheduling, recruiting, administration, job assignments, budgeting, and decision making), distinctions between hourly and salaried workers become quite blurred. Yet people are motivated by differences; they must know where they stand in relation to others, and they want their paycheck to reflect their position. Thus, while pay policies in flexible factories can no longer rely on the traditional methods of distinguishing hourly from salaried workers and having numerous job classifications, new options must still provide workers with the differentiation they need.

The third purpose of a pay policy—incentive and rewards for superior performance—has not traditionally been a priority in the pay policies of factories with conventional equipment. With AMT, incentive and reward become far more important. Since the intention of flexible automation is to enable the factory to operate at a high uptime rate, producing diverse high-quality goods with minimal scrap and rework, rewards for these several dimensions of performance must be built into the pay system.

In addition to changes in the way the three purposes of a pay policy are achieved, AMT creates other changes in pay systems. In conventional factories, rewards are primarily administered to individuals for individual performance. With flexible automation, coordinating with others is far more important. Having individuals performing at exceptional levels may not only be insufficient but counterproductive. An employee who outshines others is of no use to the integrated factory if no one wants to work with him or her. Thus, the pay policies for a factory with flexible automation will need to reward group performance or, at the very least, reward individuals for their aptitude and willingness to work with others. Yet such policies must not discourage the individual from hard work. The challenge with flexible automation is to devise a pay system that rewards both individual and group performance.

The range of rewards available to the organization with flexible automation will differ from that available to workers with conventional equipment. Traditionally, supervisors have relied on such rewards as providing overtime (where union policy did not prohibit it) or allowing workers to take time off from their jobs when production was low. Moreover, a worker on an incentive system could work hard on a particular day and substantially increase his or her take-home pay. With flexible automation, if equipment is running at three shifts, there is no overtime. Even if a firm isn't running at full capacity, a firm that needs to continue to use overtime is a firm that has not yet integrated its planning system with its production system. The more integrated the firm, the less need for unplanned overtime after the "initial" months and years of start-up. Thus, overtime as reward becomes less viable.

There is a problem with time off as a reward as well. When workers accept more responsibility for larger parts of the shopfloor and become more important in coordinating the production process, time off from the job can no longer be given often enough to constitute a reward. Finally, paying the worker on a traditional incentive scheme is not feasible because incentives are typically associated with machine activity. For example, an agricultural equipment manufacturer's FMS required the firm to end its uptime-based incentive plan (Shaiken, 1983). This was because machine downtime attributable to circumstances beyond the workers' control was having a disproportionately detrimental impact on workers' wages, and workers' control over equipment uptime and thus over their own wages was substantially reduced. For the same reasons, Wilkinson (1983) found that all of the twelve companies he studied that implemented CNC machines had to end their piecework pay systems when the CNCs were installed. Thus, with flexible automation, new rewards for a job well done will have to be identified—rewards for which there is little precedent on the shopfloor.

In sum, the implementation of flexible automation creates a need to reevaluate the pay policies used to compensate machine operators and other shopfloor personnel. This reevaluation will indicate that, while the purposes of the pay policies may be the same, their relative priorities and the ways in which they can be achieved will have changed dramatically. We now turn to options used by firms implementing flexible automation to modify their pay policies to meet these challenges.

Pay Policy Options for Flexible Automation

A pay policy for flexible automation should meet at least four, and perhaps five, criteria to confront effectively the challenges posed by flexible automation. The policy should:

1. Be equitable across individuals.
2. Balance compensation for individual and group performance.
3. Base rewards on multiple performance criteria.

4. Provide people a means to differentiate among themselves.
5. Incorporate market realities of organization where possible.

Equitability is an important criterion since a pay policy may inadvertently become inequitable unless specifically designed otherwise. For example, in one company, the earnings of the cell workers went up at such a rapid rate that dissatisfaction was created among those workers not employed in the cell (Fazakerley, 1974). The second criterion, balancing payment based on group performance with that based on individual contributions to the group task, is important because, with AMT, both group and individual performance are essential. Yet a survey by Pullen (1976) of firms implementing manufacturing cells found that while most workers were organized into teams, they were paid on an individual piecework scheme. Pullen concluded that this incongruity between group work and rewards would, in the long run, create substantial problems.

Basing rewards on multiple performance criteria is another important criterion because many kinds of performance are necessary to the success of flexible automated factories. Differentiating among people is important as well, because people are often motivated by comparing themselves against yardsticks. Finally, a pay system for flexible automation that incorporates the market realities under which the organization functions can more completely assign total job responsibility to the worker. With these criteria for AMT pay policies, then, several options for new pay policies are evaluated here.

Base Pay of Workers. The first set of options concerns how the base pay of workers with flexible automation should be computed. Four options for computing base pay are described: group performance, group plus individual, salary, and skill-based.

Group Performance. This method pays workers on the basis of the output of the group or work cell to which they belong, not the number of hours an individual works. The productivity of the work cell is often determined by both the number of parts produced by the cell and the quality of the work. Such pay systems typically have all cell members share equally in the cell's earnings, thus encouraging peer pressure on those workers who contribute less than others. Such a plan is best applied when employees of roughly equivalent skills are assigned to each group. Thus, as long as the group is composed exclusively of robot technicians or operators responsible for and able to perform approximately the same tasks, such a pay plan is a viable option. In firms that use this pay option, maintenance, engineering, and supervision are generally not considered part of the team for the purposes of pay.

Judging this option according to the five criteria of a pay policy for flexible automation, we see that, among group members, this policy is likely to be perceived as equitable; furthermore, it uses multiple performance criteria. Unfortunately, the option is weighted in the direction of group performance, providing only peer pressure to motivate individual performance. In addition, among group members, the option offers no means for differentiation; the smarter, more able members earn the same amount as those less able.

Group Plus Individual. Group plus individual is a modification of the group performance method. This option recognizes that members of a group do not contribute equally to group performance, either in motivation level or in ability. Therefore, this method, referred to as group + individual base pay, computes an individual's pay on the basis of the individual's job position, the group's output, and the contribution made by the individual to the group output. One formula described by Wagner (1985) is as follows:

individual base pay = group standard hour + (# hours individual
worked × group output × job position
evaluation points of physical and mental
effort required)

This formula allows one to determine a worker's base pay as the output of the worker's group adjusted by the skill requirements of the worker's job as well as the number of hours worked. According to a study of a firm using this formula, workers paid in this fashion increased productivity 111 percent over a base pay formula that incorporated group standard and output only, with no adjustment for individual contribution.

This option nicely captures the benefits of a group pay system while improving on the problems of a pay policy that compensates only for group performance. Thus, while still remaining equitable, the pay policy also fulfills the criterion of balancing individual and group performance, as well as differentiating among people of different abilities and skills. Maintenance workers, supervisors, and engineers can be members of a group sharing the same pay policy, permitting a more encompassing and realistic conception of how work is divided up on the shopfloor of a firm with flexible automation. Note, however, that the formula given would need to be modified to incorporate criteria of performance other than output. Note also that, in the formula, the number of hours worked serves as a proxy measure for a worker's motivational contribution. As has already been discussed, with flexible automation the number of hours is less relevant than what the person does while at work. However, including in the base pay formula a subjective judgment of a worker's contribution is likely to create a policy that is seen as inequitable. Thus, for the time being, it may be best to use the number of hours worked.

Salary. A third option for calculating individual base pay is to pay everyone a salary wage and thus end the distinction between hourly and salaried personnel. The Manufacturing Studies Board (1986) review of twenty-four flexible factories found that the most popular approach to pay was to put all workers on salary.

This method has the definite advantage of equity, particularly between the salaried staff (such as engineers) and production workers. In many ways, the symbolic value of placing everyone on salary is enormous. If everyone is paid on a similar basis, there is no reason to treat anyone differently; production workers are as valuable to the survival and growth of the organization as technical and managerial staff.

Despite the benefits, the change to an all-salaried work force by itself is not enough. First, an all-salaried pay policy fails to balance the individual with group performance needs; it encourages individual performance only, leaving group contribution only symbolically compensated. Second, paying individuals according to salary alone does not consider the performance output of the individual. While such a policy can include gradations of salary that reflect different levels of performance, many of the all-salaried pay policies fail to do this. For many, increments in salary are based primarily on seniority, rather than performance. This option fails to incorporate any performance criteria, let alone multiple criteria. Finally, this option is usually (although it need not be) accompanied by a salary compression problem. Since it is not often accompanied by a pay-oriented career development ladder, there may be little differentiation in the pay of different people, despite real differences in abilities or contributions to organizational survival. Thus, alone, an all-salaried work force appears to be insufficient to meet the pay challenges posed by flexible automation.

Skill-Based. To compensate for the problems of a pay policy based exclusively on salary, many firms moving to flexible automation have incorporated into the base pay equation the skills that an individual has acquired. Thus, while all individuals are paid on salary, their salary is determined by their skills. At a GE plant in Canada, all employees except for senior management fall into one of two grade classifications (Farnum, 1986). Pay ranges from $17,000 to $30,000 (Canadian) for one grade and from $24,000 to $45,000 (Canadian) for the other. Membership in a grade is based on skill level and degree of responsibility. In a food factory, workers are paid skill-based salaries, with salary ranges (for 1979) running from $850 a month for competence in one skill cluster to $2,000 a month for competence in all operations of the plant (Hirschhorn, 1984).

Skill-based pay systems (also called pay-for-knowledge) start with the identification of those tasks that need to be done in the organization (Lawler and Ledford, 1985). Next, the skills needed to perform those tasks are identified, and tests or measures are developed to determine whether a worker has learned the necessary skills. Wages are attached to knowledge of different tasks with total salary compensation based on the number of different tasks known, as is the case for the food factory just mentioned, or on the skill level and degree of responsibility of those tasks, as is the case at the GE Canada plant. To determine whether a person has acquired a skill or knowledge of a task, a variety of different methods have been used. Some systems assess skill competency using peer ratings of performance; other systems use supervisors' judgments or written question-and-answer tests.

Skill-based salary pay policies provide many advantages for the factory with flexible automation. They give managers substantial flexibility, since workers can be moved to different locations according to their skills and production needs rather than their job position or seniority. According to Ed Lawler and Gerry Ledford (1985), when the policy is combined with a participative approach to management and when the system encourages acquisition of upward-tending skills, employees in a skill-based pay system come to understand the entirety of the organizational operations. They thus have a much greater ability to solve systemic problems, communicate more effectively with other people, are more motivated because their job feedback is more meaningful, and can become more self-managing as employees. Staff at Westinghouse's Defense and Electronics Center in Baltimore, Maryland, claim that the skill-based salary pay policy used there helps to ease employees' concerns about being displaced by automation because they know they have the flexibility to move wherever the need arises (Julian, 1985).

A pay policy that bases pay on skill is not without its disadvantages, however. Lawler and Ledford (1985) identify several disadvantages of skill-based pay plans: (1) higher average hourly wages, since individuals tend to be more valuable, (2) larger investments in training, (3) costs associated with individuals always learning new skills rather than efficiently doing jobs they have mastered, (4) problems with equitable skill assessment practices, (5) difficulties in establishing market-based comparisons for fair wages, (6) problems of "topping out" when employees learn all the identified skills, (7) administrative burdens, and (8) problems in having employees keep a large set of skills well honed. In addition, as new technology is introduced, skills for which employees are already being paid may become obsolete. Because of these disadvantages, labor turnover may be quite high in firms with skill-based pay systems (Fadem, 1984).

Thus, despite its substantial advantages, a skill-based pay system is not without its problems. Some of these problems are particularly troublesome for the flexible automated factory. First, group output is not compensated in skill-based pay. Second, since skill is the sole basis for pay, multiple performance criteria are not considered. Finally, having workers spend a great deal of time learning new skills rather than work in efficient production is not feasible with flexible factories. Solutions to the first two problems probably lie in combining skill-based pay with other options to be discussed. The last problem—the cost of workers being less efficient while learning—may be rectified by having some tasks in the skill progression scheme and some outside of it paid on a separate basis. For example, at South Mack, a midwestern truck manufacturer, the inefficiencies of the pay system created such a problem that management eliminated the grinding and turning operations from the skill clusters so that only specialists were assigned to those jobs.

Individual Bonus Plans. Not only do pay policy options compute workers' base pay in different ways, but some pay policies also reward individual workers for work above and beyond what they would receive from their base pay—that is, with individual bonus plans. Three options for individual performance bonus plans are evaluated for their particular pertinence to plants with flexible automation: innovation rewards, group standard, and above-average multiperformance measures.

Innovation Rewards. Many firms reward workers for creative or cost-sharing ideas; AT&T and Xerox are two examples. For flexible automated factories, innovation rewards can be particularly useful when innovations in process improvements are tied to such outputs as scrap rates or met delivery schedules.

In terms of the criteria for flexible automated factory pay policies, the innovation reward option tends to be seen as equitable because typically any person or group is eligible. This option also can balance individual and group performance needs if teams as well as individuals are eligible for the bonus. Moreover, the option differentiates individuals by distinguishing between those who are motivated and able to work at an idea and those who desire to skate along and let others lead the company. Finally, when tied to performance criteria connected to the process or product improve-

ment itself, this option fulfills the criterion of meeting multiple
performance objectives.

Group Standard Rewards. In this pay policy option, a group
standard of performance is established, with the group choosing the
reward for meeting that standard. Viable rewards for flexible
automated factories might include earning extra pay, the right to
pick and choose a benefit package, or the time or tuition fee for
educational seminars.

This option takes its idea from the Earned Idle Time
program used in a Harmon International plant in Bolivar,
Tennessee, as part of the quality-of-worklife program. Earned Idle
Time referred to a pay policy that allowed work groups to select
among a set of rewards if they reached their production standard for
any particular day. These rewards included going home early with
pay for a full day's work, earning extra pay for extra work based on
group performance, and earning bonus hours for whatever a group
wanted to do at some point later on. Macy (1982) reports that this
option created substantial and positive attitudinal changes at the
Bolivar plant.

This option has the definite advantage of an equitable pay
system, since only those groups that perform above the standard are
granted the rewards. This option also helps to differentiate between
groups willing to work harder and those that are not. One major
disadvantage is in the way a group standard becomes established.
If it is based solely on quantity of group output, the pay system
becomes unidimensional and therefore of less value to automated
factories. If it is based on multiple dimensions of group output, it
becomes difficult to define a standard across different machines and
group responsibilities. Finally, this option is entirely imbalanced in
the direction of group performance and fails to take into account
the individual's need to be recognized for contributing to the group
output. Thus, alone, this pay policy option may have limited utility
for many plants with flexible automation.

Above-Average Multiperformance Measures. This option for
individual bonus plans allocates points to workers in recognition
of above-average performance in such areas as scrap rates produced

by the machines for which the worker is responsible, attendance, accident rates, machine uptime, and process improvement ideas used. For each area, thresholds of average performance are defined and the worker given points for anything above average. At the end of each year, symbolic and monetary recognition are provided to those employees with the most points for each performance measure and across all performance measures.

This option takes its idea from the bonus plan used by Diamond International in Palmer, Massachusetts, called the "100 Club." Described by Harris (1985), performance criteria at Diamond included above-average performance, perfect attendance, and working a year without industrial accidents. At the close of each year, the earned points were converted into modest prizes. Diamond boasted that this bonus plan contributed to a 16.5 percent productivity increase, a 40 percent decline in error rate, a 72 percent decrease in grievances, and a 43.7 percent decline in time lost because of accidents.

This option has the advantage of being applicable to all workers and therefore equitable. It also is the only one of the three individual bonus plan options that explicitly rewards multiple dimensions of performance. In addition, with the point system, workers can readily distinguish themselves from others as their points accumulate throughout the year. A problem with this option could arise if points were assigned only for individual performance. This problem could be avoided by giving points for above-average group achievements as well; the points could be equally divided among the group members. The other problem with this option— a difficulty in establishing the basis for determining an average performance—is less easily resolved.

Plant-Wide Pay Options. Pay policies may also allocate pay on the basis of plant-wide performance. Two types of plant-wide pay options applicable to flexible automation are discussed here: *gainsharing and profit-sharing* pay policies.

The feature common to gainsharing and profit-sharing plans is that workers' base pay is supplemented according to how well the entire plant performs. As Don Davis describes it, there are three varieties of gainsharing plans: Scanlon, Rucker, and IMPRO-

SHARE (Davis, 1986a). The three differ in the method used to allocate financial gains to employees and the degree to which participation in decision making is stressed. The Scanlon plan computes the amount of gains from the ratio of total personnel costs to total value of production and places the greatest stress on participative decision making; the Rucker plan computes gains by comparing personnel costs to value added from production; and IMPROSHARE computes gains by comparing hours of production to number of units produced, placing the least emphasis on participation. In contrast to gainsharing, profit-sharing plans pay out only when the company experiences a profit, regardless of the ratio of outputs to employee hours spent. Thus, in profit-sharing plans, employees truly become similar to stockholders, experiencing as well as influencing the company's downturns and upswings. When the company turns a profit, the compensation may reflect it handsomely. In 1985, employees at Hewlett-Packard, had received for several years between 7 and 9 percent of their base pay in pretax profits.

Both gainsharing and profit-sharing meet the optional evaluation criterion for flexible automated factory pay options of exposing the worker to the reality of the market (although profit-sharing is much closer to the market than gainsharing). Moreover, both plans assign gains and profits to employees on the basis of their existing salaries or wages. Thus, these plant-wide bonus plans tend to be viewed as equitable by plant employees. Both plans also include multiple criteria of performance in the formulas for determining how much money is returned to the employees (although the plans differ in the precise criteria used).

However, neither plan meets all the evaluation criteria. By exclusively rewarding plant-wide performance, they fail to recognize the need for individual recognition. They are difficult to administer because they do not always adequately reflect market conditions, such as when the best efforts of a highly motivated work force are negated by a slumping market or by inefficiencies in sales or management (Farnum, 1986). Employees may feel undeservedly rewarded when they see great inefficiencies at the plant and inadequately rewarded when they have worked very hard.

An additional concern with gainsharing and profit-sharing

plans is that if people are to feel rewarded, they must feel they are being rewarded for something that they understand and can control. Often, however, formulas for computing paybacks from these plans are so complicated that workers cannot relate a particular year's or month's salary supplement to what they did on the job. For example, a gainsharing plan under consideration at Volvo's Kalmar plant included a complex formula of six factors: inventory turnover, direct labor hours per car, added materials, excessive consumption of materials and supplies, spoilage and adjustments, and a quality index (Hauck and Ross, 1985). With such a complicated formula, workers may have difficulty being convinced that what they did one month has anything to do with their salary supplements. In addition, workers may not perceive that they have any control over many of the elements included in the formula. At the Volvo plant, workers were surveyed to identify which factors they felt they controlled. Results indicated that two-thirds felt they had no control over inventory turnover, 72 percent felt they had no control over direct labor hours, 71 percent felt they had no control over added materials, 48 percent felt they had no control over consumption of materials and supplies, and 48 percent felt they had no control over spoilage. The quality index (which was the result of an inspection of 3 percent of the cars) was the only element over which most (79 percent) felt they had some control. As long as the workers feel they have no control over the factors that are included in the gainsharing or profit-sharing formula, these pay options will have only limited utility for rewarding workers for outstanding performance or encouraging better performance.

Summary of Pay Options

Table 8-1 presents a summary of how the different pay policy options fulfill the different criteria for meeting the pay challenges posed by flexible automation. It is apparent from this table that no option meets all the criteria. Thus, there is no single best option. The Manufacturing Studies Board (1986) drew a similar conclusion from its twenty-four case studies: "The degree of variety [of pay options] suggests that no consensus has emerged on the best ways

Table 8-1. Evaluation of Pay Policy Options for Flexible Automation.

Options	Equity	Criteria			
		Individual-Group Balance	Multiple Performance Criteria	Differentiation	Exposure to Market Realities
Worker Base Pay					
Group Performance	Yes	No	Yes	No	No
Group + Individual	Yes	Yes	No	Yes	No
Salary	Yes	No	No	?	No
Skill-based	Yes	No	No	Yes	No
Individual or Group Bonus Plans					
Innovation Rewards	Yes	Yes	Yes	Yes	No
Group Standard	Yes	No	No	Yes	No
Multiperformance Measures	Yes	No	Yes	Yes	No
Plant-wide Bonus Plans					
Gainsharing	Yes	No	Yes	No	Yes
Profit-sharing	Yes	No	Yes	No	Yes

to evaluate and reward workers for their contributions to advanced manufacturing technologies" (p. 48).

While there is clearly no single best way, this review of options suggests that perhaps the best strategy for developing new pay options is to combine different methods that complement each other by meeting different evaluation criteria. A combination of a group performance standard and individual innovation bonus rewards will come much closer than either option alone to meeting the needs of a firm implementing flexible automation. A combination of skill-based salaries and gainsharing plans might create the needed balance between group and individual performance recognition. For example, at an agricultural equipment manufacturer implementing an FMS, consultants found that the best solution for the company's pay problems was to introduce a skill-based pay policy for individual base pay and to reward groups for machine utilization rates (Blumberg and Alber, 1982). Thus, group and individual work were rewarded, and multiple performance criteria (skill development and machine utilization) were recognized.

Career Development

A third personnel policy that is affected by the implementation of AMT is the organization's career progression scheme. In most conventional factories today, the career development progressions of both shopfloor workers and professionals (for example, engineers) are either established by the plant's job classification scheme or are left to be handled informally by concerned supervisors. For plants with AMT, however, neither method is viable.

Job classifications cannot be used as the basis for career progression because flexible automation necessitates broader job classifications that no longer define specific and gradual progressions of increasing skills and responsibilities. Leaving career progression to the ad hoc judgments of supervisors is also inappropriate with flexible automation since employees interested in career progression have no protection from capricious supervisors. Thus, in flexible automated factories, where dependency on the motivation of automation workers is so great, a formal career progression strategy that depends neither on ad hoc management nor on job descriptions needs to be established.

A formal career progression policy serves several purposes. First, it ensures a balance between the needs of the AMT factory to meet intense production pressures and the needs of the AMT workers to learn new skills. Without a clearly delineated career path, workers may find themselves always fighting fires and leave the organization out of frustration at not doing other work. For example, Hoxie and Shea (1977) describe the case of a Management Information System (MIS) manager who complained, "I've been losing one or two of my top systems people every year because I can't offer enough new development work. These guys and gals are trained professionals, and they represent a real loss to the company. . . . Yet my maintenance requirements are increasing [and these people don't want to do maintenance]" (p. 98).

Another purpose for a formal career progression policy is to motivate workers to perform well on their existing tasks because they can understand how these tasks serve as stepping stones to upgraded jobs (Butera, 1984). Thus, technicians in an engineering career track, for example, will be more willing to perform their diagnostic work, since they know their work has utility for their future engineering jobs.

A third purpose served by a formal career progression is to keep the work force from becoming technologically obsolete. Technical upgrading in flexible automated factories needs to occur every day. For example, for engineers, such technical factors as machine vision, hand grasping, tactile senses, voice recognition, interactive computer linkages, and user-friendly equipment are changing at an amazingly rapid pace. The engineer who graduated from college a few years ago is hard-pressed to be familiar with these advances today. Given this high rate of technical obsolescence, it is not to the company's advantage to maintain the work force in a steady state of knowledge. Rather, a career progression strategy is needed that allows older, stable employees to move up, laterally, or out while it brings in younger employees with a different knowledge base. Mixing the new work force with the old can be done at the production worker level as well as at the professional level. Production workers who have had experience working in teams and with engineers, for example, can serve as a valuable counterweight to more senior workers who fear such coordination.

Therefore, when flexible automation is installed, the need for a formal career progression policy increases in importance if the organization is to remain technologically current and adaptable to continuous technological change.

Many firms recently implementing flexible automation have begun to understand the need to attend to a career progression strategy for their production and technical workers (Manufacturing Studies Board, 1986). In these companies, the strategy has allowed for gradual increments in responsibilities and skills, while encouraging workers to continue to move up in the organization. As senior workers move up, new employees with fresh approaches are brought in from the outside.

One career progression option used by several companies with flexible automation complements the compensation policy of skill-based pay described earlier. Skill or task modules are defined and a progression by which more and more skills are acquired is clearly delineated. As with any progression policy, fences can be inserted that allow people to move up to the next grade of skills only when people with the higher grades have left; skill modules that become technologically obsolete can be "red-circled," requiring employees to reassert their competence with new learning.

Another career progression option used by some companies promotes the move from production machine operator to engineer. In one study of AMT plants, several companies adopted a career path strategy in which several different grades of operators progressed into several different grades of engineers (Butera, 1984). The operator grades included assembler, monitor, and technician, while the engineering grades included engineering assistant, technician, manufacturing engineer, and developmental engineer.

Another career progression option focuses on learning the technical aspects of flexible automation systems. In some organizations, this type of career progression may be applied to operators only. One organization used the categories of system attendant, system technician, and stager, with each level knowing progressively more about the technical aspects of the system (Manufacturing Studies Board, 1986). This method can also be applied to the maintenance crew. For example, some companies have differentiated a career progression for maintenance in which repairers eventually progress to preventive maintenance jobs.

Still another option for career progression includes programming jobs. One common career path has been established in which machinists eventually progress to NC programming jobs (Shaiken, 1983). In other companies, manual assemblers have the opportunity to develop into computer operators and applications programmers (Manufacturing Studies Board, 1986). In still others, career paths distinguish between the maintenance of computer systems and the development of new systems; this distinction seems essential to keep good systems people in the organization (Hoxie and Shea, 1977).

Finally, a career progression option should not discount the possibility of workers becoming supervisors and managers. A common path for work teams is to elect a team member to be a team leader responsible for the internal functioning of the group. The team leader can then become a supervisor responsible for coordinating several different teams. Finally, the supervisor can be promoted to a position similar to that of a manager with the responsibility for the functioning of a team of supervisors.

In sum, there are many different career progression possibilities with flexible automation; in fact, this variety is one of its side benefits. With broadly defined job classifications, the worker (if allowed by management) has the freedom to move in a number of different directions. An assembler can eventually become a programmer, manager, or developmental engineer. However, such a progression is possible only if it is explicitly planned for at the beginning, when AMT equipment is being selected and alternative job designs are being evaluated. Even then, without a detailed understanding of what this career progression is, and management support to ensure that career planning is carried out, the advantages of flexibility and career planning will be for naught.

Job Security Promises

A fourth personnel policy to be affected by the implementation of AMT is the layoff policy. Promises to ensure job security when new technology is installed are important to the success of flexible automation efforts. If workers fear they will be displaced by a robot, they will resist it. Resistance can easily lead to sabotage; even without open sabotage, new equipment can easily malfunction if not watched closely by motivated workers, as we have discussed elsewhere.

Promises to lay off no workers permanently are important not only because they reduce resistance to the new technology; for many companies, there is little choice in the matter. In unionized plants, layoffs due solely to technological change are often prohibited. In nonunionized plants, similar elaborate promises have often been necessary to convince workers of the need to undergo training or accept a temporary layoff. Thus, in many firms contemplating whether or not job security really needs to be promised from the outset, management should be fully aware of the severe consequences of not promising job security. Managers that decide to move ahead without such a promise may be sacrificing long-term worker motivation for short-term reductions in direct costs.

Once job security is promised, there is no reneging. One plant manager confided to me that, despite a letter written to the union promising job security when new technology was installed, he realized that the new markets he had initially hoped for were not materializing. Thus, he felt it would be necessary to undertake major layoffs in order to achieve the financial gains from the new technology. The manager went to the corporation's attorneys to find out if there was a way to be relieved of his job security promise; there wasn't. Finally, in desperation, plant management decided to lay off workers before the equipment arrived so that the connection between the layoffs and the new technology could be denied. Fortunately for the management, the plant layoff coincided with a corporate-wide layoff and market downturn; nevertheless, after that, the union mistrusted the intentions of plant management. In another example, a small company changing over to CIM discovered that it might not be able to meet its job security promises after the equipment was installed (Roitman, Liker, and Roskies, 1987). Although the management of this company did no more than inform the workers that there might be layoffs and that those able to master the new skills would be kept, substantial worker mistrust was generated because of what the workers viewed as management's reneging on a promise. Thus, once promised, job security must be achieved.

Several options have been used by firms to meet the job security challenges posed by flexible automation. These include (1) bringing subcontracted work back into the plant, (2) understaffing to reduce the likelihood of layoffs during business downturns, (3) underutilizing AMT equipment during busy times to reduce need for layoffs during slow times, (4) long-range planning prior to implementation to ensure optimal utilization of existing staff, (5) slowing down the installation of the new equipment to allow both natural attrition and transfers to take care of the supplemental personnel, (6) retraining for those jobs that the new automation will create (for example, programming, maintenance, engineering technicians), and (7) reassigning personnel to parts of the plant that typically go wanting (such as preventive maintenance, cleaning up the plant, or community work) (Manufacturing Studies Board, 1986; Skinner and Chakraborty, 1982; Kaplan, 1983; Foulkes and Hirsch, 1984). While the seventh option may not directly contribute to production output, it may add sufficiently to work force motivation to be a useful short-term strategy until the additional capacity of the equipment can be used.

The option that is selected should become a written policy against which management actions are compared. An example of such a job security policy prepared by a company implementing automation is as follows:

> Whenever practicable, regular employees whose jobs have been discontinued will be transferred to equivalent assignments for which they are qualified, and at the same rates of pay. It is recognized, however, that permanent assignments to the same rated jobs may not be immediately possible for all employees. When permanent transfers cannot be made, departments are expected to endeavor to provide the most suitable temporary work possible, anywhere in the company. It is the continuing responsibility of the department head to see that such employees are eventually placed

in permanent positions—after training if necessary
[Mann and Williams, 1960, p. 228].

Only when management's actions are held to a written policy will
workers come to believe that if they work hard and are motivated
to learn new skills, they will keep their jobs as long as management
does.

Shift Work Policies

A fifth personnel policy affected by AMT implementation
concerns shift work. Experience with flexible automation indicates
that for most firms, the installation of the new equipment
necessitates an increase in the number of shifts worked (Abbott,
1981), usually to recoup the financial investment in the equipment.
Moreover, leaving new, expensive equipment idle is far less efficient
than leaving idle thirty-year-old drill presses. The effort to run the
new equipment at full capacity often creates a need for a second
shift and in many cases a third.

Since shift work (or more of it) is introduced with flexible
automation, shift work policies are often reevaluated when flexible
automation is introduced. Most companies undertake such a
reevaluation because new job skills and designs, as well as training
needs, usually mean that old policies are inappropriate. Several
aspects of the shift work policies should be reevaluated.

First, the number of hours worked per shift should be
reassessed. There is absolutely no reason for the eight-hours-per-
shift policy to continue if workers or management determine that
a different policy would be more helpful. At a small company
transforming to CIM, each operator worked twelve-hour shifts, with
technical support continuing two shifts of eight hours each
(Roitman, Liker, and Roskies, 1987). Thus, there was technical
support overlap while at the same time workers could reduce the
number of working days.

A second aspect of shift policies that warrants reexamination
is the task responsibilities for each shift. Options are essentially
unlimited here: Workers on all shifts can be expected to have the
same responsibilities, or workers on second and third shifts can have
responsibilties that differ from those of the first shift. In one series

of case studies, two companies with essentially the same CNC equipment chose different shift assignment strategies (Wilkinson, 1983). In one company, the manager felt that third-shift operators needed to be more than mere machine tenders to be responsible for production during the night; at the other company, a night foreman was trained to deal with programming problems, keeping third-shift operators as mere machine tenders.

A third aspect of shift policies that should be reevaluated is how workers are assigned to the different shifts. The traditional method of having shift assignment dictated by management or union contract may no longer be appropriate. In some flexible automated factories, team members have been found to establish more accepted and equitable shift assignments than management or union contracts (Manufacturing Studies Board, 1986).

Finally, when flexible automation is installed, the assignment of technical support to the shifts should be reviewed. In one review of cases, a common problem with shift work was found to be the reluctance of maintenance to work the extra shifts (Gerwin and Tarondeau, 1982). For example, at a British plant implementing several NC machines, second and third shifts were run. However, because maintenance didn't want to work these shifts, downtime became high enough to cast doubt on the utility of the off-shifts. This problem is also found with CAD equipment, where drafters are expected to work second or third shifts, yet the manufacturing and design engineering staff with whom they must interact generally do not work such shifts (Majchrzak and others, 1987). Thus, in determining the optimal shift work schedule, it does little good to schedule maintenance workers for a shift they don't want, since they are likely to leave the company as soon as a better job offer comes around. A shift work strategy that provides substantial skills and responsibilities to off-shift operators, modifies shift schedules to allow for overlap of day and night shifts, or has the equipment run essentially unmanned are options to consider.

In sum, the increase in shift work with flexible automation will necessitate a reconsideration of the shift work policies in the organization—that is, who gets assigned to do what, for how many hours, and with what support. In undertaking this reexamination, it may be necessary to go back to the job design or training program to provide operators with more responsibility and more independence from technical support staff. Such an examination would signify a truly open systems approach to planning the human infrastructure of the flexible automated factory.

Union-Management Relations

The changes to the human infrastructure discussed in this book have profound effects on the relationship between the union and management. The flexibility on the shopfloor of factories with AMT—broader job classifications, complex and multifaceted pay schemes, fewer distinctions between employees, and so on—is contrary to the traditional preference of American unions for narrow job distinctions and rigid work rules. With AMT, the union's role as a defender of seniority and uniform conditions must change. New duties may include defending workers' rights in decision making, delineating specific technical issues for negotiation, acting as a clearinghouse of technical information, and training labor negotiators in the technologies and important technological change issues (Davis and Roitman, 1986; Markey, 1982; Piore, 1985). Moreover, the needed flexibility on the shopfloor is achieved only when local unions work out solutions with their own management. The national union's role in maintaining uniform rights in grievances and wages is thus seriously undermined by flexible automation (Katz and Sabel, 1985).

These changes in the role of the union clearly have dramatic effects on the way union leadership and plant management relate. Union leadership may have difficulty defining a new role for itself. If the union leadership does define a new role, it may be different from the one desired by management. For example, management may not accept workers' having decision-making rights and thus may have difficulty adapting to a union's role as a defender of those rights. Even when a union's new role is defined and accepted, coping with the tension between national and local leadership often presents substantial pressures. Finally, since union leadership and management are charting new waters both together and independently, both must learn to cope with unforeseen events in dealing with each other as the technology is implemented, as well as in predicting the effects of the technology on the workplace.

These changes to the union-management relationship will create strain. This strain need not be counterproductive for the organization, however. One success story of a plant effectively coping with the changes to union-management relations when automated technology was implemented is described by Williams (1985). The strain faced by management was related to how to negotiate a change where workers from four different bargaining groups (production, craft engineering, supervision, and staff) were involved. Management's strategy included working out its own proposals before opening negotiations, setting up a joint forum of all the union representatives to discuss the changes, offering similar costs and benefits to each union group, conveying management trust by committing only to those matters that management was willing to implement, and exercising extreme care in the timing and presentation of information to acclimate the union groups to the new ideas. The initial responses of the four unions to management's proposals showed extreme concern; but when management challenged the unions to come up with a better proposal, the unions, after two weeks of deliberations, determined that they could not. Implementation of the changes then proceeded smoothly.

Experience with flexible automated factories suggests several ways to help foster a constructive union-management relationship during the process of technological change. These suggestions are described here.

Advance Notice. Perhaps the first rule of working with unions is to provide them with advance notice of the impending technological change. A large proportion of major labor contracts already provide for advance notice. For example, Fadem (1984) reviewed 100 union contracts and found that 31 percent had such a provision. Advance notice is important not only because it illustrates management's goodwill by not hiding information from workers but also because it provides time to bargain about how and when to discontinue nonautomated operations—negotiations that could affect layoffs. Allowing adequate time to bargain about this issue has been identified by the *California Lawyer* trade journal as the key future legal fight in the robotics controversy (Hanauer, 1984). By providing between six and twelve months of advance notice, as the trade journal recommends, the employer can never be seriously accused of preventing negotiations.

Union Technology Representatives. Several observers of union-management relations suggest that trade unions should establish a union subcommittee separate from the shop committee to discuss and present to the shop committee a union strategy on the introduction of new equipment (Clark, Jacobs, King, and Rose, 1984; Poza, 1983; Fadem, 1984). The 1979 United Auto Workers–Ford agreement recognizes this need for the union to focus on the technology issue by suggesting that local-level union committees identify a single person or set of persons who would be responsible for discussing anticipated introductions of new technology and evaluating their impact. By not using the people who are on the shop committee, an atmosphere of collaboration rather than bargaining can be created. Moreover, a union representative who focuses exclusively on technology will be able to devote the attention needed to understand the system and its implications without being constantly concerned about solving workers' grievances and other unrelated matters. In fact, the British Trade Union Congress has developed a training program for unionists specifically focused on new technology agreements. Included in the training are checklists and guidebooks for negotiation (Markey, 1982). In another example, Westinghouse management permitted the union to choose one welder to spend six weeks with R&D personnel developing a new robot (Foulkes and Hirsch, 1984). Senior local management and union officials then flew to Japan for a two-week tour to view robots at work in plants. One purpose of the trip was to show union leaders the competition facing U.S. industry and Westinghouse.

Multiple Union Work Rule Options. Michael Piore (1985) suggests another approach to constructive union-management relationships during technological change. In this approach, management and the union bargain not over specific work rule changes but over work rule options available for coping with the effects of the technology on the human infrastructure. Some of these union options are presented in Table 8-2. The range of options for each effect illustrates the fact that when bargaining does occur, it need not be focused on one contractual issue. Finding those issues less central to the integrity of the bargaining contract that still cope sufficiently with the technology effects will prove a more fruitful strategy than hammering away at a single contractual issue until either side gives in.

Union Membership Surveys. Another suggestion for constructive union-management relationships is the liberal use of union membership surveys. Local union leaders have been elected to represent their membership. Their election conveys to the leaders that the membership abides by the leaders' principles and priorities. When new technology is implemented, new priorities often must be established. When the implementation of new technology does not coincide with a union election, the membership may not have a formal means for sharing its views because new information is released from management. Thus, the leadership may occasionally find itself espousing one view about certain human resource issues when a majority of the membership espouses another view. For example, in one firm, the unions had claimed seven to eight years ago that shift work would be "socially unacceptable" to the work force (Abbott, 1981). Since management kept pressing the issue, the union finally balloted its members and found that a majority of the work force preferred to work a twelve-hour shift, despite the union's claims to the contrary. Thus, as human resource options are considered during the planning for the new technology, the joint management-union committee should consider conducting periodic surveys to assess the views of the members on these issues. If the union leadership has correctly assessed the views of the membership, such surveys will only serve to strengthen their position. If the leadership has misinterpreted the members' views, it is better to find that out prior to election time.

Shared Vision and Values. Union-management relationships are most constructive when both union and management share clear visions and values about the desired effects of technolog-

Table 8-2. Work Rule Options with Technological Change.

Type of Work Force Effects of New Technology	Illustrative Types of Union Responses to Potential Effects
1. Employment effects	Advance notice
	Attrition versus layoff
	Slow down rate of introduction
	Influence proposed staffing plans for new technology
	Retraining for displaced employees to qualify for other jobs
	Expanded bidding rights
	Job placement and counseling
	Pressure for job-creating investments by company
	Shorter workweek
2. Relocation effects	Expanded job transfer rights at same location and retraining to qualify for other jobs
3. Health and safety effects	Request studies; access to studies
	Grieve conditions
4. Bargaining unit effects	Assurances precluding "transfer of work"
	Challenge management actions
5. Skill and income effects	Challenge appropriateness of lower ratings
	Assurances that revised jobs will pay as much as the jobs they replaced
6. Job qualification effects	Training for new job
	Longer period to demonstrate mastery
	Burden of proof for disqualifying
7. Job advancement effects	Training
	Bidding rights
8. Job control and job pressure effects	Assurances that new system will not be used to monitor individual performance
	Constraints on load and other job conditions
	Grieve conditions and direct action
9. Job satisfaction effects	Influence on job design
	Employee involvement

Source: Walton, 1983, p. 11.

ical change (Walton, 1983). The shared vision should indicate, in writing, the general types of work force effects that are to be promoted and those that are to be avoided by the move to flexible automation. Also specified should be the institutional procedures for information sharing and technology assessment, as well as the mechanisms for implementing the policies. With these issues in writing, an accountability mechanism is established and the joint union-management committee can get on with the task at hand of developing an optimal human and technical system.

Conclusions

Given the open systems model adopted by this book, the effect that flexible automation will have on each of the policies described in this chapter will depend to a large extent on the choices that have been made thus far. Operators who will have robot technician jobs will have broader job classifications than operators whose sole responsibility will be machine tending. A training program developed for continuous learning will make a career progression policy more feasible. Redesigning marketing jobs so that marketing personnel become knowledgeable early on about the capacity of the new technology will increase the chances that new markets can be identified for the new capacity and that no-layoff promises can be met.

For policies to be congruent with the organization and with other aspects of the technological implementation, substantial advance planning is needed. If the company is unionized, union representatives need to be involved in planning job designs to be convinced of the need to reduce the number of job classifications. For no-layoff promises to be kept, substantial advance planning for implementation is needed so that the decision to slow down the purchase and installation of the new equipment can be made if new markets are not found for the increased capacity. Again, the reader is reminded that options are options only as long as the environment does not become too constrained. Management must not wait until the equipment has been selected and installed before considering options for personnel policies.

9

Altering the
Organizational Structure
to Enhance Performance

Every organization, in order to maintain control, must divide its staff, functions, and processes into distinguishable units. This is called differentiation. Yet it is also necessary for these people, functions, and processes to be closely coordinated. This is called integration. Maintaining the balance between integration and differentiation is a central dilemma for organizing with AMT. The need for integration is so great that any distinction between units seems to create problems in coordination.

Faced with this dilemma, nine solutions that AMT plants have used are presented, as follows: (1) Adding a CAD/CAM coordinating unit (2) Having coordinating units report to the same boss (3) Developing task forces and standing committees (4) Grouping units by common products (5) Grouping units by common processes (6) Utilizing matrices (7) Decentralizing (8) Downsizing, and (9) Fostering an organizational climate that encourages coordination.

Each solution is evaluated for its merits and the problems it poses. From this evaluation, no solution is found to be without problems. Thus, combining the most successful aspects of several solutions seems to be the best answer. One such combination that maintains the necessary balance between integration and differentiation includes grouping units by flow production processes, introducing committees, matrixing workers to both the flow process and their function or committee, decentralizing some decisions while centralizing others, and creating an organizational climate with the message, "Integrate! Coordinate! Communicate!"

Organizational Dilemma of the Flexible Automated Factory

The installation of AMT equipment facilitates the electronic linking of people, processes, and functions. AMT provides the opportunity for management to develop an integrated and comprehensive plan for manufacturing products of high quality, delivered at low cost and on time. An essential element of this plan is determining how to organize the people, functions, and processes for the ideal amount of coordination and integration. Since the management of an organization requires that people, functions, and processes be grouped in some way and since any grouping creates, by definition, distinctions between groups, a dilemma of the flexible factory arises: how to group units to foster more integration and coordination than differentiation. The frustration posed by this dilemma is aptly described by the plant manager of a petrochemical plant designed to have the most advanced computer-controlled equipment in the world: "Management had experienced something of a dilemma in reconciling the organizational convenience of separately organized units on the one hand and the technological imperatives of a very highly integrated system of processes on the other. In this event, technology had to be sacrificed to organizational requirements. If we had been clever enough, we would have been able to devise an organization set-up to make full use of the technological possibilities" (Abbott, 1981, p. 64).

This dilemma is often acutely experienced by design and manufacturing engineering. While design and manufacturing engineering clearly have different purposes and use different methods to achieve those purposes—and thus should be divided— successful products are only possible when there is effective coordination between them. With CAD/CAM or CIM, effective coordination between manufacturing and design engineering becomes even more crucial. Since a part can now be designed on a CAD system by the R&D engineer and immediately transferred to an NC tape, careful review by manufacturing engineers and skilled trades must be explicitly built into the organizational structure; otherwise, the expertise of these individuals will be inadvertently ignored. Thus, while design and manufacturing must remain separate organizational entities, they must simultaneously be integrated. How much of the integration can occur with the technology itself? Very little. For example, in a study on the implementation of CAD, the influence of different factors on the effectiveness of the liaison between manufacturing and engineering was examined (Mosher and Majchrzak, 1986). The results indicated that effective liaison was attributable not to such CAD system factors as the capability to share and modify drawings more easily but rather to such organizational factors as management's encouragement to work with manufacturing, accessibility of manufacturing staff to engineers' overtures, and language similarities between manufacturing and engineering staff. Thus, these barriers to coordination are not the type to be reduced by the introduction of new automation such as CAD/CAM. Other mechanisms to enhance coordination and yet maintain differentiation are needed.

The dilemma of grouping units in a way that encourages coordination over differentiation cannot be solved in similar ways for all organizations. Rather, each organization must define the solution most suitable to its particular circumstances. Because of the unique nature of each organization's solution and the fact that the solution cannot be found in the technology, this chapter describes a range of solutions used by different organizations with AMT. While much research remains to be done on when each of these solutions is likely to be most suitable, advantages and disadvantages documented for each solution can be identified. From the discussion below, researchers will be able quickly to identify the research questions yet to be answered while managers will have the benefit of a review of solutions potentially applicable to their own organizations.

Adding New Departmental Functions

With AMT, perhaps one of the least disruptive ways to encourage coordination while simultaneously maintaining traditional functional groups is to add a new function to the CAD/CAM support group. This option is also the one most frequently used by flexible automated factories (Manufacturing Studies Board, 1986; Shaiken, 1983). For example, when a set of CNC machines was implemented in one company, a unit responsible for NC program-

Figure 9-1. Structure of Manufacturing Organization with CNC Machine Implementation. A. Before Implementation.

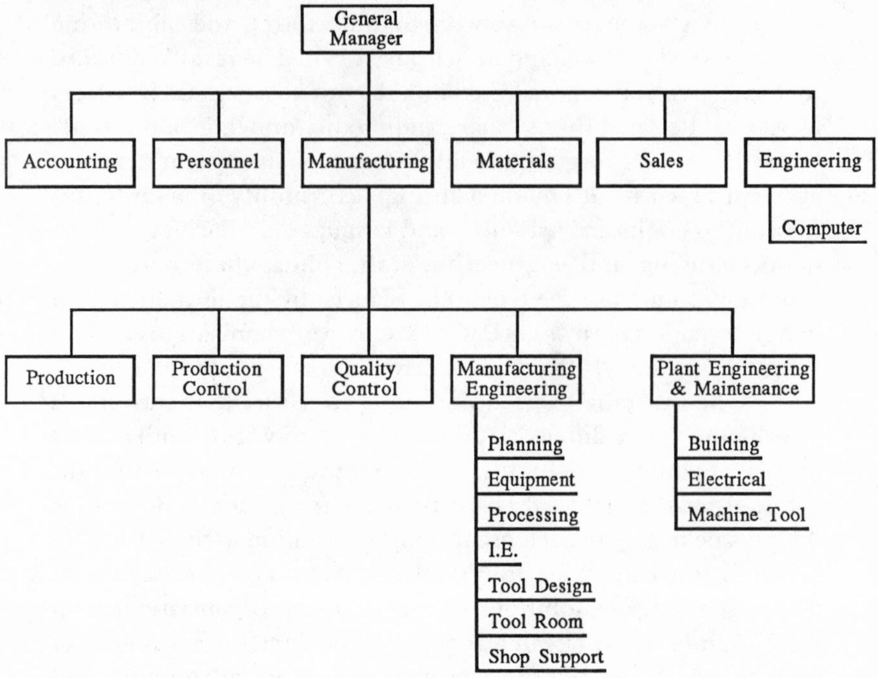

(A.) Before Implementation

ming, equipment selection, and maintenance was added (Risch, 1971). Figure 9-1 presents the formal organizational structures of the firm before (A) and after (B) implementing the CNC machines.

The new function may consist of an entire unit of staff or involve only one person (called a CAD/CAM coordinator) responsible not for actually developing the system but for coordinating the work of different departments in their system development efforts. This person or unit might serve as a conduit of information as well as a facilitator of interdepartmental meetings and efforts. Like a product manager, the CAD/CAM or CIM coordinator can be quite

Figure 9-1. Structure of Manufacturing Organization with CNC
Machine Implementation. B. After Implementation.

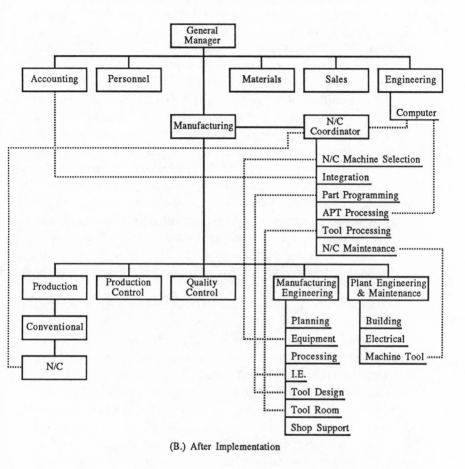

(B.) After Implementation

Source: Risch, 1971, pp. 12–23.

effective at identifying cross-departmental problems, finding
organizational resources for solving certain problems, and ensuring
that system development efforts proceed in the same direction.
Unfortunately, many organizations assign the CAD/CAM coordinator position to a senior-level technical person close to retirement

who has long since lost touch with the shopfloor. Such a person spends considerable time learning about new systems from external sources and conveying that knowledge to higher levels in the organization; however, the usefulness of that person for actual system work in the trenches is questionable at best. A CAD/CAM coordinator clearly must serve as a coordinator at the levels where specific system development decisions are made.

The addition of a new AMT unit to a plant's organization chart has both advantages and disadvantages. The addition of a new function requires little change in the organizational structure, thus minimally disrupting it at a time when it least needs disruption. The new function can also serve as the central coordinating unit for AMT, fostering technical as well as organizational linkages between the different parts of the organization. As such, it can encourage the design and use of common data bases and standards, something unlikely to occur without a centralized function. It can also help to attract and retain technical people specifically trained on the system, and identify and resolve common problems across the different uses of the system.

Despite the advantages of defining a new function when flexible automation is installed, arguments against such a function abound. One stems from a fear that if a new function is created, managers in other units will not have to accept any responsibility for the automation project. Another argument is that the new function may become removed from the local needs of different parts of the organization. An organizational unit out of touch with the shopfloor, for example, runs the risk of encouraging a system that is seen as irrelevant by the shopfloor users. A third argument is that if ultimate integration and coordination are really to occur, the line and support managers should be expected to do it themselves rather than relying on another organizational unit to take responsibility. This argument has been summarized thus: "This kind of organization works, but one wonders if in setting up this czar or high priest [of AMT] you will really accomplish anything that can't be accomplished just as well by encouraging people in the functional departments to figure out what NC is all about and what they have to know to work with it" (Risch, 1971, p. 12). With such a perspective, the solution to the dilemma would not be to create a new department. Rather, strategic decisions for integration and system development would be assigned to a team of existing managers with technical system development staff placed within the existing grouping of units.

Arguments both for and against a centralized function responsible for CIM are convincing, and thus it is difficult to recommend whether or not to introduce such a new function when flexible automation is implemented. Therefore, it appears that the decision should rest not on the implementation of flexible automation per se but rather on organizational factors. Is the organization likely to be able to attract talented CIM experts without a title and specific function listed on the organization chart? If not, a separate function is needed. Is the organization likely to encourage integration and coordination by having a special coordinating unit, or can it assign responsibility equally to all relevant managers? If the former is the case, a new function is useful. Is a new function necessary in order to give flexible automation sufficient visibility and priority, or will implementation proceed smoothly simply by CEO edict? If visibility will suffer, a new function (even if temporary) may be necessary. Will a new function create jealousy and misunderstanding, as well as convey to workers another faddish project that management has decided to focus on for a while? If so, it should not be introduced. By addressing such questions as these, the decision of whether or not a new function should be created with flexible automation will be made more easily.

Reporting to the Same Boss

One of the most straightforward ways to encourage interdepartmental coordination in an organization is to have the units that need to be coordinated assigned to report to the same higher-level manager. For example, *Business Week* ("High Tech to the Rescue," 1986) reports that at a PPG Industries Inc. $30-million glass plant, the implementation of automated equipment was coupled with an organizational structure that promoted a mode of coordination different from that traditionally used by PPG. In this plant, the plant manager had both sales and manufacturing reporting to him rather than having sales reporting to a higher level of management. The rationale for this structure was to encourage better coordination between sales and manufacturing; by giving both functions to the same boss, better coordination than before was much more likely to occur.

The advantages of such a solution are apparent. Units that report to the same boss are likely to try to resolve their own conflicts without taking them up a level. Unit managers are therefore more likely to coordinate with each other, whether they want to or not. The disadvantages of such as solution, though, indicate that the solution is only a partial one at best. Simply having two units with the same boss doesn't necessarily mean that the correct issues will be integrated across the units. Sales and manufacturing may not share any more information than before or collaborate more frequently on customer orders. Additional solutions are needed, such as an organizational climate that identifies key issues for integration, task forces, and so on.

Committees

A third solution for the differentiation-integration dilemma is the use of standing committees and task forces. This is perhaps the most popular model of liaison when flexible automation is implemented. It does not necessitate creating a new position or restructuring the organization to have people report to new bosses. An example of one type of standing committee is presented in Figure 9-2. This organization chart illustrates the new structure of an automobile components factory that was built with substantial amounts of flexible automation equipment. The superintendent of the plant heads the Plant Operations Committee, which is made up of shift representatives, finance, manufacturing, engineering, electronic systems, and union representatives. Reporting to the Plant Operations Committee is the Shift Operations Group (one group for both shifts), which is a committee composed of the production and support personnel.

Standing committees have become popular in plants with flexible automation in part because they can allow workers to

Figure 9-2. Organizational Structure at an Automobile Components Plant.

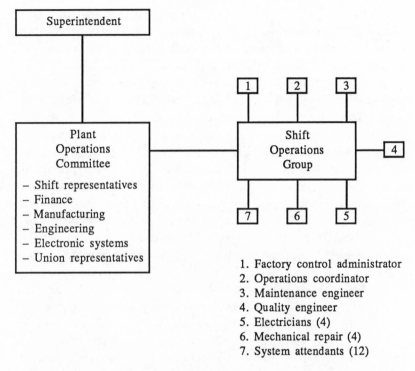

1. Factory control administrator
2. Operations coordinator
3. Maintenance engineer
4. Quality engineer
5. Electricians (4)
6. Mechanical repair (4)
7. System attendants (12)

Source: Manufacturing Studies Board, 1986, p. 28.

remain in the same positions, merely adding to their duties. Thus, in Figure 9-2, electricians are still electricians, operators are still attendants, and the manufacturing manager is still manager of manufacturing. The difference, of course, is in their need to coordinate with others in other areas; there is no need to structure their own departments differently. Another reason for the popularity of standing committees as liaison devices is that they tend to work so well in many organizations. For example, in a study of a food processing plant installing flexible automation, the frequent reliance on interdepartmental working parties was found to increase flexibility within the organization (Dickson, 1981): "[It] has given rise to greater integration within the organization and tends to discourage tendencies towards overspecialization, rigid role definition and hierarchical attitudes. Such working parties tended to aid the company's attempts towards participative management, and it did appear that their existence, and the participative management practices used, facilitated the introduction of the new technology, both physically and psychologically" (p. 178).

While standing committees may be successful in some organizations, they can easily lead to feelings of impatience about time wasted in meetings, frustration at the amount of time that group consensus takes, and anxiety at never finding committee members when they're needed. Some of these feelings stem from ill-run meetings and possibly from not having the right people as members of the committee. The latter anxiety comes from not scheduling meetings at appropriate times (for example, all companies should have times when key people are at their desks or at other specified places) and possibly including too many of the same people in committees rather than spreading the knowledge about.

In order to make standing committees work with flexible automation, committee leaders should be appointed, partly on the basis of their team-building and meeting skills. Leaders should be chosen for their abilities to facilitate effective and efficient group discussion, to serve as role models who confront members with hidden agendas and conflicts, and to help the committee to subordinate individual interests for the purpose of integration and coordination. In addition, any committee in a flexible factory needs to have a clear delineation of its responsibilities since, without that, the committee can easily get bogged down in the realities of an open systems approach where everything is connected to everything and thus anything should be discussed. The organization may decide to have multiple committees on different topics: quality control, supplier contracts, new product development, scheduling, training, process improvements, and so on. Membership of the different committees should overlap—for example, a representative of the supplier contract committee should be on the scheduling committee, and a member of the product development committee should be on the process improvements committee. In a flexible factory, coordination will be effective only if it is multilayered, focuses on multiple topics, and provides for communication that is both horizontal (between committees) as well as vertical (from committees to workers and back).

Grouping Common Products Together

A fourth way of ensuring adequate coordination with AMT is the *focused factory,* a term coined by Skinner (1974). A focused factory is one in which a plant groups its units into different product lines, perhaps one for old, standardized products and another for new, customized products. In some plants implementing flexible automation, grouping by products may be equivalent to grouping according to whether or not a machine is automated— that is, the flexible machines may be responsible for customized products while other machines are responsible for standardized products. In other plants, grouping by products may be equivalent to grouping by distinctly different production processes that correspond to unique product families.

Grouping production units by product has received substantial attention in automated factories of late (see, for example, Kolodny and Armstrong, 1985; Susman and Chase, 1986). While such a basis for grouping has merit, particularly when it corresponds to meaningful differences in the marketplace, several conditions of the factory must be met for "product shops" to be effective. First, the product mix must be fairly limited in order for highly integrated factories to be managed adequately. Given the current level of technology, factories organized by products may not be able to cope with simultaneously high levels of variety, uncertainty, and interdependence. Second, a product shop must possess its own resources for administration, service, and maintenance to avoid conflict between the shops (Aguren and Edgren, 1980). Moreover, the manufacturing chain in the shop must be uninterrupted so that parts are not sent elsewhere for supplementary machining and semifabricated goods are not needed from other organizational units. Thus, grouping by product is certainly an option that many firms are considering when implementing flexible automation. Research has indicated, however, that this option for grouping production units may need to be used with some caution.

Grouping Common Processes Together

A fifth solution to the coordination-differentiation dilemma posed by AMT is to group common processes together. People and functions that share similar production needs thus can be more easily coordinated. Three alternative ways of grouping common processes for AMT are discussed.

The first alternative is the most traditional one, whereby units are defined by convenient stopping points in the production process. Each distinct organizational unit typically signifies a separate step in the sequential production process. Examples of this process grouping alternative include differentiating a printed circuit board (PCB) plant manufacturing department into fabrication, assembly, and test, or separating a different plant's operations into machining, forging, and pinch and roll.

In this approach, steps in the production process are defined to optimize coordination among those people and functions involved in each step of the process. Moreover, since unit distinctions are often made at clearly separate steps in the production process, the organizational structure is not complicated by attention to the less essential coordination between steps. Thus, the advantages of this option are apparent. With flexible automation, however, many of the basic assumptions of this option—such as a sequential production process and little need for coordination between production steps—are no longer appropriate. Often, flexible production flows in a reiterative fashion, such as to correct errors or add multilayered components; this reiteration necessitates coordination between definable production steps as frequently as within any single step. Thus, for factories with AMT, this option of differentiating units by convenient stopping points in the production process seems short-lived at best.

A second alternative is to recognize that the production process of flexible equipment is inherently different from that of conventional equipment. Thus, if a plant has not completely automated all of its operations (as many do not), the organizational chart may be differentiated by operations performed by automated and conventional equipment. In a new organization chart of a plant moving toward CIM, for example, operations were differentiated not by convenient stopping points in the process but by whether the equipment consisted of the new NC machining centers or the conventional manual equipment (Roitman, Liker, and Roskies, 1987).

This approach to process grouping has definite advantages over the previous one because it recognizes the inherent differences in producing with automated and nonautomated equipment and encourages coordination appropriately. However, since many companies implement islands of automation rather than integrated lines, expensive AMT is often expected to serve multiple production lines, some of which consist of automated equipment and some of which do not. Thus, distinguishing between automated and nonautomated operations is often unrealistic and misleading. This option probably has the most utility when the distinction between automated and nonautomated operations precisely coincides with a distinction between different types of product lines—a solution already discussed.

A final alternative for process grouping with AMT is referred to as flow or parallel production. In this approach, units are defined as having similar complete production processes. Thus, a unit will be responsible for both the insertion and testing of a group of PCB components or for the entire assembly of a car body. Units may be differentiated because they use different equipment, manufacture different products, or proceed through different complete sequences of the production process. By grouping units in this fashion, all those people and functions necessary to complete an entire production process (whether using automated or nonautomated equipment) are brought together to optimize coordination.

A machine shop that reorganized in this fashion when CNCs and group technology were introduced illustrates this alternative to process grouping (Jasper and Vapor, 1979). When the new technology was first implemented in the machine shop, units were split with one foreman responsible for all drilling operations and another foreman responsible for all CNC operations. The company decided that this structure was not encouraging effective utilization of either the CNC machines or the group technology. The units were therefore regrouped so that a single foreman was now responsible for all those machine tools capable of completing parts requiring similar production processes. One foreman was responsible for all complex milling and drilling (which included CNC maching centers as well as conventional drills) and another foreman was responsible for common milling and drilling operations. Each group foreman was also made responsible for the timely completion of the entire process within a budget.

For AMT, grouping units by flow or complete production processes has the particular advantage of ensuring coordination throughout the entire production sequence. Thus, the possibility of truly integrated production is enhanced. Such a solution has other benefits as well. In the machine shop reorganization just described, performance data were obtained before and after the reorganization. The results indicated an improvement in the percentage of schedules met, a decrease in the number and amount of cost overruns, an improvement in communications (since foremen had more control over the entire process), improved time standards, improved management information (because the foremen knew the progress of all parts throughout the process), and greater foreman job satisfaction.

As with all of the solutions discussed thus far, this alternative carries with it certain cautions. Grouping units by common processes requires the equipment to be selected and installed to encourage a flow-type of production process. Thus, the more integrated the equipment for a particular process, the better. Moreover, the less that the same equipment needs to be used by more than one production line, the better; otherwise, process managers may find themselves in conflict over the use of the equipment. Assuming these criteria are met, grouping by distinctive flows may be more commonly used for process grouping in flexible factories than it has been in the past.

Matrix

A sixth method of encouraging coordination with AMT is the matrix structure. In a typical matrix, people are assigned to two types of responsibilities, such as functional and product, committee and function, project and function, or project and process. Thus, a maintenance worker may report to a maintenance supervisor as the "home" supervisor but also be expected to report to the leaders of committees on process improvement and quality control. FMS system attendants may have their performance reviewed by both the manufacturing cell supervisor and the manager of FMS operations. When the links and reporting hierarchies are stable, the structure is referred to as a matrix. When the links are fluid such that projects, functions, and committees are shuffled around at frequent intervals, the structure tends to be referred to as an adhocracy (Mintzberg, 1979).

Many manufacturing managers do not like matrix or adhocracy-type structures. They find them too difficult to manage because supervisors may compete with their counterparts for services, workers often prefer more role clarity than a matrix allows, and the inevitable time and pressure conflicts that arise with matrices can only be settled through negotiation and adjustment— interpersonal techniques not frequently used by manufacturing managers. Thus, most manufacturing plants prefer a different solution, such as standing committees. Nevertheless, several plants are beginning to realize that some form of a matrix structure is probably on the horizon for most flexible factories. Assigning production engineers to both the functional group of manufacturing engineering and to a specific work cell is becoming more and more popular as a form of matrix. Several AMT plants have temporarily deployed to manufacturing cells those personnel normally assigned to functions (for example, maintenance, quality control, engineering), thus creating a matrix structure (Manufacturing Studies Board, 1986). Therefore, a plant implementing flexible manufacturing may want to begin experimenting with certain early forms of matrices in order to prepare the work force for what may become the coordination device of the future flexible automated factory.

Decentralization

The seventh solution for increased coordination is to decentralize responsibility for such important decisions as scheduling, customer contact, recruiting, and process improvements. When shopfloor supervisors and workers are responsible for these decisions, the people closest to the production operations are free to coordinate as they need to in order to make the decisions.

While a firm may decentralize to encourage coordination at the lowest levels, in reality some decisions will be centralized and some will be decentralized. For example, at the Kalmar Volvo plant, three computer systems were established to enhance decentralization or worker control (Hedberg, 1975). The process control system informed work groups of the activity of those earlier in the line so that the work groups could get a picture of their future work load. The production control system delivered written specifications for each separate car concerning equipment, options, and so on. Finally, the quality control system reported errors on their cars. In addition to decentralization, the same systems provided greater centralization of decisions about problems in the production process. Rather than relying on workers to pinpoint problems or waiting for manufacturing engineers to investigate problems, the supervisor received information over time on 3,000 control points per car and detailed performance figures in terms of error rates, error types, and rates of work. With computer software provided to compute such statistical analyses as regression equations and correlations, the supervisors could analyze for themselves problems they thought were occurring and their possible sources. Thus, at this plant, decisions about workers' immediate future and jobs were decentralized, while supervisors were given more control over process problem detection and improvements.

The introduction of a decentralized structure often yields rather interesting organization charts. At Sherwin-Williams' Richmond, Virginia, plant using advanced technology to produce automotive coatings, production teams were given total responsibility for different parts of the production process. The organization chart, presented in Figure 9-3, illustrates the flatness of a hierarchy that is composed primarily of teams, team leaders, and selected technical experts.

Decentralization as a solution has the distinct advantage of encouraging coordination at the lowest level. Moreover, coupled

Figure 9-3. Organization Structure at Sherwin-Williams' Richmond Plant.

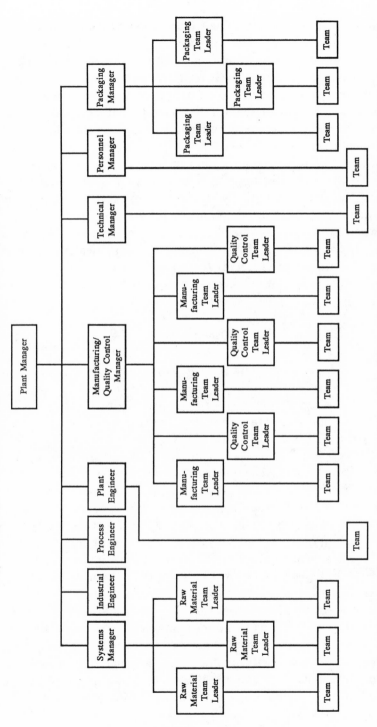

Source: Reprinted, by permission of the publisher, from "Success Story: The Team Approach to Work Restructuring," by Ernesto Poza and Lynne Markus, *Organizational Dynamics*, Winter 1980, p. 16, © 1980 American Management Association, New York. All rights reserved.

with centralization of appropriate decisions, this approach can help to ensure that the right levels in the organizational hierarchy are making the right decisions. In a flexible integrated factory, the information needs are so great that decisions will be made correctly only when made at the level with the appropriately specific or broad perspective. Thus, this solution helps to ensure approriate management of decision making with AMT.

On the cautionary side, decentralization is an effective tool only when it is coupled with an organizational climate and structure that foster coordination and information sharing between decentralized groups. The Sherwin-Williams organization shown in Figure 9-3 works only if teams and team leaders actively communicate among themselves. Thus, lateral communication lines are as essential to a decentralized solution as are the vertical reporting lines.

Downsizing

An eighth solution to coordination problems with AMT, and one useful only to larger businesses, is downsizing. The average size of manufacturing plants is shrinking, as Figure 9-4 shows. With CIM, the upper limit of the size of a plant has been suggested to be somewhere between 500 and 800 employees. Tom Gunn (1982) suggests 500 to be the maximum. Hay Management Consultants recommend 600 as the maximum ("Small Is Beautiful . . . ," 1984). Farnum (1986) describes a manager at GE's Bromont plant, which has only 400 workers and manages its advanced technologies with teams, business units, and skill-based salary structure, who stated that a plant of more than 800 people would be difficult to manage with this system. Regardless of the specific maximum size, 500 to 800 workers per plant is far smaller than the typical production operations of many plants today.

Downsizing has been identified as a particularly useful strategy in CIM plants because communication and coordination are thought to be simpler and more efficient when fewer people are involved in any one self-contained organizational unit. In addition, it is easier to have a sense of responsibility and ownership over the production when fewer people are involved. Moreover, when all the

Figure 9-4. How Plant Size Is Shrinking.

Average size of plants measured
by number of employees
for 410 major manufacturers

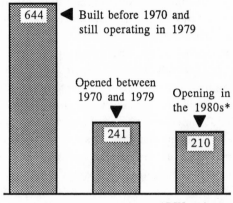

*BW estimate

Data: Roger W. Schmenner, Duke University

Source: "Small Is Beautiful . . . ," 1984, p. 156.

employees know each other, peer pressure for high performance can be enhanced.

The disadvantages of downsizing are equally clear. For existing plant facilities with 3,000 to 8,000 workers, identifying ways to create plants of 800 workers is difficult, if not impossible. Production processes may not be separable into different plants, or the building may not have been constructed for easy separation. Moreover, simply having fewer workers to manage does not necessarily mean that the workers will coordinate better. Unless management establishes a climate and job design for integration, having fewer people is not enough. Thus, this solution alone is probably insufficient and when combined with other solutions may be too difficult to achieve.

Organizational Climate

A final solution to the dilemma of fostering integration while maintaining differentiated units is an organizational climate that encourages coordination at multiple levels. Organizational climate can encourage coordination at the job level, so that a worker will be willing to work closely with another to complete a task. The organizational climate can also encourage coordination in upward and downward information exchange so that employees will be willing to invest the time to inform and learn from others above and below them. Finally, the organizational climate can encourage coordination to fulfill the plant-wide mission of survival and growth so that individuals will be willing to go out of their way to help make the workplace a better place for others.

The organizational climate can encourage coordination in a variety of ways. Rituals, symbolic actions by managers, management speeches, recognition awards, posters, and company-sponsored nonproduction-related activities (lunches, sports teams, and so on) can all be structured to convey the message, "Integrate! Coordinate! Communicate!" Some features of the organizational climate that can convey this message are as follows:

- Retreats where groups of employees report and discuss with managers concerns about the technological change
- Impromptu award ceremonies when a work group has "really pulled together" during a production crisis
- Sports events encouraging teamwork
- Supervisors role-modeling how to work with others to complete a task
- Management sharing business data with workers in exchange for workers' suggestions for process improvements
- Undermining status differences by "equal work-equal privileges"
- Specifying to each individual how he or she can contribute to coordination.

Creating the appropriate organizational climate has the obvious advantage of building a rallying point around which employees can revolve. When that rallying point is clearly and unequivocally understood to involve coordination of all types, employees will be motivated to perform in the direction that an integrated factory needs. Moreover, over time, informal channels and networks for communication and coordination can become so central to the integrated factory that the employees can essentially manage themselves. Formal structures become far less necessary to keep such an organization functioning effectively.

As a solution to the integration-differentiation dilemma, though, reliance on an appropriate organizational climate is both risky and perhaps insufficient. It is a risky strategy because messages that are intended to be conveyed are rarely conveyed with complete accuracy. Supervisors may not adequately role-model working with others; improperly managed retreats may turn into gripe sessions; and status differences, mistrust, and misperceptions die hard. Thus, the intended organizational climate may be only partially created, or created only in the minds of the managers. Moreover, changing the organizational climate alone is probably not enough. Even assuming adequately conveyed messages, it is questionable whether, without decentralized authority, standing committees, or a CAD/ CAM coordinating unit, the needs created by the technical change can be met. Thus, while the organizational climate is a very important solution to the dilemma posed in this chapter, its utility is probably most dramatically enhanced when it is combined with other solutions.

Conclusions

In this chapter, the basic dilemma posed by AMT for organizational structure was described. Several options for resolving this dilemma were presented. It is apparent from this review that few of the solutions alone will effectively encourage enhanced integration with AMT while maintaining manageable and distinguishable units. Decentralization must be coupled with an organizational climate that encourages coordination among decentralized units; having different units report to the same boss must be coupled with standing committees to ensure appropriate lateral coordination; grouping production processes by common work flows often coincides with grouping by common products; and adding a new CAD/CAM organizational unit may produce a structure much like a matrix.

In mixing and matching the solutions, the open systems

approach to organizational effectiveness should be applied. The formal structure established by delineating separate units, reporting hierarchies, and decision-making authority must match with the informal organizational climate. Thus, if bottom-up coordination is desired, both the climate and the formal structure must convey the same message. Similarly, the structural solution must match with the system constraints. A corporate philosophy that espouses participative management and yet has a rigidly defined formal structure is incongruent and will generate either hostility or confusion, but not motivation and commitment. Finally, the structural solution must match with other elements of the human infrastructure. A plant organized by flow production is not effectively matched to operators' job responsibilities when those responsibilities are focused solely on monitoring. Decentralization must be coupled with a pay policy that rewards for correct decisions. Members of task forces need training in team building, the language of other disciplines, and an overview of the production process—old and new. In conclusion, the choice of the organizational structural solution must be made within the context of other human infrastructure decisions.

10

Overcoming Resistance to Factory Automation

The work force, ranging from managers to unskilled workers, frequently resists AMT at first. Research indicates that this resistance can severely limit the success of the implementation process. A review of the causes of this resistance indicates that many of them have to do with a lack of information about the technological change, such as information about the plant's plans concerning job security, job design changes, or new personnel policies. This chapter examines several approaches to countering the resistance. From this examination, two approaches appear to be the most appropriate: (1) extensive communication about the changes through training, orientation programs, and periodic information exchanges and (2) worker participation in the technological changes, through consensus, direct consultation, and/or worker representatives.

Resistance to Change

There's a radio commercial in which Winkler, a young management superstar, is called to the boss's office for a promotion. "We've been watching you," says the boss. "You're very together, very cool." He goes on to tell Winkler that his next assignment is to visit a client who faces imminent danger from a volcano. "No problem," Winkler says with smug self-assurance. "And then," the boss continues, "you'll come back and change our phone system." Winkler goes berserk. "Change the phone system!" he shouts hysterically. "They'll chew me to pieces!" New technology has that effect on a lot of people [Darlin, 1985, p. 90c].

247

In this chapter, problems of resistance to flexible automation are discussed. Evidence for the existence of such resistance is first described and sources of that resistance are identified. Options for managing resistance are then presented.

Resistance to Flexible Automation: Is There Any?

The research evidence to date clearly indicates that there is resistance to flexible automation among the work force and that this resistance has serious detrimental effects on the successful implementation of AMT. For example, in one study of twelve CIM plants, the second most frequently mentioned reason for slow progress to CIM was resistance to change (Fossom, 1985). Other studies by Hyer (1984), Margulies and Colflesh (1985), and Chen and others (1984) report similar results. Much of the resistance is not necessarily among production workers. The problems of managerial resistance have already been described in Chapter Five. In addition, resistance can be found among professionals as well. For example, a major obstacle to the successful use of group technology (GT) has been convincing designers and manufacturing engineers to use the GT codes; designers often think GT limits their creativity, while manufacturing engineers reportedly fear that GT will eliminate their jobs (Houtzeel and Brown, 1982). Clearly, there is sufficient resistance to AMT to warrant an examination of how to reduce it.

Sources of Resistance

To understand how to reduce resistance, we must identify its sources. Studies of resistance to AMT have identified a laundry list of reasons that an employee may resist: demands of retraining, actual or feared loss of status, fear of job loss, breakup of work groups, dilution of skills, loss of intrinsic job satisfaction, erosion of pay differentials, fears about actual losses in earnings, erosion of craft boundaries and trade union demarcations, unfavorable experience with similar changes, unfavorable attitudes of peers toward the new technology, lack of general knowledge about the new technology, and fears about management's ability to handle the change (Abbott, 1981; Chao and Kozlowski, 1986; Roitman, Liker, and Roskies, 1987; Leonard-Barton, 1986a; Nieva, Gaertner, Argoff, and Newman, 1986).

Interestingly enough, these fears do not seem to be related directly to age (Nieva, Gaertner, Argoff, and Newman, 1986). The often-quoted relationship between age and resistance appears to depend more on the level of job experience with nonautomated equipment than on age (Majchrzak and others, 1987). That is, experienced workers tend to be more productive with the old production process than less-experienced workers and thus are more doubtful that the new technology will provide the same benefits that they are capable of achieving with the old equipment.

Union and nonunion workers also seem to share similar fears. That is, both union members and nonmembers are frequently unconvinced of the need for technological change and feel ill-informed about how the change will affect their jobs. Markley Roberts (1982) describes a 1979 survey by Doris McLaughlin in which union officials and management were surveyed about the impact of unions on the rate and direction of technological innovation. The results indicated that "willing acceptance" was the most common response American labor unions made to the introduction of new technology. The next most common response was "initial opposition," followed by "adjustment" with an effort to control the use of the technology. The Office of Technology Assessment's (1984) study of programmable automation found that a fear of organized labor is an unjustified reason for not automating. "Most unions have in fact displayed only modest resistance to factory modernization," asserts an OTA spokesperson (Brody, 1985, p. 45).

What are the fears behind this modest union resistance? First, unions express a concern about whether change is needed. In a 1985 University of Oregon doctoral dissertation by Roger Anderson, determinants of union workers' attitudes toward work innovations were examined. It was found that the most important determinant of union attitudes was the extent to which management had clearly and convincingly articulated the need for change. Second, unions are often concerned that they are not being provided with all the information about the change. For example, Chamot and Dymmel (1981) describe a technology agreement reached between the

Norwegian Federation of Trade Unions and the Norwegian Employers' Federation, in which a large part of the agreement centered on the need for management to keep its employees informed of all matters related to the new technology.

Background factors of the individual, such as age and union status, are thus not necessarily the source of resistance to new manufacturing technology; in view of the laundry list of concerns raised by users of new technology, the underlying source of resistance to AMT becomes apparent. That source appears to be a lack of information about the change. If the worker had specific information about the plant's plans concerning job security, the technology itself, how management is planning to implement and use the technology, and how precisely the worker's job will change, major concerns would dissipate. In one study cited by Fadem (1984), interviews were conducted with 200 employees in automated and nonautomated settings in the automobile manufacturing industry. The researchers found that the workers were more favorably disposed toward technological change if they felt that management was concerned about their welfare, communicated openly with them, and ran the operations efficiently. The most important aspect of management concern was open, two-way communication. Of those workers who felt adequately informed in advance of techno- logical changes, 51 percent endorsed automation. Of those who felt that they had not been adequately informed, only 31 percent endorsed automation. Nieva, Gaertner, Argoff, and Newman (1986) found similar results in their survey of 192 workers anticipating the introduction of flexible automation in their workplace; those employees who attended communication meetings about the equipment, saw notices about the technology, and spoke to supervisors and managers about the equipment had more optimis- tic attitudes about the effect of the technology on their jobs. These results suggest that the implementation process should provide workers with this information so their resistance can be alleviated.

Options for Managing Resistance to Change

Two main strategies are described for reducing resistance to change by providing workers with information. The first strategy is to communicate the needed information about the change directly to the workers. The second strategy is to involve the workers themselves in the decisions being made about the new technology.

Communication. One way to communicate information that will alleviate the fears that cause resistance to technology is through training. Training reduces fears in multiple ways. First, workers retrained for new jobs will have their fears about job security laid to rest; even if they lose their current jobs, they will be more qualified to get another job someplace else. Thus, for example, Westinghouse retrained all eight of its conventional welders, even though only two were needed to run the new robot (Argoff, 1983–84). Second, training reduces workers' fears about losing control over the production process. For example, Cincinnati-Milacron reports that in its customer training program for computerized machine tools, the instructors explicitly address the concern about losing control by stressing that the operators' knowledge of traditional machining operations will enable them to anticipate machine motions and functions once they become used to the controller and its operations. With this knowledge, CNCs can give operators more, not less, control of the machining process.

Another way to communicate information and alleviate fears is through orientation programs. Orientation programs typically explain the new technology through visual aids or demonstrations. Their purpose is to impress upon the audience the benefits of the new equipment. It should be noted that in such a program, different audiences may perceive or want different benefits from the same equipment. For example, senior management may look for strategic benefits, such as public image; middle management may look for operating benefits, such as work flow control; foremen may look for the benefits of minimal disruption; and operators may look for job security and pay assurances (Leonard-Barton and Kraus, 1985; Boddy and Buchanan, 1986).

AMT orientation programs have taken many different forms to convey the necessary information. Some of the programs have taken place as formal, on-site meetings between management and workers. One example of such an orientation program was at Westinghouse's Center for Defense and Electronic Systems (Argoff,

1983–84) where a one-half-day orientation was given two months before the welding robot was installed. The orientation was given to the eight welders, the chief union steward, the welding foreman, NC programmers, the area manager, and several other management and engineering personnel. The orientation included discussions of what a robot is, its function, the future of robotics at the center, the workers' role in the development of the robots, and programming procedures. The discussions were followed by demonstrations of how the robot works, with the participants allowed to type in commands to put the robot through its paces.

Other programs have used videotapes, such as these examples described by the Manufacturing Studies Board (1986, p. 20): In an electronics equipment plant, employees were shown videotapes that linked automation to making employees more effective and jobs easier. The tapes stressed that, given changing worldwide competition, impending plans to automate were a natural and necessary extension of the plant's nearly thirty-year history of automation. Managers described the tapes as effective in allaying fears and linking the future of the plant to automation.

In a second plant, the videotapes portrayed superintendents holding "cross-talks" with ten to twelve people at a time, and arranging career-oriented discussions between individual supervisors and employees.

Some companies have held their orientations off-site. For example, at one engine company, announcement of the new technology program was accompanied by off-site meetings with representatives of a variety of different groups (inspectors, skilled trades, operators, union officials, management) to discuss all aspects of the FMS installation.

Another means of alleviating fears is the periodic provision of information over time. Regular talks given by the plant manager in formal meetings or on videotape are one popular mechanism used by AMT plants. Regularly published information reports are another. At Hylsa, a steel manufacturer, the reports contained information on the manufacturing cost (per ton of steel) in each plant in the corporation compared to competing U.S. and foreign manufacturers, tons per employee, labor costs, and direct/indirect labor ratios (Poza, 1983). A third mechanism for continuous communication of information is having supervisors periodically provide information to subordinates. The supervisor is often the most frequently mentioned source of information about new technology, followed by demonstrations and written reports (Argote and Goodman, 1986; Leonard-Barton, 1986b). Despite the frequency with which they are used as sources of information, supervisors should be used with caution: they may not know much more than the workers, they may have poor communication and listening skills, and they may (inadvertently or not) misinform subordinates out of anger and frustration with the planned changes.

When should the periodic communication start? Research by Billings, Klimoski, and Breaugh (1977) has found that workers report changes in their perceptions of their jobs prior to any technological change. Thus, communication must start before the new equipment arrives at the plant. But how much before? At Westinghouse, all workers at the Center for Defense and Electronic Systems (regardless of whether or not they would be directly affected by the new technology) saw a film on the use of robots and what workers' jobs would be like two years before the first robot was installed (Argoff, 1983–84). At Ford, meetings about the new technology were started with the hourly workers a year ahead of time (Chen and others, 1984). The point, then, is to start the training, orientation, and periodic information exchange early.

Participation. A second strategy for providing information to workers in a way that will help to alleviate some of their resistance to new manufacturing technology is through employee involvement or participation. Participation has three primary advantages over one-way information sharing. First, it solicits employee input; employees may identify unforeseen problems and derive their own solutions. At Westinghouse, for example, users' inputs were solicited during the final design stages of a computerized inspection data entry station, a computerized device used in quality control to isolate faulty components on printed circuit boards (Argoff, 1983–84). As a result of the users' suggestions, the location of the menu was modified and the work area elevation made adjustable so that an operator, regardless of size, could be comfortably close to the work.

A second advantage over one-way communication is that, through participation, workers are likely to acquire a greater knowledge about the department and system. This greater knowledge may give them the patience to understand why management has chosen certain courses of action, as well as the ability to solve problems in more realistic ways. A steelworker for thirteen years at Jones & Laughlin Steel Corporation, for example, described to *Business Week* ("A Work Revolution," 1983) the benefits he derived from being a member of a labor-management participation team: "I've been exposed to the company's problems, and I know if they're not solved, I won't have a job" (p. 102).

Finally, research has found that participation is superior to one-way communication because, if carried out correctly, it can lead to greater job satisfaction and a greater sense of ownership (see review by Cotton and others, forthcoming). For example, at one manufacturer of fluid-handling equipment that implemented CNC machines, the management informed the employees about the CNC machines but did not solicit their input (Abbott, 1981). "The management experienced no problems in gaining acceptance of the idea of new machinery but it experienced considerable difficulties in obtaining efficient use of the tools. The operators placed unilateral restrictions on the kinds of tasks that could be performed on the new machines, and it was a full year to eighteen months before these restrictions could be overcome. Moreover, even when the tools did come to perform the full range of intended tasks, productivity did not come up to expectations and it was only in a minority of cases that shortfalls in output could be attributed to technical difficulties" (p. 42).

Participation is not without its detractors, however. It is a very time-consuming process. It is cumbersome to involve everyone in direct participation or even to involve only the key members of different groups. Moreover, involving workers who do not have the technical background to easily understand the technological system or the communication skills to function well in a group will present major obstacles to creating a sense of sharing and consensus building. Finally, research by Hiltz (1984) indicates that people's goals for systems change over time, particularly as they use the system more. Thus, a goal that a worker might have established for the system at one point may change when the system is installed.

Therefore, while participation as a means to convey information has numerous advantages over one-way communication, a participation system that overcomes some of the problems needs to be designed. In designing this system, four decisions must be made: (1) when to involve the workers, (2) whom to involve, (3) how to involve them, and (4) about what decisions to solicit their involvement.

Case examples indicate that workers have been involved at virtually any time, sometimes as early as the minute when management begins to sense that new technology may be needed, sometimes not until initial design specifications have given the workers a better-defined target for comments (see, for example, case descriptions by Gyllenhammar, 1977; Manufacturing Studies Board, 1986). Given the range of alternatives, the decision about when to involve workers must take into account the preferences of top management, the complexity of system plans, and the speed with which implementation plans are proceeding. As long as involvement occurs before plans are solidifed, workers will be able to reap some of the benefits of participation.

The question of *whom* to involve is one of breadth. If an integrated system is being installed, chances are that it will affect multiple departments and multiple occupations. In one plant studied by the National Academy of Sciences (Manufacturing Studies Board, 1986), inspectors, skilled trades, operators, union officials, and management were involved in initial decisions about aspects of an FMS installation. At General Dynamics, over twenty departments were identified as being involved in the implementation of a robotics systems. Building a broad constituency base rather than a narrow one is far better for enhancing the development of a truly integrated system.

The third decision is one of means: *How* should participation be solicited in decisions about the new technology? Several options are available here. First, the organization may prefer the consensual involvement of all those directly affected by the new technology. This option, referred to as consensus participation, may be feasible for a small robot system where only a few workers, skilled trades, one supervisor, some engineering personnel, the production manager, and a human resource professional need to be involved. In such a situation, working as a team with consensus about major system decisions may be the best way to ensure that the system is properly planned and executed. Such a strategy quickly becomes unwieldy for larger systems involving more people; it can be feasible, however, if some modifications are made. A nominal group technique can be used, for example, in which groups of workers, after some initial training and explanation, are asked to provide opinions about different aspects of the technology. With the nominal group technique, these opinions can be solicited in a fairly structured manner, such as by providing the workers with criteria for evaluating opinions (for example, worklife, quality of product, scrappage, machine uptime) and the opportunity to weight those criteria. In a large plant, this strategy might be time-consuming initially and might need to be redone as technology plans are modified. The feeling of direct input that it gives the workers, however, may be necessary or preferred in some plants. A plant with a long history of labor strife, for example, may need to turn to such a strategy in order for management to convince labor of its good intentions.

Because of its cumbersome and time-consuming nature, many firms preferring a direct approach to participation do not use consensus participation. An alternative to consensus that still promotes direct involvement in decisions is consultative participation. Markus (1984) refers to this type of participation as evolutionary system development, where designers present limited prototype systems with which users can experiment. A similar notion is advanced by others, such as Boddy and Buchanan (1986). Examples presented earlier in which workers are asked for their input concerning decisions on quality inspection workstations and lighting systems describe the consultative option. Consultative participation may occur in a variety of ways. In five plants studied by the Manufacturing Studies Board (1986), skilled workers accompanied managers on visits to equipment vendors and then were asked what they thought about the new technology and its effects. In another organization, described by Guest (1982), a mock area was set up where supervisors and workers could examine new equipment and make suggestions for changes. At a GM plant, a similar arrangement was used in the training laboratory (Argoff, 1983-84). The way in which workers are consulted clearly depends on the point in the implementation process at which consultation is requested. The later they are consulted, the more constrained their input will be and the less consulted they will feel.

Both consensus and consultation are direct forms of participation. As such, they both involve some extra time on the part of the automation project team in order to reach consensus or obtain the input. Many firms find this extra time to be so costly or inconvenient that they avoid this degree of worker involvement. Instead, many adopt a method, called here representative participation, in which groups of workers are represented in participative committees by elected group members. The union bargaining committee is a classic example of representation; when a joint management-labor committee is established for the purpose of collaboratively designing a new technical system. While this method is much more efficient than the other two methods in terms of time and resources, research comparing the two has concluded that it is significantly less effective in providing information than direct participation methods, since workers do not feel as involved (Cotton and others, forthcoming; Rubenowitz, Norrgren, and Tannenbaum, 1983). It might be concluded that the reason for this feeling of noninvolvement is that the representatives are not doing an adequate job of conveying information and soliciting inputs directly from the workers. If this is indeed the case, management can encourage the representatives to spend more time in such pursuits by, for example, freeing them from some of their production responsibilities. Nevertheless, one should be aware of the problems inherent in representative participation as a solution to resistance to change.

The final decision to make when determining the appropriate method of participation is about the set of issues for which worker input is sought. In selecting the issues, one consideration should be the technical knowledge that the workers need to participate effectively in decisions. If they do not have the necessary knowledge (for example, computer language or electronic systems), attempts to involve them in decisions about the technical system

Figure 10-1. Flowchart Showing Laypersons' Influence
on Expert Solutions.

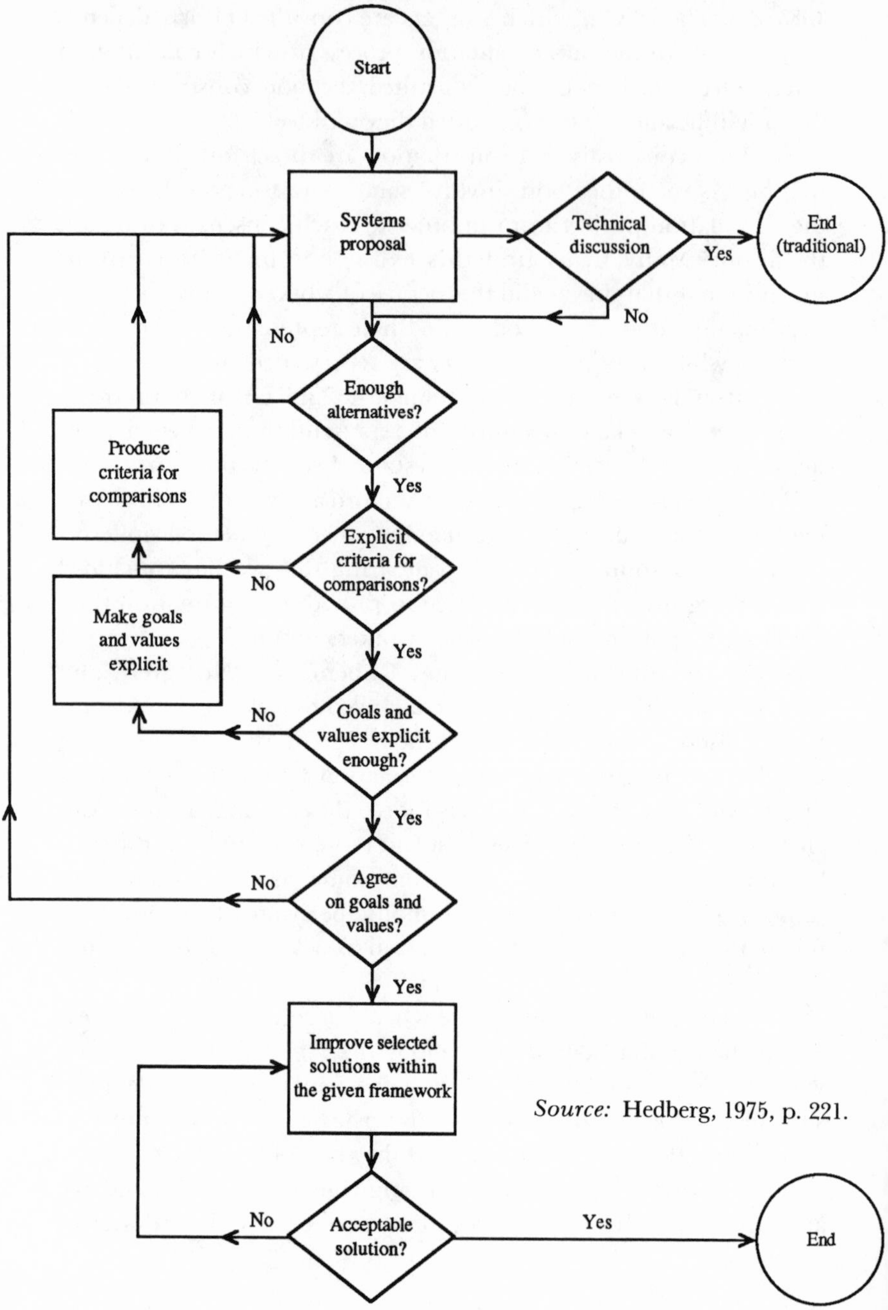

Source: Hedberg, 1975, p. 221.

may be frustrating for all concerned. To remedy this problem, lower-level decisions related to the technology system development can be categorized into either strategic and tactical or technical decisions (Hedberg, 1975; Mumford and Sackman, 1975). Strategic decisions are those in which objectivҽs, strategy, and values of the system are established, such as the job design of operators, control and responsibilities of shopfloor versus those of management, and training requirements of the new systems. The technical decisions are those that concern the specific equipment features that are necessary to ensure that the strategy is carried out. To avoid the frustration of a lack of technical knowledge, workers should participate in strategic decisions only. Figure 10-1 offers a flowchart for channeling their participation into strategic, rather than technical, decision making.

Conclusions

Resistance is a problem that impedes the successful implementation of AMT. To avoid resistance, two-way communication and participation must be introduced before the equipment is selected. Unfortunately, communication and participation take time. Nevertheless, according to a GE Bromont plant spokesman, where decisions are made by participative committees, "We trade time for communication, consensus, and a feeling of ownership" (Farnum, 1986, p. 92).

Participation and information dissemination do not provide all the answers, however. "Without participation the worker may never exercise creativity or imagination or put out an outstanding job. But on many jobs, management has no use for outstanding performance. . . . Participation is useful in a great many fields. But it is not a sovereign remedy for all management" (Strauss, 1966, p. 6). Thus, other aspects of the implementation process must also be appropriately planned if flexible automation is to be successfully used. It is one of these aspects of the implementation process that we turn to next.

11

Structuring Automation
Project Teams
and the Change Process

In 1982, Westinghouse's Construction Group Human Resource Council examined four plant locations where at least one robot had been installed. Results of the study cited by Chao and Kozlowski (1986) indicated that according to operators, engineers, supervisors, and managers, the management of the implementation process was a critical factor in the successful installation of the robots. The effective management of AMT implementation involves both managing automation project teams and efficiently moving through the three essential stages of any planned change effort.

An important aspect of managing automation project teams is the selection of the team's mission and members. Project teams should have a mission that is as broad-based as possible. It should include not only specifications of technical requirements but the development of the specifications for the human infrastructure and the implementation of the project as well. Team members should be selected to represent a range of functions, disciplines, and personal philosophies about worker motivation; they should include vendor representatives, members with implementation experience, and worker representatives (if appropriate). The team should be managed so that a vision and excitement about the company's use of new technology are encouraged, high visibility is discouraged, leaders are neither autocratic nor laissez-faire, members are trained in group process skills, and team membership is stable. Finally, the team should (1) conduct a needs analysis of both production process and human infrastructure that includes visits to other organizations, (2) perform a feasibility assessment of preliminary alternative automation *designs that weighs such criteria as their match with management's human resource philosophy, (3) prepare a project proposal that describes both technical and human infrastructural effects of the selected automation system, and (4) develop an implementation plan for both human infrastructure elements and equipment installation.*

Successful implementation also involves effective movement through the three stages of any planned change process: unfreezing, moving forward, and refreezing. To move effectively through the unfreezing stage, management must communicate the need for change in general before communicating the benefits of the purchased equipment, present a clear vision of the range of changes to occur with AMT, involve "key workers" in the implementation process, and involve top management in providing strategic, not directional, support. To prepare effectively for the moving forward stage, management must be cautious about continuing to purchase new technology in an evolutionary or piecemeal fashion, failing to develop implementation plans that allow flexibility before the equipment arrives, and failing to provide supervisors adequate support if they are expected to be responsible for implementation. Finally, to achieve success in the refreezing stage, management must continually motivate the work force to maintain its interest and commitment to the new technology. Motivational techniques include continuously evaluating progress toward high expectations, rebuilding enthusiasm when those expectations are not initially met, and periodically reassessing the congruence between the technical, human, and organizational subsystems as they mature independently and together.

Management of Automation Project Teams

An important aspect of any firm's implementation effort is the selection and activities of the automation project team. An automation project team is the group of individuals responsible for preparing the CAD/CAM project proposal and purchasing and installing the equipment. Four management issues are relevant to the success of an automation project team: purpose, composition, structure, and activities.

Purpose

Because of the complexity of computerized technology, an organization considering the purchase of new manufacturing technology will find it necessary to have the selection and installation of the new equipment handled by a team of individuals. At a minimum, the automation project team will be responsible for the identification of the plant's equipment requirements, selection of a vendor, design of the equipment, development of software for the system, preparation of the plant facility for the new equipment, and installation and burn-in (not necessarily implementation) of the equipment. Typically, the project team's responsibilities end after start-up problems have been resolved and the equipment has been turned over to production. Depending on the complexity of the system envisioned, an automation project team may be together for anywhere from six months (for the purchase of a simple robot) to several years (for the purchase of CIM equipment).

In addition to its largely technical responsibilities, an automation project team may serve other purposes. In order for the human infrastructure to be adequately planned, the team should also be responsible for changes to the human infrastructure posed by the new equipment. The team should therefore prepare options for job designs, training, and personnel policies as well as select the equipment parameters. Having the same team responsible for both the technical and human infrastructures will greatly facilitate the design of AMT that meets the complete requirements of the entire organizational system.

Another purpose served by automation project teams can be the enhancement of worker involvement. The automation project team may actually include members of the work force and thus serve as a vehicle for representative participation. Or the team may be given the task of ensuring involvement by soliciting worker input at critical points in the design process.

Finally, the team may also be given the responsibility of managing the entire implementation process—a process that involves training, overcoming resistance to change, and evaluation as well as equipment installation. For example, the automation project team engineers at Westinghouse were responsible for training supervisors (who then trained the workers). Many organizations may find that if they do not assign the responsibility for implementation to the automation project team, implementation activities occur in an unplanned, haphazard fashion.

In conclusion, the purposes of the project team should be as broad-based as possible, including not only technical requirements specifications but human infrastructural specifications and implementation as well.

Team Composition

Regardless of the precise purposes specified for the automation project team, several criteria should be considered in choosing project team members. First, the members should represent multiple disciplines and functions. The multiple functions are necessary because flexible automation integrates, or at least affects, many different areas of the plant. Multiple disciplines are necessary because no single type of educational background provides the systems knowledge needed to understand the diverse impacts and implications of flexible automation. Some disciplines that should be represented might be design engineering, design/drafting, engineering analysis, industrial engineering, tool design, numerical control programming, data processing, financial analysis, and human resources. In addition, the needs of the user community should be represented by the workers or managers of these functional areas. Finally, if the project team is to serve as a vehicle for representative participation, representatives from major worker groups, such as inspectors, setters, operators, shipping, maintenance, and other skilled trades, may need to be included in the team.

It is apparent from this list of team members that the automation project team can quickly become too large for effective decision making. Therefore, it may be necessary to create a two-tiered team. The upper tier, which could be called the CAD/CAM steering committee, would consist of the larger group of representatives and would review plans and make strategic recommendations. The second tier, which could be called the CAD/CAM technical committee, would involve the smaller set of people who have the skills to make the technical design decisions. Even the smaller group, however, still needs to maintain a cross-functional, interdisciplinary nature.

Cross-functional teams can also present problems in collaboration because language is different, decision-making styles differ, and stereotypes of other fields and areas reign. To overcome these barriers to collaboration, Honeywell, for example, ensures that some team members have cross-functional experience, that each team has an external facilitator for the initial stages of team development, and that the management of the functional groups represented in the teams provides time and rewards for cross-functional collaboration (Bowman, 1986).

Team members should be selected on the basis of their models of worker motivation as well as their disciplines and functions. For example, research by Taylor (1979), Hedberg and Mumford (1975), and Zuboff (1982) has found that the specific design selected tends to reflect not only technical requirements but also the system developers' model of worker motivation. Thus, a team composed of designers who unanimously agree that workers are not motivated by the challenge of their jobs would design a system that is unlikely to fit the needs of workers who are challenged by their jobs. A team composed solely of those who feel everyone wants challenge is equally unlikely to be compatible with the needs of the entire work force. Thus, in addition to multiple disciplines and functions, varying views of how workers are motivated should be represented on the team.

Members of automation project teams may also include vendor representatives. Typically, manufacturing plants treat the CAD/CAM vendor like any supplier—the less seen of the vendor, the better. With flexible automation, however, a vendor held at arm's length about the production process and company plans for the equipment cannot be very helpful in suggesting alternative designs and equipment configurations (Ettlie, 1973, 1986a). Few firms have the expertise that a vendor has and thus are wasting this expertise when the vendor is not fully involved. Obviously, there are concerns about confidential plans and processes, but it is shortsighted to let those concerns influence the design of an expensive system that may not be suited to the organization's needs.

Finally, since there is no substitute for experience, automation project teams should have at least one or two people experienced in implementing automation (Westcott and Eisenhardt,

1986; Susman, Dean, and Porter, 1986). This experience should not, however, be allowed to be the basis for the individuals to become prima donnas, since prima donnas will seriously damage the effectiveness of the team's efforts (Susman, Dean, and Porter, 1986).

Team Structure

As with any work group, the structure of the team (its leadership, its source of motivation, and so on) is essential to its effectiveness. Ensuring adequate team effectiveness through the structure of work groups in general has already been discussed in Chapter Three. Research is beginning to accumulate about the structure of successful automation project teams in particular. One research finding is that teams organized by "grass-roots" principles appear to be more successful than teams organized by "top management" principles (Westcott and Eisenhardt, 1986). Grass-roots teams are those that are not given high visibility in the organization, in which members are not paid more than the norm for their occupational group, and in which the incentive for the team members is the intrinsic excitement and vision about flexible automation rather than visibility or large budgets. In contrast, top management teams have clear top management visibility and have sizable budgets to control. Apparently, the grass-roots teams are more successful because the lower-level users tend to be actively involved with such teams, team members tend to have more experience with manufacturing and not just engineering, and the team is small and thus more manageable.

The structure of the team is also determined by whom the team reports to. AMT organizations have adopted several different reporting arrangements. Some organizations have the teams report to an engineering manager. Occasionally, this has created concern among members of other functional areas about the team's ability to operate in a truly cross-disciplinary, cross-functional mode. Moreover, when they must report to an existing function, it can be difficult for team members to remove themselves from the daily pressures of the production line. As a result, some organizations have directed the teams to report directly to the production manager or CEO. For example, in the Roitman, Liker, and Roskies (1987) study of a firm introducing CIM, a new group called Automation Management was created to plan for the CIM transition. The group reported to the CEO without functional ties. Other organizations have gone so far as to create a new company or move the team completely off-site. Ettlie (1986c) describes Frost Incorporated, which created a new firm called Amprotech for the sole purpose of implementing Frost's CIM. Amprotech drastically overhauled Frost's employee compensation plan, removed most of the layers from the firm's organizational hierarchy, took out all time clocks, and installed a completely integrated factory. Ettlie concluded that Frost probably could not have made such major changes if the automation project team had reported to any manager in the normal hierarchy. Of course, creating independent companies and off-site project teams runs the risk that the team will create plans that nobody adopts. This danger can be offset, however, by the inclusion of the right people on the team.

Since project teams must work effectively as a group, principles of group dynamics apply here. The team must feel like a working group; thus team-building exercises might be needed as well as training in group problem-solving skills. A group structure that is less formalized and more decentralized tends to be better suited to the complex, innovative decision-making process that the team must undergo (White, Dittrich, and Lang, 1980). There should also be a recognition that over time, the team may progress through different stages of evolution (for example, creation of norms must be done before effective problem solving can occur). Because of this need to evolve, there must be a core group of team members that stays with the team throughout most of its activities. Otherwise, the team may remain in the early stages of evolution and be unable to progress to more productive stages.

Finally, the leadership of automation project teams must be managed to foster innovation. From research on innovation team leaders we know that automation project team leaders must have at least four competencies: problem solving (including the ability to think conceptually and systematically and to gather and synthesize information), management (including self-confidence, flexibility, and comfort with being a manager), achievement-mindedness (being results- and business-oriented), and an ability to influence others through interpersonal astuteness, team building, developing others, and exercising self-control. As such, leaders of automation project teams are not autocrats; rather, they are self-assured persons who allow the team to function on its own, while introducing direction and group process skills as needed.

The structure of the automation project team should encourage a vision and excitement about the company's use of new technology; it should not necessarily be high in visibility. The team should have a leader who is neither autocratic nor laissez-faire, members trained in group process skills, and a sufficiently stable membership for it to evolve quickly into an effective functioning unit. It may be organizationally located within one function or separately, as its own unit.

Activities

The specific activities of an automation project team will, of course, depend on its purpose. If it has been given responsibility for implementation, its range of activities will be broader than if it has been given responsibility only for equipment installation. If the team is to serve as a vehicle for worker involvement, its activities will be more complicated than those of a team that has left those responsibilities to management. In this section, a plan is presented for performing the activities expected of all automation project teams, regardless of team mission. For those teams given greater responsibilities than the minimum, the activities needed to fulfill those responsibilities will naturally evolve from the discussions in other parts of this chapter and this book.

At a minimum, the automation project team needs to undertake the following activities: needs analysis, feasibility assessment of preliminary alternative designs, project proposal and design, and development of a minimum implementation plan. Each of these activities is described here as an open systems approach would dictate.

Needs Analysis. Needs analysis is undertaken for the purpose of identifying technical and human infrastructure opportunities for flexible automation applications. A needs analysis might also be called the current system audit. To conduct a needs analysis, data are obtained about the following issues:

1. Existing conditions, such as those listed in the HIIS for elements of the human infrastructure
2. Areas of suboptimal performance in production processes and human infrastructure
3. Which of these areas could benefit from the application of a combined technical and human infrastructure change
4. Existing constraints on system development, such as those listed in the HIIS
5. Technical and human infrastructure options that exist at large that might meet the application needs identified.

For each of these five issues, data must be obtained from multiple sources. A first source is, of course, one's organization. Data should be obtained from an examination of the work flow and records (for example, absenteeism, scrappage). In addition, the opinions of workers, managers, and professionals should be solicited concerning all five issues. Not only will this solicitation help to generate new ideas that the team alone may not have considered, but it will involve more employees in the process.

A second source of data can be the vendors. By asking the vendors for information and advice at this early date, the team can begin to assess which vendors are likely to be effective team members if they are selected as the equipment supplier. A third source of data about these five issues, particularly about available options, is, of course, conferences and the literature. Little needs to be said about the benefits of these sources.

Another important source of data is other sites that have already implemented the type of flexible automation that a team is considering, or that have had some of the same process problems that have stimulated the organization to automate. Several sites should be visited at this stage of the team's activities. The purpose of these visits is to build up a repertoire of options and experiences for optimizing requirements specifications as well as system selection and design. Site visits can also be used for other purposes. They can provide union representatives with real-world examples of what their jobs might be like in the future and thus reduce some of the resistance among the work force. They can provide management with realistic appraisals of what the equipment can and cannot do, and what changes to the human resource systems will be necessary. They can excite and regenerate the team when it gets bogged down in seemingly endless discussions on the same issues. Thus, site visits should be dispersed throughout the planning process, and site visitors should be judiciously selected to optimize benefits from each visit.

Where does the team find the sites? Often vendors, to show off their latest successes, will arrange site visits for their customers. At conferences, contacts can be made with colleagues at other companies that can later lead to swapping visitors. Local community business round tables often provide a mechanism for identifying other companies struggling with the same problems. University professors and consultants are another source of sites. And firms are often more than willing to show off their latest attempts at beating the competition. Rarely is proprietary information essential to the success of a company's market share identified in these site visits.

Having compiled a list of potential sites, careful consideration should be given to deciding which of the sites to visit and when. Obviously, the more similar the production processes and problems, the better. In addition, having a tour leader at the site who is articulate and knowledgeable about the changes the company has undertaken can make the difference between a wasted trip and an enlightening experience. Finally, sites should represent different stages of implementation. One site just beginning to install the equipment after a year of planning may be visited; such a visit might focus on planning and preparation activities. Another site that recently declared its equipment fully operational may then be visited. Finally, a site may be visited that has had its original flexible equipment so long that expansion problems are beginning to be confronted. In this way the team can benefit from snapshots of other companies' experiences all along the implementation road.

Site visits not only involve some care in the selection of the site, they also involve care in the preparation of the site visitors. Unless team members (and workers or managers along for the show) are adequately prepared for what to look for and what questions to ask, they may derive very little new information from the visit. All too often, site visitors complain that the site is experiencing the same problems as their own and has no new solutions, and thus the visit was a waste. An examination of the preparation of these site visitors indicates, however, that unsatisfied visitors often go to a site with a very specific question: How did you handle this specific problem? Since every organization uses unique problem-solving processes, the site is unlikely to have defined problems in the same way as the visitor's organization. Thus, the site representatives are often unable to answer questions in more than general or noncommittal terms. Instead of expecting specific answers to specific questions, the site visitor should arrive at the site with the team's own problems put aside for the moment in an effort to understand what that site has done to address its own definitions of its concerns. The knowledge acquired at the site can be applied to the team's own problems back in the team's workroom after the visit is over. Because the preparation of site visits is essential to their effectiveness, a list of questions has been provided in Table 11-1 to be asked by site visitors.

The final step in the needs analysis is to take the data gathered from the site visits, the conferences, the literature, the vendors, and the organization's people and records and synthesize it into the requirements of the new technical and human infrastructure system. Functional specifications (that is, user-specific performance requirements), applications requirements, information requirements, and human infrastructure requirements of the new system should be identified as a result of this needs analysis. Synthesizing the information and obtaining team consensus on these requirements is not easy. Yet if the team moves ahead to the next activity without consensus, it may leave behind hidden concerns, hostilities, and agendas that will only surface after the equipment arrives—when it is too late.

Feasibility Assessments. The information gathered in the needs analysis will have pointed the team in the direction of a range of potential technical and human infrastructure solutions. In the second phase of activity, these potential solutions are combined into several alternative preliminary designs. A variety of designs ranging

Table 11-1. Sample Site Visitation Questions.

System Features and Design Characteristics

- Describe your organization's major CAD/CAM system use and key applications.
- Describe system configuration and cost. Is the system turnkey or unbundled?
- From a general perspective, describe the system's intelligence and flexibility in handling design and manufacturing control information.
- Does the system support high-level languages (for example, FORTRAN, C, Pascal)?
- Is the CAD/CAM system required to communicate with other systems? Have any interfaces been effected?
- Does the system support remote workstations? For which applications or users?
- Is the system upgradable? Give the range.

System Performance and Operational Characteristics

- How many workstations can be operated before moderate degradation occurs? Unacceptable degradation?
- Can application program development occur concurrent with routine system operation? Does this produce any significant degradation in routine operations?
- Have you experienced data translation problems when interfaces have been implemented? What kinds of problems?
- What is the system's rate of downtime?
- Describe data input sources and forms and data output flexibility.
- What data security controls can be used between different CAD/CAM user groups?
- How often are data backups required for adequate protection against data base degradation?

Vendor Support

- Does the vendor supply good system documentation? Describe any problems in this area. Are new software releases adequately debugged before they are issued?
- Does the vendor provide hardware maintenance? Describe the overall quality and responsiveness of maintenance.
- Does your CAD/CAM vendor have an active user group?
- Describe the vendor's user training program. How long does it take to train an operator on the system to reach beginner, intermediate, and expert skill levels?
- Describe sources of applications software. Indicate satisfaction.

General Impacts

- How has CAD/CAM affected information flow and business practices within your organization?

Table 11-1. Sample Site Visitation Questions, Cont'd.

- What considerations had to be made regarding the location of equipment and workstations and the design of the surrounding environment?
- How has the system affected turnaround and error rates?
- Provide any additional insight into the CAD/CAM system's strengths and weaknesses.

Human Resource Impacts

- What human resource changes have you made in conjunction with the technological implementation in:
  Machine operators' job responsibilities
  Job responsibilities of support functions
  Jobs of supervisors
  Jobs of managers
  Skill requirements of jobs
  Selection
  Training
  Personnel policies
  Organization structure?
- At what point in the implementation of the flexible automation system were these changes made?
- How essential to the success of the flexible automation system do you feel each of these changes was?
- Were any changes made to the technical equipment features in order to accommodate to human resource changes?
- What steps did you use in the implementation change process; how did you reduce resistance to change?
- What lessons have you learned about human resource changes if you were to implement flexible automation again?

Source: All but "Human Resource Impacts" adapted from Montgomery, 1984, p. 6.

from those yielding the most conservative to the most far-reaching changes should be developed. Each design is then studied for its feasibility. Feasibility is defined by three criteria: (1) how well the design meets the system requirements developed in the needs analysis, (2) likely acceptability of the changes to the existing human infrastructure and technical system, and (3) costs relative to benefits.

    In conducting a feasibility assessment of each preliminary design, there is a tendency among project teams to select designs on the basis of the aggregate assessment across all three criteria rather than a separate examination of each criterion and its components. Aggregation clearly leads to a simpler decision; however, the decision may be the wrong one. Let's say that a design gets low marks because it demands more responsibility of workers than top management would prefer. The same design may also receive high marks for meeting both technical requirements and costs. If the team were to equally weight the three criteria, the design would be given an overall moderately high score. However, the implementation of the new system might fail if management were unwilling to alter its notions of work force responsibility. If the team recognized the importance of the responsibility issue and weighted this criterion more heavily, the design would be given an overall low score and dropped from further consideration. This might be unfortunate, given its other advantages. The point here is that by evaluating the different alternatives separately on each criterion, the team is in a much better position to understand what parts of the organization have to change for the design to work. Thus, in our example here, the team might choose to present its design to management, pointing out the need for management to decide whether or not to maintain its attitudes about worker responsibility. If management chooses not to go forward with the design alternative, at least it has been made aware of the consequences of its value preferences.

Project Proposal. Having selected a design, the team develops a project proposal that provides the more detailed design specifications of the selected alternative. These specifications should be those related to both technical and human infrastructure issues. Technically, the design should describe the hardware and software configuration, the data base design, system operation and support, system integration and interfaces, and expandability of the system. The human infrastructure issues should include the job responsibilities of personnel involved directly (for example, maintenance and operators) and indirectly (managers, supervisors) with the new equipment, personnel policies that must be changed to match the job designs (for example, pay, job transfers), and skill requirements.

Implementation. The automation team must then prepare an implementation plan. Traditionally, this plan includes an exclusive focus on the technical aspects: software development, facilities preparation, modification of information systems, burn-in dates, and target dates for turning the equipment over to manufacturing. In addition, however, the plan should consider the human infrastructure issues: selection (how, by whom, and when), training, communication of information, participation of work force, critical decision points to involve management, and continued follow-through after the equipment is turned over to manufacturing. These are critical issues in any implementation plan, but particularly in one that involves the implementation of such unfamiliar equipment as flexible automation. After preparing this plan, the team will be ready to carry it out. In the following section of this chapter, suggestions for effectively working through the human infrastructure aspects of the implementation change process are discussed.

Steps in the Change Process

In this section, techniques for enhancing the change process as flexible automation is implemented are discussed. These are described in terms referred to by Kurt Lewin (1951) as the three essential stages through which every successful change effort proceeds: unfreezing, moving forward, and refreezing.

Unfreezing Stage

Unfreezing is the stage during which people are convinced of the need for change in technology. A common mistake of many organizations is to ignore this stage or assume that the workers and other managers are as convinced of the need for change as the automation team and the CEO. For example, Robey and Zeller (1978) compared a department successfully implementing new technology with one that rejected it. The researchers found that a major factor accounting for the difference between success and failure was that the unsuccessful department had perceived less urgency in the need for the technology. Even if the firm acknowledges this stage by disseminating information to the work force, too often the information focuses on the need for the particular equipment before the workers have been convinced that any change is necessary and that new technology is the solution. When new technology is being considered, the work force must first be convinced of the need for a change from current operations. Information and discussion must then ensue about the need for a new technological/human resource system as a partial answer to this need for change. Then, and only then, will discussions or announcements about the specific technology (for example, the robot or FMS) be appreciated.

A company that followed this progression had the executive vice-president, executives, and managers write a detailed argument describing the need for change (Zager, 1982). This argument was then reviewed with the entire work force meeting in small groups. Each meeting ended with a secret ballot concerning the need for change. Ninety percent of those attending the meetings voted in favor of change and created an ad hoc committee to work out a plan. It was only at that point that the plant work force was ready to accept the possibility that new technology was the answer, as well as the specific equipment. Another example of a company using this progression in its information program was described by Boddy and Buchanan (1986, p. 185):

> When a new automated facility for Babcock Power was to be constructed near Glasgow, three television programs, each 25 minutes long, were made for the workers at the old facility. It is important to note that management had themselves to understand clearly the nature of their plans and proposals and the nature of their own commitment. . . . The first program explained management's assessment of the problems confronting the company, the proposed survival plan, the need for radical change, and the need for full commitment to the plan to make it work. It identified the company's successful history, the threat of competition, and illustrated how the machine and assembly factory would be rebuilt. . . . The program was shown to the workforce in small groups of around 25 people

at a time to collect and assess as many individual reactions to the proposals as possible. This meant that the individual managers and foremen present at these showings had to understand the proposals well enough to be able to assess their impact on their areas and to answer questions. . . . Everybody was asked to present further written questions. Over a thousand questions and comments were received. They were analyzed by a joint union-management committee. The second television program was based on a selection of these issues. This second program took the form of a televised debate with senior managers on the platform being questioned by employee representatives on the floor. . . . The third program had a similar purpose and format. All three programs were shown before the new technology arrived. Two years later, the new factory was completed largely free of industrial relations problems.

Another common problem associated with the unfreezing stage of technological change is that too often the need for change is not accompanied by a clear vision and value statement of the future. Ed Lawler (1985) has found from his extensive experience with implementing work innovations that a clear vision and value statement is of particular importance when the change is implemented in existing rather than greenfield sites. With such a statement, the workers can compare the vision of the future to the past, reduce their anxieties about the change, and settle in because they know where they are headed. If a manager presents to the work force a plan for the first installation of CIM without discussing the vision of what the truly integrated plant will look like in the year 2010 and how each installation will get the plant one step closer to CIM, the work force will be hard pressed to appreciate the first step or to accept the problems associated with it. Moreover, without making clear value statements about the change (for example, retraining, more worker responsibility, and so on) and showing how those values will be incorporated into the system designs, fears will abound about job displacement, deskilling, and lack of management concern for the workers' plight.

Another activity that must be undertaken during the unfreezing stage is the solicitation of top management support. Top management should be involved in developing ultimate goals and values for the system, as well as intermediate steps to reach those goals. For example, research by Ettlie (1973) has indicated that organizations with higher success rates in implementing innovations were those in which top management was committed to the concept rather than the specifics of the innovation.

A final activity to be accomplished during the unfreezing stage is the identification of "key players" (Tornatzky and others, 1983; Leonard-Barton and Kraus, 1985). Key players (or stakeholders) are those individuals in the organization whose involvement in implementation will help others to be convinced of the credibility and utility of the automation. These people may be particularly well-respected supervisors and shop stewards, well-liked engineers and managers, and shopfloor workers who seem to be "spokes" in the workers' communication network. These people do not necessarily earn the respect of others by their position in the organization; instead, the respect is often attributable to their fair and concerned view of the world and their willingness to go to bat for unfairly treated people. If these individuals are identified early on, ways to solicit their commitment or involvement in the automation project can be explored.

Moving Forward

The moving forward stage of the technological change process is the stage in which the specific technical system and human infrastructure are identified, the equipment is purchased, and all the changes are implemented. Most of the content of this book has focused on this part of the change process. Three issues still remain to be discussed: evolutionary versus revolutionary change, programmed versus adaptive implementation plans, and the supervisor's role during implementation.

Evolutionary Versus Revolutionary Change. A question that has often been raised by plants contemplating the purchase of flexible automation is whether the purchase and planning of the equipment can be done in a piecemeal fashion or whether it should be done all at once as the budget permits. The first strategy is essentially an evolutionary and incremental one in which "islands of automation," pilot automation projects, or stand-alone equipment are installed. The second strategy is referred to as the revolutionary strategy, in which CIM is planned for all at once. Aside from the technical problems of an evolutionary strategy (for example, interfacing islands), research has found that the evolutionary strategy creates management problems as well. For example, while organizations experienced in new technology may obtain earlier success in implementing more technology than organizations without any experience, for the evolutionary strategy to work, the accumulated experience must be useful in adapting the organization to new equipment. Yet, as discussed earlier in this book, research evidence indicates that the human infrastructures for integrated and stand-alone equipment are quite different. Thus, plant managers who implement only stand-alone equipment and think that they have built up a store of knowledge to prepare them for the integration of that equipment are wrong.

Since most plants do not have the finances to implement their new technology all at once in a revolutionary fashion, they will continue to use the evolutionary approach. However, this approach should be used with some caution. If new technology is added that is substantially different from the old—for example, if integrated equipment is added to stand-alone equipment—management should not assume that its experience base will make implementation any easier. In fact, on some issues (for example, interdepartmental coordination), the organization may be back to square one.

Programmed Versus Adaptive Implementation. A second issue involved in the moving forward stage concerns the specificity of implementation plans. Should implementation plans be carefully and explicitly programmed before the equipment arrives (a programmed strategy), or should there be only very general plans with the specifics adapted as the events and decisions unfold (an adaptive strategy)? Many observers of the change process have argued for the use of adaptive strategies (McLoughlin, Rose, and Clark, 1985; Lawler, 1985). Not prescribing details too early gives people room to adjust to the change as it unfolds.

With an adaptive strategy, preinstallation plans should be quite general, leaving the specifics until the equipment arrives. However, with AMT, the selection of certain equipment features may rest on decisions about job design; thus, it would appear that a specific plan about job design needs to be developed early. Moreover, for many manufacturing organizations in which rigid hierarchies traditionally dictate a plan by which people perform, the programmed strategy would be far superior (Berman, 1980). Thus, for AMT, while general plans should be developed, these plans should probably by adapted before rather than after the technology arrives, so that by the time the equipment is operational, the organization has a programmed plan to live by.

Supervisors' Role During Implementation. There are many different opinions among technology researchers about how much responsibility should be assigned to supervisors during the implementation process. For example, in a study of twenty companies implementing information technology, Rothwell (1985) found that supervisors' roles in implementation varied. In some companies supervisors were responsible for keeping the old system running concurrently with the new one, while in other companies they became involved in training and communication. On one side of the argument are those who feel that supervisors are already overburdened with production pressures and thus should also not be expected to be responsible for AMT implementation (see case descriptions by Manufacturing Studies Board, 1986; Fazakerley, 1976). On the other side of the argument are such cases as Westinghouse, which gave supervisors the responsibility to provide all training to their workers. This was obviously not a case of protecting the supervisor from the dual responsibilities of meeting production schedules and implementation.

Apparently, the conclusion to be reached is somewhere in between. Supervisors probably should be involved in the change effort because that is how they learn about the change, adapt to the equipment, and adapt the equipment to their production line.

However, supervisors cannot be expected to take responsibility for the change unless they have been appropriately prepared for it and have the proper support services to help them. If they have been involved since the beginning, if they have been training an assistant to handle many of the day-to-day production responsibilities, and if they have a vision of what the future production line will look like, their role in the implementation process can be a major one.

Refreezing Stage

The refreezing stage of change focuses on ensuring that, once implemented, the changes in the human infrastructure and technology continue to operate smoothly. Maintenance of the change can be accomplished both by evaluation of the change and by continual reassessment of system matches.

Evaluation. The Manufacturing Studies Board (1986) found in their case studies that better implementation efforts were accompanied by high performance expectations—major improvements in design for producibility, quality, inventory reduction, cost performance, and so on. They concluded that the high performance expectations were required not only to justify the major capital investment but also psychologically to drive the process of organizational innovation. Examples of clear goals cited by Boddy and Buchanan (1986) include getting stock turnover back up to five times per year and increasing output by 25 percent. In one study of thirteen companies implementing AMT, three-quarters of those without clear goals ended in failure.

In addition to these high performance expectations, there must be evaluation efforts to determine if the expectations have been met. While the initial expectations may help to drive the innovation, feedback about how well the organization is doing against those expectations is needed to maintain motivation. The workers need to be provided continually with information about how their performance is meeting both process and outcome goals. Process data may include uptime, work-in-process inventory, cycle times, rework and scrap, and average numbers of jobs waiting. Outcome data may include periodic job satisfaction surveys, number of new customers, number of new products, and market share.

While expectations must be high and evaluations must be provided that reflect movement toward these goals, immediate achievement of expectations is unlikely. During the first years of flexible automation, 15 to 20 percent downtime is not unusual (Shaiken, 1983). Accident rates also do not usually decrease immediately because of more production problems and complicated machinery. Unrealistic expectations are a constant source of complaints from workers and supervisors responsible for operating the new equipment. Ken Knight (1985) describes the case of a steering committee of managers who were trying to determine when the equipment would be fully operational. When the robot system had been operated under ideal circumstances by the development engineers themselves, it had met a 50 percent improvement in chip component placement time. On the basis of these data, the steering committee discussed ways of pushing the operators and the system harder to guarantee quick accomplishment of throughput improvements. This strategy of excessive production pressures, however, would have eliminated worker time to experiment and test the equipment on variations to identify sources of possible problems. As a result, the pressure might have caused accidents, tool breakage, and higher stress, rather than the 50 percent improvement desired. In considering these consequences of pushing the operators too hard, Knight's steering committee finally decided to release the robot system to manufacturing with no time standards or output goals.

Thus, a way to ensure refreezing is to assure the work force that high expectations are unlikely to be met initially; however, over time, performance data feedback should eventually reflect closer and closer achievement of those expectations.

Continual Reassessment. Within the open systems framework, another method of ensuring refreezing when flexible automation is implemented is to continually reassess the match of the technical system with both changing production requirements and changing human infrastructure elements. Production requirements that may have been appropriate initially may not be appropriate after the system has been in place for a year. Elements of the human infrastructure may change as well; there may be a substantial amount of turnover among the work force one year that may lead to workers wanting more challenge on their jobs than the equipment permits. Or top managers may have decided that increased worker responsibility is a more acceptable human resource strategy than originally envisioned. A plant's assumption that the system that was initially installed is still appropriate a year or two later may prove to be incorrect. Unfortunately,, "few companies have made formal provisions for the kind of continued experimentation and adaptation that the FMSs require to achieve their full potential," two researchers concluded from their study of FMS implementation in eight firms (Graham and Rosenthal, 1985, p. 9). Thus, there must also be a plan for how continued assessment will occur and how the company will respond to what it finds.

Conclusions

Even if the suggestions offered throughout this chapter are followed, an otherwise successful implementation effort will not be sufficient if the new technology presents too great a challenge to the existing technical, human infrastructure, and organizational systems. Thus, the challenging nature of the technology should be assessed to determine how successful the implementation effort will be. The new technology can be assessed along five dimensions, as proposed by Zaltman, Duncan, and Holbek (1973): its relative advantage, compared to the existing state of affairs; its compatibility with existing values, experiences, and organizational needs; its complexity, or the ease with which it can be understood and used; its trialability, or the extent to which it can be experimented with; and its observability, or the extent to which the results of the innovation are visible to others. Research on these characteristics by Rogers (1983) and Zaltman, Duncan, and Holbek (1973) has found that the higher the innovation's score on each of these characteristics, the more successful the implementation is likely to be. Thus, a new flexible automation system is likely to be successfully implemented if it is substantially better than the organization's current equipment, it is compatible with the way things are done at the organization, it is not too difficult to understand, it can be tried and modified if need be, and it has highly visible results.

High scores on these characteristics, though, should not fool anyone. The manager implementing new technology needs to remember that even with a compatible technological innovation, the ultimate success rests with people. And as we all know, working with machines is often much easier than working with people.

Realizing the Potential
of Factory Automation:
Key Strategies
for Success

An organization has one bottom-line reason for implementing auto-mated manufacturing technology (AMT)—to maintain or regain its competitive advantage. There really are no other reasons. AMT helps the company achieve this goal by providing the technical capability for efficient yet flexible production. Simply possessing the technical capability does not guarantee success, however; management must know how to use it.

AMT will not yield low WIP inventories, high met delivery schedules, and low-cost, high-quality products. AMT will succeed only at changing the technical and human infrastructure. Whether these changes result in any of the potential yields of AMT depends on management decisions and commitment—not the technology. The level of management commitment to AMT will be evidenced by the appropriateness of decisions being made about first-order effects on job designs, second-order effects on human infrastructure, means of matching first- and second-order effects to create an infrastructure that harmoniously supports the potential yields of AMT, and steps to implement the technology so that the change process proceeds in a manner acceptable to a majority of those involved.

These decisions are made—whether explicitly or implicitly, planned or unplanned, intentionally or unintentionally. In the interest of controlling our own destinies, it is far better to make fully informed decisions intentionally than to have them made for us by default.

Therefore, managers implementing AMT should plan the decision-making process to ensure that the potential yields of AMT are realized.

Managing First-Order Effects

Three first-order human infrastructure impacts of flexible automation must be considered: effects on the functions and jobs of machine operators, effects on technical support, and effects on supervisors and managers. These effects are labeled as first-order because they are the ones most likely to be directly affected by technological design choices.

Managing Changes to Operators' Jobs. Jobs of operators are greatly affected by the implementation of flexible automation. The new equipment takes over many of the manual jobs formerly performed by people, and the operator is less often required to intervene physically in the machine operations. As a result, less direct labor time is needed to do what the operators once did.

Decisions about how the operators should now spend their free time must be made. At a minimum, managers will have operators spend more time monitoring operations to ensure adequate fault detection and response to variations in work flow. In addition, managers often have operators handle the inputs and outputs to the manufacturing cell, such as feeding the machine and removing completed parts.

These two simple and minimal decisions about operators' jobs—having operators monitor production and handle materials—strongly affect the plant's ability to achieve the benefits desired from AMT. Having operators spend more time monitoring and less time physically manipulating equipment means that the operators' activities can no longer be determined solely by the machine, supervisors, or work rules. Within limits, the operators alone determine precisely what aspects of the production process are watched and what information is sufficiently important to prompt them to intervene in the production process. Thus, the act of attending to the equipment and freedom from the immediate pacing of the machine allow the operators themselves, to a much greater extent, to determine their own behavior. The implication of such a simple decision as having operators monitor is that if operators are not motivated to closely examine a production process, the benefits expected from the new equipment will not be achieved.

Management's decision to have operators handle materials may also affect the realization of AMT's potential benefits. Since often the various cells of flexible equipment are integrated or will soon become integrated, the responsible handling of inputs and outputs frequently necessitates coordination with others in the production process. Moreover, since it is the operators who feed and watch the new equipment, their familiarity with it often surpasses that of technical support personnel. Operators are often thrust into the role of helping engineers and technical support staff to diagnose complex problems associated with equipment breakdowns or production flaws. If management fails to encourage the necessary coordination, valuable information will not be exchanged and downtime will increase, reducing the yields of AMT.

Finally, in making the basic decision to implement flexible as opposed to dedicated equipment, management has intentionally or unintentionally altered the priorities of the operator's job. Often, operators are now held accountable not just for the amount produced but also for the quality of the product and the scrap generated by the production process. High-quality products will not be manufactured if management has failed to develop a system to support such new accountability needs.

As consequential as these decisions about operators' jobs are, such choices and their implications are the minimum disruption to be expected from flexible automation. To enhance the operators' fault detection capabilities, managers may decide to involve the operators in other facets of the production process, such as scheduling and performing minor maintenance. Moroever, if operators are to be held accountable for quality, management may decide to provide the operators with discretion over events that affect quality, such as inspecting inputs and machine setups and proofing computer programs. Thus, beyond making the minimal decisions about what AMT operators will do, managers must consider additional activities that will have serious consequences for AMT.

Decisions about what the operators do on their AMT jobs do not necessarily translate directly into a particular job design. Managers are wrong if they assume either that the existing traditional job design is correct or that any one job design is appropriate for most applications of flexible equipment. There are many feasible job designs and it is the managers' task to understand these options sufficiently to choose among them. For example, as discussed in Chapter Three, one option for meeting the task needs of AMT operators' jobs is to enlarge the jobs—have each and every operator personally and individually responsible for maintenance. An equally plausible option, but one with a different approach to meeting the task need, is to apply an ergonomics framework to job design, wherein jobs are created that are best suited for optimal performance by both human and machine. Thus, materials-handling equipment would be placed at the correct height, while information gauges would be presented in a fashion optimal for signal recognition and processing. Finally, the most radical option for meeting operators' task needs is to apply a synergistic perspective in which the technical structure and human infrastructure are analyzed simultaneously with multiple priorities of quality, fault detection, and output in mind. Each of these options is based on different assumptions about what is to be accomplished by using the new technology, the type of work force existing at the plant, the type of work force desired, and the vision of management about how the technical structure and human infrastructure should interface. The equipment does not dictate which of these options to apply; it only makes them possible.

Managing Changes to Technical Support Jobs. In addition to decisions about AMT operators' jobs, flexible automation creates a need to make decisions about the jobs of technical support staff. A critical effect of AMT on technical support functions is the addition of NC, FMS, or CAM parts programmers. The introduction of AMT parts programmers often creates power and control conflicts between operators and programmers. The question of which group can proof and modify computer programs often initiates a symbolic war over who has ultimate control over the shopfloor. Management must decide the outcome of this war. Those job designs that will help to achieve AMT benefits are those that clarify the programming responsibilities of the two groups so that there are no obvious losers and the sharing of learning and information is promoted. Otherwise, downtime and order slippage are incurred while symbolic battles are fought.

Another critical technical support function affected by flexible automation is engineering, both R&D and manufacturing. For CAM and CIM to yield higher-quality products efficiently, management must ensure that both R&D and manufacturing engineers increasingly coordinate with others—with other engineers, with marketing (for designers), and with shopfloor staff (for manufacturing engineers). If management allows R&D engineers to focus on design solely for innovation rather than for manufacturability as well, the valuable opportunities offered by CIM will be wasted. Similarly, for manufacturing engineers, less time needs to be spent bidding jobs (since centralized computer systems can now do that), and process improvements no longer need to be their exclusive responsibility (since operators and others more involved in the daily operations of such complex systems are often in as good a position to suggest and implement process changes as the manufacturing engineer). If management fails to replace these traditional engineering tasks, it will unnecessarily underutilize valuable manufacturing experience at a time when this experience would be most useful. Manufacturing engineers can be reassigned to fill essential roles as technological superstars, members of permanent automation project teams, or engineering consultants to operating teams, marketing teams, or strategy teams.

A third technical support function affected by AMT is the skilled trades. Managing the maintenance of flexible equipment is naturally more sophisticated than managing maintenance in conventional factories. Maintenance problems take longer to diagnose with flexible equipment because the equipment is more complex. Since maintenance problems typically involve more than one control mechanism (for example, electrical and mechanical), knowledge of only one type of control mechanism is insufficient. Moreover, the demands of preventive maintenance are different from those of corrective maintenance. The complexity of the systems requires working with others to solve problems; the time of the lone "Maytag repairman" working by himself to solve every problem with the machine is over. Thus, a manager who fails to create AMT maintenance departments that cross disciplinary boundaries will all but ensure high equipment downtime rates and fewer AMT benefits.

A fourth group of technical support functions affected by AMT is production and quality control. Shopfloor personnel will assume many daily tasks of control and scheduling. This freed-up time, if management so desires, can then be used by production control for master scheduling and planning to optimize the delicate balance between equipment capacity and customer demand. As for quality control personnel, the greater emphasis on a high-quality product will increase their power. Increased power will not necessarily translate into a more centralized staff. Rather, management may decide that inspection activities are best performed by machine operators, leaving quality control staff to provide such essential support as training, follow-up checking, quality problem diagnosis, and general coordination. Such a support network would then help to ensure the production of high-quality, low-cost products.

Accounting personnel, a fifth technical support function, also experience some changes with flexible automation. The traditional assumptions used by accountants about the variability of direct labor and its use as a basis for cost are wrong. Multiple dimensions of performance, both financial and nonfinancial, need to be added to cost-accounting practies to reflect the multiple reasons for purchasing the equipment in the first place and the multiple dimensions upon which the company is judged in the marketplace. While these changes may not translate into a different job design for the accountant, management must still rethink the priorities of accountants' jobs and their need for continuing education and development.

Finally, the role of marketing personnel in achieving the potential of AMT is unfortunately often overlooked. The marketing department is ultimately responsible for finding the markets for the additional capacity provided by the equipment; otherwise, the machines' ability to take over operators' tasks will lead to layoffs, and payback periods will be unnecessarily lengthened. Thus, if

AMT is to yield its potential benefits, marketing managers need to become involved early in the equipment planning to ensure that the appropriate customer base has been sought. Moreover, they must stay involved with R&D and manufacturing to keep the plant's customer base in line with its equipment capacity.

Managing Changes to Managerial and Supervisory Jobs. The implementation of AMT affects not only the jobs of professional and shopfloor personnel, but also those of supervisors and managers. For the first-line supervisor, the increased ability of operators to determine their precise work activities means that operators should no longer be as closely supervised as before. Therefore, a main activity—and, in some sense, the identity—of first-line supervisors is eliminated. Management must decide what activities should take its place. Supervisors in a flexible automated factory may be encouraged to engage in proactive planning and problem solving to ensure that opportunities offered by integrated computerized equipment are grasped and potential problems avoided. The supervisor may be given greater responsibility for the business, usually in terms of authority over support functions and a greater number of machines. This broader responsibility usually results in more complex information-gathering activities, often with contradictory information from multiple inputs about different, seemingly interconnected problems. More coordination with peers and support staff is required. If management fails to clarify the supervisors' new role responsibilities, important information will not be conveyed, and potential AMT yields will be jeopardized.

For higher-level managers, the effects of flexible automation are not as dramatic as for supervisors and thus necessitate fewer decisions about new job functions. Nevertheless, managers of flexible factories must learn to operate in an integrated setting. They need to exercise a systems orientation in setting objectives, solving problems, supervising staff, staffing committees, allocating resources, and coordinating with other managers. In addition, as the first-line supervisor acquires more responsibility for routine decision making over a greater part of the business, the manager will have time freed up from this routine decision making. As a result, some companies will eliminate higher-level management jobs, while other companies will provide higher-level managers with the valuable time they need to become opportunity-seekers and champions of new ideas.

Managing Second-Order Effects

Once decisions about how to deal with the first-order effects of AMT on job designs are made, decisions about the second-order effects that flow from the job designs can be considered. Decisions must be made about five second-order effects: skill needs, selection, training, personnel policies, and organizational structure.

Skill Requirements. If the benefits of AMT are to be realized, the specific skills needed to adequately perform particular jobs must be identified. While the specific skills will obviously depend on the job design and a detailed task analysis of each new job, there are certain general skills needed on an AMT shopfloor. There will be less need for skills involving manual dexterity and greater need for perceptual, conceptual, and human relations skills. The perceptual skills required include an increased ability to concentrate and observe, for fault detection. Conceptual skills needed include an increased ability to diagnose complex problems, and increased knowledge of manufacturing systems and circuitries. Finally, the human relations skills needed to complement the increased coordination and interdependence of AMT jobs include group problem solving, communication, and conflict resolution. Without these skills on the shopfloor, the work force will be unable to utilize the new equipment appropriately.

Selection Policies. With the new skill requirements, policies for selecting workers for the AMT shopfloor must also change. Management's first consideration with these policies is the amount of job displacement expected with AMT. An analysis of the cases to date indicates that predictions of substantial job displacement with the implementation of flexible automation are false. Thus, purchasing new equipment for the primary purpose of reducing direct labor costs is misguided. Rather, the extent of job displacement seems to have as much to do with the design of the operators' jobs, top management's human resource philosophy (for example, about training), and the speed with which the equipment is introduced as with the advent of the flexible factory itself. If the existing work force is to retrain for other jobs using the new equipment, little job displacement will occur.

Training. A second consideration is the criteria upon which AMT worker selection should be based. Since not all workers can meet skill-based selection criteria or can effectively work with the new equipment even after having met the selection criteria, the issue of training for flexible automation is essential. The traditional approach to training used in manufacturing firms with conventional equipment—relying on equipment vendors or unstructured on-the-job training (OJT)—will not work with flexible automation. The skill needs, the job designs, the technical equipment, the systems thinking, and the integration create such different demands on the labor force that only a structured, in-house training program will suffice. Such an in-house training program needs to allow for an individualized curriculum, since the existing work force will start the training with different levels of knowledge—some will barely be able to read and write, while others have been unofficially reading engineering blueprints for years. The precise curriculum will depend on the skills needed for the different occupations. However, given the general conclusions about skills required with flexible automation, generic courses for all occupations will need to be offered. These generic courses include human relations training, such as interpersonal skills, communication skills, problem solving, and decision making; knowledge of the manufacturing process and how the new equipment fits into that process; and basic skills in economics (to understand the effect of the marketplace), math, and reading.

The amount of training needed will depend on the extent to which new skills are required by the new job designs. Nevertheless, it is clear that the in-house training program must be continuous; it must repeat some courses (as refreshers or for new personnel) as well as offer advanced courses to allow the work force to enhance its skill development over time. The training should allow for active learning, preferably through simulations of equipment operation, and combine off-the-job training with on-the-job learning to optimize real-world applications of classroom teaching. The training should be started and possibly completed prior to the arrival of the equipment in production. Finally, the training should be periodically evaluated in the light of its initial purposes. Obviously, a training program primarily intended only to reduce resistance to change should be evaluated according to very different criteria than a training program intended to take the work force from the Dark Ages to the twenty-first century. Without a well-considered, multifaceted training program, the work force will be inadequately prepared to meet the challenges posed not only by the newly purchased AMT but by the equipment yet to be purchased as the company carries its modernization effort forward into the future.

Personnel Policies. The implementation of flexible automation also obliges management to make decisions about at least six personnel policies: job classifications, pay, career development, job security, shift-work, and union-management relations. Managers of flexible automated factories will have to redefine job classifications; these will be fewer and broader to reflect the new job designs for the work force. Pay in flexible factories is based on very different assumptions from pay in conventional factories. Basing pay primarily on hours worked and company loyalty, rewarding only for individual performance—with performance being judged solely by output—and differentiating between employees on the basis of minor differences in job classifications: these standards no longer constitute an appropriate pay system. Because the flexible automated factory has new expectations of its workers—quality, commitment, teamwork, and motivation, as well as output—using a conventional pay system will essentially promote worker behavior that is at odds with the needs of AMT. Instead, flexible automation requires pay systems that reward both team and individual effort, differentiate between people based more on performance than on job classifications, and reward workers more for quality of work than for simple attendance. Management must then choose from among a variety of different options for paying workers to meet the priorities of the flexible automated factory. These new options include hourly pay formulas that incorporate individual and team performance, salaries that are linked to minimal skill requirements, bonuses for innovative ideas or exceptional performance, and gainsharing or profit-sharing plans.

Management must also pay greater attention to formal career development policies. Such policies increase in importance with AMT because with fewer job classifications, a career development policy may be the sole means by which motivated employees will determine that their career objectives can be met at the company. An automated plant cannot long endure excessively high turnover among the employees who are knowledgeable about AMT. Fortunately, certain career ladders are created with AMT that have not existed before. With AMT it is possible for operators to progress to engineering or for maintenance personnel to learn programming. Moreover, such career progression within the organization creates new room for fresh minds and fresh experiences, which are essential in a technologically changing environment to keep people motivated and innovative.

Another personnel policy that management must consider is the guarantee of no layoffs due to technological change. While most companies would prefer not to guarantee no layoffs, the cases indicate that job security must be promised for either contractual or motivational reasons. Workers who fear for their jobs or who do not have management's assurance about their future with the company are not likely to willingly meet the shopfloor challenges of AMT. Thus, management's decision is actually how to ensure that job security promises are met. Slowing down the implementation of new equipment, returning subcontracting to the organization, and instituting massive retraining efforts are examples of possible options.

Shift-work policies also are often affected by the introduction of AMT. The cost of the new equipment typically necessitates adding shifts to reduce payback periods. The decision to increase the number of shifts often marks the point at which management reevaluates its shift policies. Should the third-shift operators have the same responsibilities as the first shift? If so, where is the support staff for them? If not, how can the off-shift be staffed? There are multiple possibilities, including the decision not to add additional shifts after all. If the company cannot find adequate support staff to work with the off-shift, running an off-shift may not be cost-effective.

Finally, AMT changes the ways in which union and management interact. As job classifications broaden and work rules become less rigid in the flexible factory, local unions will find it necessary to redefine their role so that they can adequately represent the concerns of their members. Such a role may focus on defending workers' rights to decision making rather than rights to uniform treatment. National unions also must find new issues as uniform national solutions give way to unique local solutions. With the changing union roles, management and the union have the opportunity to create a constructive relationship where one did not exist before or to preserve a constructive relationship into the future. If there is to be a constructive relationship following the implementation of AMT, management will need to provide advance notice of technological change, unions should have specially appointed technology representatives, both sides will bargain less on specific contractual work rules than on work rule options for coping with the effects of the new technology, liberal use will need to be made of union membership surveys, and written principles should be promulgated describing a shared union-management vision of the types of work force effects to be promoted or avoided with the new technology. The overall goal of these suggested changes is a relationship in which AMT is fully utilized to maintain the organization's competitive advantage; and in the long run competitive advantage is maintained in a flexible automated factory only with motivated and committed workers.

Organizational Structure. One of the central management dilemmas for organizing with AMT is how to achieve a balance between integrating different people, functions, and processes in an organization while simultaneously differentiating among these elements to allow for manageable-sized units. With AMT, the need for integration is overwhelming, yet units must still be differentiated in some way. To resolve this dilemma, management must choose from a number of different solutions. One solution is to add a CAD/CAM coordinating unit in which personnel are assigned responsibility for system development and coordination. Other solutions include appointing task forces; restructuring the organization to reflect different complete sequences of production processes; establishing matrix-type reporting hierarchies; and fostering an organizational climate that promotes coordination. A review of the advantages and disadvantages of each indicates that no one solution is without problems. Combining the best of multiple solutions seems to be the answer. For example, management could try a combination of (1) reorganizing manufacturing operations into distinct flow production processes; (2) introducing committees on such issues as quality control and software development; (3) integrating workers simultaneously into the flow process, their functional area, and committees; (4) decentralizing decisions that demand immediate attention while centralizing planning decisions; and (5) creating an organizational climate with the message: "Integrate! Coordinate! Communicate!" All these changes to the organizational structure may be essential to ensure that the work force, paperwork, and mission continue to reflect the needs of AMT.

Managing the Matches

According to the open systems approach, one must never ignore the multiple aspects of the system. The time a supervisor devotes to close supervision should be freed up only when that person is given something else to do and if the workers have the skills and authority to direct their own work. Examples of companies' failing to adopt an open systems approach unfortunately abound. For example, at Simmonds Precision Products, "a savings of $18.6 thousand was projected for NC programming, but the enormous printed circuit and graphics work loads effectively preempted the manufacturing engineers from spending any appreciable time on the system during the first 20 months of operation. Savings were nil; in fact, a net loss resulted" (Van Nostrand, 1984, p. 13).

Firms with the open systems approach often regard the implementation of flexible automation as the occasion to adopt administrative innovations simultaneously with the new technology. John Ettlie (1985) interviewed 100 managers in thirty-nine plants implementing FMSs and found that 56 percent of the firms simultaneously instituted quality circles, eliminated first-line supervisors, or made other administrative changes. Ettlie also found that the more radical the technology for the organization, the more radical the administrative innovation (such as STS work redesigns, broadened job descriptions, or an all-salaried work force). Thus, in planning for new technology, remember that the human infrastructure must be constructed in such a way that its important elements are congruent with each other. Otherwise, both the technology and the human resource opportunities are wasted.

Advocating congruence is not meant to imply that certain changes, independently assessed, are better than other changes. Rather, it is the complete configuration of interrelated changes and decisions that determines whether the system will fulfill the promise of AMT. Thus, while a synergistic approach to operator job design may theoretically be valuable, it will have detrimental effects if used in an organization where equipment is selected by an off-site group of engineers lacking any knowledge of the nuances of the actual production runs on the shopfloor.

Configurations of elements of the human and technical infrastructure are virtually infinite in their variety. Any of them can be successful as long as the elements are matched. A highly bureaucratic manufacturing organization can be as successful as a team-based organization, provided it has matched elements. The matched elements of a bureaucratic organization may include narrowly defined operator jobs allowing for little exercise of discretion, substantial numbers of maintenance and manufacturing engineering staff, an integrated computerized system to do quality inspections and routing, operators trained primarily in specific machine skills and the importance of following instructions, and an organizational structure in which the lines of responsibility for a flexible automated factory are clearly demarcated, for example by process flow. The team-based organization would have a different configuration, possibly with a matrix structure, broad job designs, cross-training, and a group-based reward system. Again, the point in this book is not to recommend a particular configuration of management decisions; rather, as long as the configuration is appropriate to both the technical requirements and the human infrastructure, it should be successful.

Finally, in matching the technical requirements and human infrastructure, implementing AMT may not always be the best way to maintain a competitive advantage. For example, the New United Motor Manufacturing Inc. (NUMMI) plant in Fremont, California, the GM-Toyota joint venture, uses "out-of-date technology" to assemble Chevrolet Novas. *Business Week* ("High Tech to the Rescue," 1986) describes its productivity as higher than most of GM's new plants. "The key, experts say, is Toyota's management style, which emphasizes thorough training and participative management, lean layers of middle management, and decision making pushed as close as possible to the assembly line" (p. 104). The answers cannot always be found in the technology because they are not always there. Examining the existing factory first and building the desired infrastructure—both technical and human— before new technology is added may be a far more beneficial strategy in the long term.

Implementation

The final set of decisions management must make concerns the implementation process itself. The best human and technical options will be wasted if the implementation is inappropriately planned and executed. At a minimum, implementation plans should take into consideration resistance to change, automation project teams, and the change process.

The problems of resistance to flexible automation are tremendous. Since resistance stems in large part from a lack of communication and involvement, management must decide among various options for promoting communication and/or involvement. Options for enhancing communication about flexible automation can include training, formal orientations, and ongoing information dissemination. Options for enhancing involvement include encouraging consultative participation—for example, through simulation labs for the new equipment, promoting indirect participation through worker-elected committees, providing for direct participation through town hall meetings, and developing more sophisticated participation systems that allow for two-tiered (strategic and technical) involvement.

Automation project teams plan for the new equipment. For the automation team to select the best equipment and develop the implementation plan that is best suited to the organization, management must design the team to promote open systems thinking. Such a team is composed of multiple disciplines and interest groups and is structured to optimize team cohesiveness and effectiveness. Substantial thought must be given to the selection of the leader and the conduct of team business. Such a team must also undertake its mission in a way that promotes systems thinking. A multiple-step approach for the automation project team has been suggested.

Finally, management must consider the change process when planning for implementation. The first step in the change process, unfreezing, should concentrate on convincing the work force (including other managers) of the need for change before the notion of new technology is introduced. The second step, moving forward, should be the step during which the human resource and technical changes are introduced. A key consideration in this stage is whether change should be introduced incrementally or all at once; there are pros and cons to both strategies. The final stage, refreezing, is the stage in which, after the changes have been introduced, they must be solidified to ensure that slippage back to old ways does not occur. A primary vehicle for refreezing change is constant evaluation and feedback. A little movement in the direction of the goal goes a long way toward assuring people that they are on the right track to help the company regain its position in the marketplace.

Closing

In summary, the desired benefits of AMT are achieved as a result of decisions made by management, not as a result of the technology itself. A review of possible decisions leaves a long list of do's and don't's for managers implementing AMT. Some of the more important ones are listed here:

- Don't regard automation as a quick fix for basic manufacturing or human resource problems; look to the entire infrastructure as the fix.

- Don't assume that human resource problems can be resolved after the equipment is installed, since some of the problems may have to do with the specific equipment selected.
- Do expect that multiple different configurations of matches of technical and human infrastructure elements are equally effective, as long as the organization can undergo all the needed changes.
- Do expect to redesign jobs of operators, technical support staff, and supervisors.
- Do involve marketing staff in equipment planning to ensure that equipment capacity can be fully utilized.
- Do not look for broad-brushed deskilling or skill upgrading of the work force with AMT; rather, some new skills will be required and others will no longer be needed.
- Don't make direct labor the prime economic target of flexible automation, since the displacement of direct labor is such a small part of the economic benefits of AMT.
- Do expect a substantial increase in training costs.
- Do expect that the existing pay system is likely to become obsolete.
- Do expect that the union-management relationship will change dramatically.
- Do begin facing the dilemma of changing the organizational structure to meet both coordination and differentiation needs.
- Do expect resistance; begin convincing managers and the work force of the need for change before installing the new equipment.
- Do use a multidisciplinary automation project team to implement AMT.
- And finally, do remember a passage written by Saint-Exupéry, an observer of society, in the 1930s (cited in Walker and Guest, 1952, p. 6):

> But the Machine is not an end; it is a tool . . . like the plow. If we believe that it degrades Man, it is possibly because we lack the perspective for judging the end results of transformations as rapid as those to which we have been subjected.

Appendix

Human Infrastructure
Impact Statement

Instructions

Exhibit 2-1, which appears on page 42, describes the staged model of human infrastructure impacts of AMT. The model identifies nine elements of the human infrastructure that are affected by AMT equipment parameters. From this model, the Human Infrastructure Impact Statement (HIIS) has been developed. The HIIS contains multiple pages, with each page representing a different element of the human infrastructure. Thus, the first page assesses the impact of equipment parameters on operators' jobs, the second page assesses the impact on technical support jobs (using the operator's job dimensions), and so on. Moreover, following the discussion in this book, each element of the human infrastructure and the equipment parameters have been further broken down into dimensions. For each human infrastructure element, there are particular dimensions for which assessments should be made. For example, for AMT operators' job activities, the impact of AMT on the four dimensions of the jobs (including, for example, information needs and areas of discretion) is assessed. Similarly, for equipment parameters, the impact of each of the six parameters identified in Chapter Two is assessed separately. Finally, in keeping with the staged model, the impact of the equipment parameters on the first-order elements of the human infrastructure (jobs) only is assessed. For the second-order elements, the impact of first-order changes is assessed, while for the third-order elements, the effect of second-order changes is assessed.

First Assessment: Equipment Parameters

To complete the HIIS, first consider the impact of each equipment parameter on each of the first-order human infrastructure elements. For a particular human infrastructure element, assess the degree and type of change caused by each equipment parameter to each dimension of the element. A box to mark each assessment has been provided. For example, if the AMT equipment's high need for feedback affects machine operators' jobs by increasing their information and coordination needs, both of those boxes could be marked with an up-arrow (↑). Then continue the assessments for each equipment parameter. To facilitate use of the HIIS all the terms in the statement are defined at the end of this appendix.

As discussed throughout the book, simply assessing the effect of each equipment parameter on each dimension of each human infrastructure element separately is not sufficient. Additional assessments must be made as well. First, the existing conditions (prior to AMT installation) of the human infrastructure element should be assessed. For example, are the information needs of conventional equipment operators' jobs high? If there are no comparable existing conditions, this place on the HIIS would be left blank. However, when existing conditions can be assessed, it is possible to use this assessment to determine the extent of change in the operators' job created by AMT.

Second Assessment: Constraints on
Impacts of Equipment Parameters

The second additional assessment concerns the effects of constraints on impacts of the equipment parameters (or first- and second-order changes). In Chapter Two, four constraints on human infrastructure changes were identified. These four include (1) work force (for example, preferred job challenge or skill level), (2) control over resources (for example, supplier agreements), (3) marketplace conditions (for example, market growth), and (4) management human resource philosophy (for example, priorities and decision-making style). For each of these constraints, a judgment should be made for each human infrastructure element about the way that the constraint will limit options and equipment impacts. For example, for machine operators' jobs, union status may limit the amount of discretion that workers can have, or management decision-making style may limit the amount of information the workers can have. With this assessment of the constraints, one can compare the assessed impacts of equipment parameters (or first-order changes) to the assessed constraints in order to identify possible conflicts, problems, or limits on changes to the human infrastructure. For example, if increased information were identified as being necessary with unreliable AMT equipment and management's decision-making style discouraged giving information to the workers, a potential problem would have been identified and should be resolved before equipment installation.

Third Assessment:
Effects on the Change Process

The third additional assessment to make is the effects of the changes to the human infrastructure elements on the planned change process. Four assessments need to be made here:

1. Are specific changes likely to create resistance to change?
2. If so, what counterresistance activities should be undertaken?
3. Are specific changes likely to have implications for the activities of automation project teams?
4. Are specific changes likely to have implications for how the equipment is initially implemented and continually accepted?

These assessments may be made for each dimension of each human infrastructure element. For example, the increased information needs of the machine operator's job may be found to reduce worker resistance while greater worker discretion is found to increase management's resistance. Or the planned change assessments can be made across all dimensions of the human infrastructure element. With this planned change assessment, problems that are likely to occur during implementation can be identified early on.

Final Assessment:
Effects on Other Elements

The last additional assessment concerns the effects of the changes to a particular human infrastructure element on the other eight elements. For example, increased worker discretion may mean that workers have discretion over areas formerly decided by supervisors. If so, the probable impact on supervisors should be noted.

The final category on each page of the statement is the conclusions. In this space, conclusions about the likely impacts, problems, and options—given a review of the assessments made on that page—should be noted.

In summary, the HIIS consists of assessments of the:

- Impact of equipment parameters on first-order human infrastructure elements (and impact of first-order on second-order elements, and so on)
- Existing conditions of the human infrastructure element
- Effects of constraints on equipment parameter impacts
- Effects of changes to the human infrastructure element on the planned change process
- Effects of changes to the human infrastructure element on other elements
- Conclusions about problems, impacts, and options for each element.

I. FIRST-ORDER IMPACTS: Machine Operator Functions

	Coordination Needs	Information Needs	Human-Machine Redundancy	Areas & Degree of Discretion
A. IMPACT OF EQUIPMENT PARAMETERS				
Integration				
Rigidity				
Reliability				
Work Unpredictability				
Feedback				
Safety				
B. EXISTING CONDITIONS				
C. EFFECTS OF CONSTRAINTS ON IMPACTS				
WORKFORCE				
-Desired job challenge				
-Management trust				
-Union status				
-Skill level & experience				
CONTROL OVER RESOURCES				
-Plant autonomy				
-Supplier agreements				
-Laborforce mobility				
MARKETPLACE				
-Entry into new markets				

- Recent perf gaps
- Market growth

MANAGEMENT HR PHILOSOPHY
- Model of worker motivation

- Decisionmaking style

- HR priorities

D. EFFECTS OF IMPACTS ON PLANNED CHANGE PROCESS

Resistance to change

Counter-Resistance acts

Autom project teams

Implementation steps

E. EFFECTS OF IMPACTS ON OTHER ELEMENTS

Technical support jobs

Management/Supervision

Skill requirements

Selection

Training

Personnel policies

Organizational structure

Outcomes

F. CONCLUSIONS

II. FIRST-ORDER IMPACTS: Technical Support Functions

	Skilled Trades	Quality & Production Control	Programming	Engineering	Accounting and Marketing
A. IMPACT OF EQUIPMENT PARAMETERS					
Integration					
Rigidity					
Reliability					
Work Unpredictability					
Feedback					
Safety					
B. EXISTING CONDITIONS					
C. EFFECTS OF CONSTRAINTS ON IMPACTS					
WORKFORCE −Desired job challenge					
−Management trust					
−Union status					
−Skill level & experience					
CONTROL OVER RESOURCES −Plant autonomy					
−Supplier agreements					
−Laborforce mobility					
MARKETPLACE −Entry into new markets					

-Recent perf gaps

-Market growth

MANAGEMENT HR PHILOSOPHY
-Model of worker motivation

-Decisionmaking style

-HR priorities

D. EFFECTS OF IMPACTS ON PLANNED CHANGE PROCESS

Resistance to change

Counter-Resistance acts

Autom project teams

Implementation steps

E. EFFECTS OF IMPACTS ON OTHER ELEMENTS

Machine operators' jobs

Management/Supervision

Skill requirements

Selection

Training

Personnel policies

Organizational structure

Outcomes

F. CONCLUSIONS

III. FIRST-ORDER IMPACTS: Supervisory Functions

	Supervising People	Supervising Pro-duction Process	Coordination	Planning & Scheduling	Staffing & Training
A. IMPACT OF EQUIPMENT PARAMETERS					
Integration					
Rigidity					
Reliability					
Work Unpredictability					
Feedback					
Safety					
B. EXISTING CONDITIONS					
C. EFFECTS OF CONSTRAINTS ON IMPACTS					
WORKFORCE					
-Desired job challenge					
-Management trust					
-Union status					
-Skill level & experience					
CONTROL OVER RESOURCES					
-Plant autonomy					
-Supplier agreements					
-Laborforce mobility					
MARKETPLACE					
-Entry into new markets					

-Recent perf gaps

-Market growth

MANAGEMENT HR PHILOSOPHY
-Model of worker motivation

-Decisionmaking style

-HR priorities

D. EFFECTS OF IMPACTS ON PLANNED CHANGE PROCESS

Resistance to change

Counter-Resistance acts

Autom project teams

Implementation steps

E. EFFECTS OF IMPACTS ON OTHER ELEMENTS

Machine operators' jobs

Technical support jobs

Skill requirements

Selection

Training

Personnel policies

Organizational structure

Outcomes

F. CONCLUSIONS

IV. FIRST-ORDER IMPACTS: Management Functions

	Routine Decision-making	Objective-setting	Coordination With Other Departments	Supervisory Needs

A. IMPACT OF EQUIPMENT PARAMETERS

Integration				
Rigidity				
Reliability				
Work Unpredictability				
Feedback				
Safety				

B. EXISTING CONDITIONS

C. EFFECTS OF CONSTRAINTS ON IMPACTS

WORKFORCE				
-Desired job challenge				
-Management trust				
-Union status				
-Skill level & experience				
CONTROL OVER RESOURCES				
-Plant autonomy				
-Supplier agreements				
-Laborforce mobility				
MARKETPLACE				
-Entry into new markets				

-Recent perf gaps

-Market growth

MANAGEMENT HR PHILOSOPHY
-Model of worker motivation

-Decisionmaking style

-HR priorities

D. EFFECTS OF IMPACTS ON PLANNED CHANGE PROCESS

Resistance to change

Counter-Resistance acts

Autom project teams

Implementation steps

E. EFFECTS OF IMPACTS ON OTHER ELEMENTS

Machine operators' jobs

Technical support jobs

Skill requirements

Selection

Training

Personnel policies

Organizational structure

Outcomes

F. CONCLUSIONS

V. SECOND-ORDER IMPACTS: Skill Needs

	Perceptual	Conceptual	Manual Dexterity	Discretionary	Human Relations
A. IMPACT OF FIRST-ORDER CHANGES					
Operator jobs					
Technical support jobs					
Management/Supervisors					
B. EXISTING CONDITIONS					
C. EFFECTS OF CONSTRAINTS ON IMPACTS					
WORKFORCE					
-Desired job challenge					
-Management trust					
-Union status					
-Skill level & experience					
CONTROL OVER RESOURCES					
-Plant autonomy					
-Supplier agreements					
-Laborforce mobility					
MARKETPLACE					
-Entry into new markets					
-Recent perf gaps					

- Market growth

MANAGEMENT HR PHILOSOPHY
- Model of worker motivation

- Decisionmaking style

- HR priorities

D. EFFECTS OF IMPACTS ON PLANNED CHANGE PROCESS

Resistance to change

Counter-Resistance acts

Autom project teams

Implementation steps

E. EFFECTS OF IMPACTS ON OTHER ELEMENTS

Machine operators' jobs

Technical support jobs

Management/Supervision

Selection

Training

Personnel policies

Organizational structure

Outcomes

F. CONCLUSIONS

VI. SECOND-ORDER IMPACTS: Selection

	Number of Workers Needed	Definition of Recruiting Pool	Selection Criteria
A. IMPACT OF FIRST-ORDER CHANGES			
Operator jobs			
Technical support jobs			
Management/Supervisors			
B. EXISTING CONDITIONS			
C. EFFECTS OF CONSTRAINTS ON IMPACTS			
WORKFORCE			
-Desired job challenge			
-Management trust			
-Union status			
-Skill level & experience			
CONTROL OVER RESOURCES			
-Plant autonomy			
-Supplier agreements			
-Laborforce mobility			
MARKETPLACE			
-Entry into new markets			
-Recent perf gaps			
-Market growth			

MANAGEMENT HR PHILOSOPHY
-Model of worker motivation

-Decisionmaking style

-HR priorities

D.   EFFECTS OF IMPACTS ON PLANNED CHANGE PROCESS

Resistance to change

Counter-Resistance acts

Autom project teams

Implementation steps

E.   EFFECTS OF IMPACTS ON OTHER ELEMENTS

Machine operators' jobs

Technical support jobs

Management/Supervision

Skill requirements

Selection

Training

Personnel policies

Organizational structure

Outcomes

F.   CONCLUSIONS

VII. SECOND-ORDER IMPACTS: Training

	Source of Training	Use of Off- vs OJT	Stdized vs Individ'zed Training	Amount	Timing	Curriculum
A. IMPACT OF FIRST-ORDER CHANGES						
Operator jobs						
Technical support jobs						
Management/Supervisors						
B. EXISTING CONDITIONS						
C. EFFECTS OF CONSTRAINTS ON IMPACTS						
WORKFORCE						
-Desired job challenge						
-Management trust						
-Union status						
CONTROL OVER RESOURCES						
-Plant autonomy						
-Supplier agreements						
-Laborforce mobility						
MARKETPLACE						
-Entry into new markets						
-Recent perf gaps						

-Market growth

MANAGEMENT HR PHILOSOPHY

-Decisionmaking style

-HR priorities

D. EFFECTS OF IMPACTS ON PLANNED CHANGE PROCESS

Resistance to change

Counter-Resistance acts

Autom project teams

Implementation steps

E. EFFECTS OF IMPACTS ON OTHER ELEMENTS

Machine operators' jobs

Technical support jobs

Management/Supervision

Skill requirements

Selection

Personnel policies

Organizational structure

Outcomes

F. CONCLUSIONS

VIII. SECOND-ORDER IMPACTS: Personnel Policies

A. IMPACT OF FIRST-ORDER CHANGES

	Job Classifications	Pay	Career Development	Job Security	Shift Work	Union Management Relations
Operator jobs						
Technical support jobs						
Management/Supervisors						

B. EXISTING CONDITIONS

C. EFFECTS OF CONSTRAINTS ON IMPACTS

	Job Classifications	Pay	Career Development	Job Security	Shift Work	Union Management Relations
WORKFORCE -Desired job challenge						
-Management trust						
-Union status						
CONTROL OVER RESOURCES -Plant autonomy						
-Supplier agreements						
-Laborforce mobility						
MARKETPLACE -Entry into new markets						
-Recent perf gaps						
-Market growth						

MANAGEMENT HR PHILOSOPHY

-Decisionmaking style

-HR priorities

D. EFFECTS OF IMPACTS ON PLANNED CHANGE PROCESS

Resistance to change

Counter-Resistance acts

Autom project teams

Implementation steps

E. EFFECTS OF IMPACTS ON OTHER ELEMENTS

Machine operators' jobs

Technical support jobs

Management/Supervision

Skill requirements

Selection

Training

Organizational structure

Outcomes

F. CONCLUSIONS

IX. SECOND-ORDER IMPACTS: Organizational Structure

	Adding new Departments	Committees	Grouping Departments by Products	Grouping Departments by Process	Matrix	Decentralization	Organizational Climate
A. IMPACT OF FIRST-ORDER CHANGES							
Operator jobs							
Technical support jobs							
Management/ Supervisors							
B. EXISTING CONDITIONS							
C. EFFECTS OF CONSTRAINTS ON IMPACTS							
WORKFORCE							
-Desired job challenge							
-Mgmt trust							
-Union status							
-Skill level & experience							
CONTROL OVER RESOURCES							
-Plant autonomy							
-Supplier agreements							
-Laborforce mobility							
MARKETPLACE							
-Entry into new markets							

- Recent perf gaps
- Market growth

MANAGEMENT HR PHILOSOPHY

- Decisionmaking style
- HR priorities

D. EFFECTS OF IMPACTS ON PLANNED CHANGE PROCESS

Resistance to change

Counter-Resistance acts

Autom project teams

Implementation steps

E. EFFECTS OF IMPACTS ON OTHER ELEMENTS

Technical support jobs

Management/Super-vision

Skill requirmnts

Selection

Training

Personnel policies

Outcomes

F. CONCLUSIONS

X. THIRD-ORDER IMPACTS: Outcomes

	Process	Growth	Innovation	Employee Satisfaction

A. IMPACT OF SECOND-ORDER CHANGES

	Process	Growth	Innovation	Employee Satisfaction
Skill requirements				
Selection				
Training				
Personnel policies				
Organizational structure				

B. EXISTING CONDITIONS

C. EFFECTS OF CONSTRAINTS ON IMPACTS

	Process	Growth	Innovation	Employee Satisfaction
WORKFORCE				
-Desired job challenge				
-Management trust				
-Union status				
-Skill level & experience				
CONTROL OVER RESOURCES				
-Plant autonomy				
-Supplier agreements				
-Laborforce mobility				
MARKETPLACE				
-Entry into new markets				

-Recent perf gaps

-Market growth

MANAGEMENT HR PHILOSOPHY
-Model of worker motivation

-Decisionmaking style

-HR priorities

D. EFFECTS OF IMPACTS ON PLANNED CHANGE PROCESS

Resistance to change

Counter-Resistance acts

Autom project teams

Implementation steps

E. EFFECTS OF IMPACTS ON OTHER ELEMENTS

Machine operators' jobs

Technical support jobs

Management/Supervision

Skill requirements

Selection

Training

Personnel policies

Organizational structure

F. CONCLUSIONS

Glossary

Equipment Parameters

INTEGRATION. The extent to which components of the production process are inextricably linked.

RELIABILITY. The actual degree of dependability with which the equipment performs (note: actual, versus hoped-for).

RIGIDITY. The inability of the production process to reroute around equipment if breakdown occurs.

WORKFLOW UNPREDICTABILITY. Degree to which the anticipated inputs, processes, and outputs to the human-machine system are unpredictable.

FEEDBACK. Degree and type of feedback needed by the equipment about a variety of different factors, such as tolerance, temperature, density, and so on.

SAFETY. Likelihood that use of the equipment will not cause worker accidents.

Work Force Constraints

PREFERRED JOB CHALLENGE. Extent to which some or all members of the work force want challenge in their jobs.

LEVEL OF SKILL. Average skill level and experience with AMT of the work force at the plant.

PLANT'S DEGREE OF AUTONOMY. Degree to which plant management (as opposed to corporate management) controls decisions involving in-house resources such as personnel, capital expenditures, R&D, and so on.

PLANT AGREEMENTS WITH SUPPLIERS. Written agreements in place that specify quality and delivery time of materials provided by suppliers.

LABOR FORCE MOBILITY. Availability of alternative jobs outside the organization to which members of the work force can turn if dissatisfied with plant management.

RAPID ENTRY INTO NEW MARKETS. Extent to which the plant can take advantage of its new production capacity with AMT to enter new markets quickly.

PERFORMANCE GAPS. Situations in which the organization's recent performance fails to meet expectations.

MARKET GROWTH. Predictability of market swings that affect long-term expectations and decision making.

MANAGEMENT MODEL OF WORKER MOTIVATION. Extent to which managers feel workers are motivated by the challenge of the job, as opposed to money.

MANAGEMENT DECISION-MAKING STYLE. Extent to which management prefers that decisions in the organization be made using a consultative, consensus, delegative, or authoritarian style.

MANAGEMENT HR PRIORITIES. Top management's attitudes about the importance of such human resource (HR) issues as training and group process skills for workers.

AMT Operators' Jobs*

COORDINATION NEEDS. Extent to which operators must work with others to obtain the information necessary to perform their jobs.

INFORMATION NEEDS. Type, source, and amount of information that operator must have to operate equipment effectively.

HUMAN-MACHINE REDUNDANCY. Extent to which operators should be involved in tasks performed by machines as a check on machine operation.

DISCRETION. How and to what extent operators exercise autonomy.

*The same assessments are to be made for technical support jobs.

Skills

PERCEPTUAL SKILLS. Degree to which AMT jobs demand vigilance, concentration, attention, and judgment.

CONCEPTUAL SKILLS. Degree to which AMT jobs require knowledge of the subject matter as well as the ability to interpret, abstract, and infer.

MANUAL DEXTERITY SKILLS. Degree to which AMT jobs require the motor abilities of material handling, picking, and placing.

DISCRETIONARY SKILLS. Degree to which AMT jobs demand autonomous problem-solving ability.

HUMAN RELATIONS SKILLS. Degree to which AMT jobs demand the ability to communicate, engage in group interaction, and coordinate with others to solve problems.

Selection

RECRUITING POOL. The group of workers from which AMT workers will be chosen.

SELECTION CRITERIA. The degree to which work force choice, machine skills, human relations skills, and individual interest are used as criteria in selecting AMT workers.

Training

SOURCE OF PRIMARY TRAINING. Use of either vendors, corporate training departments, consultants, local educational institutions, or in-house training programs as the primary source of AMT training.

Structure

GROUPING DEPARTMENTS BY PRODUCTS. An organizational structure where the main departments of the organization are grouped by major product lines.

GROUPING DEPARTMENTS BY PROCESS. An organizational structure where the main departments of the organization are grouped by distinctly different production processes—for example, by technology, flow, or parallel processes.

DECENTRALIZATION. The extent to which the organizational structure allows lower-level workers to make decisions about their jobs, work flow, and work activities.

Selected Guide
to Empirical AMT Literature

Listed here are references for studies written in English describing either research on the effects, or pertaining to the effects, of AMT on elements of the human infrastructure. The studies have been grouped into three categories:

- Qualitative Case Descriptions, in which statistical analyses were not done; included in this category may be studies of more than one case, provided that no statistical analyses were performed.
- Quantitative Analyses, which may include case studies in which statistical analyses were done, as well as surveys, interviews, or experiments.
- Research Reviews, varying from reviews that have been undertaken to primarily support the author's perspective to informal "meta-analyses" of the literature.

Qualitative Case Descriptions

Aguren, S., and Edgren, J. *New Factories: Job Design Through Factory Planning in Sweden.* Stockholm: Swedish Employers' Confederation, 1980.

Allred, J. K. *Computer-Integrated Robotic Assembly Systems and Their Potential for the Factory of the Future.* MS 85-533. Dearborn, Mich.: Society of Manufacturing Engineers, 1985.

Argoff, N. J. *Report to the Office of Technology Assessment on Training for Programmable Automation.* Washington, D.C.: Office of Technology Assessment, 1983-84.

Argote, L., and Goodman, P. S. "Investigating the Implementation of Robotics." In D. D. Davis and Associates (eds.), *Managing Technological Innovation: Organizational Strategies for Implementing Advanced Manufacturing Technologies.* San Francisco: Jossey-Bass, 1986.

Birn, S. A. "Improving Motivation Through Job Design in the GT Work Cell." Paper presented at the CASA/SME Group Technology Seminar, Detroit, Mich., 1978.

Bowman, B. L. "Cross-Functional Collaboration: Teaming for Technological Change." In O. Brown and H. W. Hendrick (eds.), *Human Factors in Organizational Design and Management.* Vol. 2. New York: Elsevier Science, 1986.

Brody, H. "Overcoming Barriers to Automation." *High Technology,* May 1985, pp. 41-46.

Buss, D. "Winners and Losers: On the Factory Floor, Technology Brings Challenge for Some, Drudgery for Others." *Wall Street Journal,* Sept. 16, 1985, p. 1.

Butera, F. "Designing Work in Automated Systems: A Review of Case Studies." In F. Butera and J. E. Thurman (eds.), *Automation and Work Design.* New York: Elsevier Science, 1984.

Bylinsky, G. "The Race to the Automatic Factory." *Fortune,* Feb. 21, 1983, pp. 52-64.

Chamot, D., and Dymmel, M. D. *Cooperation or Conflict: European Experiences with Technological Change at the Workplace.* Washington, D.C.: AFL-CIO, 1981.

Chauvin, B. "Training NC Maintenance Personnel." In Numerical Control Society (ed.), *Striving for Technological Excellence in Manufacturing.* Princeton, N.J.: Numerical Control Society, 1981.

Chen, K.; Eisley, J. G.; Liker, J. K.; Rothman, J.; and Thomas, R. J. *Human Resource Development and New Technology in the Automobile Industry: A Case Study of Ford Motor Company's Dearborn Engine Plant.* Ann Arbor: University of Michigan, 1984.

Darlin, D. "Coping with Technofright." *Wall Street Journal*, Sept. 16, 1985, 90C.

Davis, D. B. "Apple: Harvesting the Macintosh." *High Technology*, May 1985, pp. 39-40.

Davis, D. B. "Renaissance on the Factory Floor." *High Technology*, May 1985, pp. 24-25.

Dawson, P. and McLoughlin, I. "Computer Technology and the Redefinition of Supervision: A Study of the Effects of Computerization on Railway Freight Supervisors." *Journal of Management Studies*, 1986, *23*, 116-132.

DeYoung, H. G. "GE: Dishing out Efficiency." *High Technology*, May 1985, pp. 32-33.

Dickson, K. "Pet Foods by Computer: A Case Study of Automation." In T. Forester (ed.), *The Microelectronics Revolution*. Cambridge, Mass.: MIT Press, 1981.

Farnum, G. T. "An Experiment in Management." *Manufacturing Engineering*, Mar. 1986, pp. 91-92.

Fischer, R. E. "Training Needs of Associate Degree Graduates." In Numerical Control Society (ed.), *Striving for Technological Excellence in Manufacturing*. Princeton, N.J.: Numerical Control Society, 1981.

Foulkes, F. K., and Hirsch, J. L. "People Make Robots Work." *Harvard Business Review*, 1984, *62*, 94-102.

Fraade, D. J. "Some Aspects of In-House Training for Computer Control of Batch Processing." *Computer Control of Batch Processes*, Fall 1979, 38-39.

Freedy, A., and Lucaccini, L. F. "Adaptive Computer Training System (ACTS) for Fault Diagnosis in Maintenance Tasks." In J. Rasmussen and W. B. Rouse (eds.), *Human Detection and Diagnosis of System Failures*. New York: Plenum Press, 1981.

Gerwin, D., and Tarondeau, J. C. "Case Studies of Computer Integrated Manufacturing Systems: A View of Uncertainty and Innovation Processes." *Journal of Operations Management*, 1982, *2*, 87-92.

Gibson, J. E., and Richards, L. G. "Redirecting Engineering Education: Computer Graphics and CAD/CAM." In P. Wang (ed.), *Automation Technology for Management and Productivity*

Advancements Through CAD/CAM and Engineering Data Handling. Englewood Cliffs, N.J.: Prentice-Hall, 1983.

Groebner, D., and Merz, C. M. "An Empirical Study of the Benefits of Japanese Manufacturing Techniques to Hewlett-Packard." Paper presented at the American Institute of Decision Sciences meetings, Las Vegas, Nev., Nov. 1985.

Houtzeel, A., and Brown, C. S. "A Management Overview of Group Technology." Paper presented at the Computers and Automated Systems Association/Society of Manufacturing Engineers, Westec 82 conference, Detroit, Mich., Mar., 1982.

Hymowitz, C. "Manufacturing Change: Automation Experts Explore the Promise and Problems of the Factory of the Future." *Wall Street Journal,* Sept. 16, 1985, pp. 10C-12C.

Jasper, W. A., and Vapor, J. C. "GT Approach Proves Out." *American Machinist,* Feb. 1979, pp. 86-89.

Jelinek, M. "Rethink Strategy or Perish: Technology Lessons from Telecommunications." *Journal of Production Innovation Management,* 1984, *1,* 36-42.

Julian, K., "Westinghouse: Building a Better Board." *High Technology,* May 1985, pp. 36-38.

Kinnucan, P. "Flexible Systems Invade the Factory." *High Technology,* 1983, *3,* 32-42.

Kinnucan, P. "IBM: Making the Chips Fly." *High Technology,* May 1985, pp. 34-35..

Knight, K. A. "Socio-Technical Engineering: An Approach to Technology Integration." Paper presented at the Society of Manufacturing Engineering Autofact Conference, Detroit, Mich., Nov. 1985.

Levin, D. P. "Pitfalls of High-Tech Field." *Wall Street Journal,* May 14, 1984, p. 16C.

Liker, J., and Thomas, R. J. "Prospects for Human Resource Development in the Context of Technological Change: Lessons from a Major Technological Renovation." In D. Kocacglu (ed.), *Handbook of Technology Management.* New York: Wiley, 1987.

Love, J. H., and Walker, J. "Problems of New Technology Deployment in the Mechanical Engineering and Printing Industries: A Case Study." Paper presented at the Managing

Advanced Manufacturing Technology conference, London, Jan. 1986.

Mackulak, G. T. "Planning Techniques for Computer-Integrated Manufacturing." *National Productivity Review*, Summer 1984, pp. 315–333.

McLoughlin, I.; Rose, H.; and Clark, J. "Managing the Introduction of New Technology." *Omega*, 1985, *13*, 251–262.

Manufacturing Studies Board (MSB), Committee on the Effective Implementation of Advanced Manufacturing Technology, National Research Council, National Academy of Science. *Human Resource Practices for Implementing Advanced Manufacturing Technology*. Washington, D.C.: National Academy Press, 1986.

Markey, R. "New Technology, the Economy and the Unions in Britain." *Journal of Industrial Relations*, 1982, *24*, 557–577.

Markus, M. L. "Implementation Politics: Top Management, Support and User Involvement." *Systems, Objectives, Solutions*, 1981, *1*, 203–215.

Nag, A. "Automakers Discover Factory of the Future Is Headache Just Now." *Wall Street Journal*, May 13, 1986, pp. 1, 26, and 27.

National Center for Productivity and Quality of Working Life (NCPQWL). *Productivity and Job Security: Retraining to Adapt to Technological Change*. Washington, D.C.: National Center for Productivity and Quality of Working Life, 1977.

Nulty, L. E. "Case Studies of IAM Local Experiences with the Introduction of New Technologies." In D. Kennedy, C. Craypo, and M. Lehman (eds.), *Labor and Technology: Union Response to Changing Environments*. University Park: Department of Labor Studies, Pennsylvania State University: 1982.

Perrow, C. *Normal Accidents*. New York: Basic Books, 1984.

Risch, R. P. "NC Is a Business Tool." In M. A. DeVries (ed.), *Management Guide to NC*. Princeton, N.J.: Numerical Control Society, 1971.

Roitman, D.; Liker, J. K.; and Roskies, E. "Birthing a Factory of the Future: When Is "All at Once" Too Much?" In R. H. Kelmann and T. M. Covin (eds.), *Corporate Transformation: Revitalizing Organizations for a Competitive World*. San Francisco: Jossey-Bass, 1987.

Saari, L. M. "Human Resource Issues at Two Computerized Sawmills." Paper presented at the Academy of Management meeting, Los Angeles, Aug. 1985.

Sepheri, M. *Just-in-Time, Not Just in Japan: Case Studies of American Pioneers.* Falls Church, Va.: American Production and Inventory Control Society, 1986.

Shaiken, H. *Automation and the Workplace: Case Studies on the Introduction of Programmable Automation in Manufacturing.* Cambridge, Mass.: MIT Press, 1983.

Shaiken, H. *Work Transformed.* New York: Holt, Rinehart & Winston, 1984.

Stricharchuk, G., and Winter, R. E. "Second Thoughts: Experience with Robots Shows They Can Be More Costly and Complicated Than Expected." *Wall Street Journal*, Sept. 16, 1985, p. 14C.

Tucker, J. B. "GM: Shifting to Automatic." *High Technology*, May 1985, pp. 26-29.

Van Nostrand, R. C. "CAD/CAM Justification and Follow-Up: Simmonds Precision Products Case Study." In K. M. Dunn and B. Herzog (eds.), *CAD/CAM Management Strategies.* Pennsauken, N.J.: Auerbach Publications, 1984.

Wilkinson, B. *The Shopfloor Politics of New Technology.* London: Heinemann Educational Books, 1983.

Williams, R. "Snakco: Negotiation over the Introduction of High-Speed Equipment:" In E. Rhodes and D. Wield (eds.), *Implementing New Technology.* Oxford: Basil Blackwell, 1985.

Zuboff, S. "New Worlds of Computer-Mediated Work." *Harvard Business Review*, 1982, *60*, 142-152.

Zukowski, R. "Retraining Existing Human Resources to Meet Tomorrow's Technology Needs." Paper presented at the National Science Foundation conference on Industrial Science and Technological Innovation, Raleigh, N.C., May 1984.

Quantitative Analyses

Argote, L.; Goodman, P. S.; and Schkade, D. "The Human Side of Robotics: How Workers React to a Robot." *Sloan Management Review*, 1983, *24*, 31-41.

Ayres, R. U., and Miller, S. M. *Robotics: Application and Social Implications.* New York: Harper & Row, 1983.

Billings, R. S.; Klimoski, R. J.; and Breaugh, J. A. "The Impact of a Change in Technology on Job Characteristics: A Quasi-Experiment." *Administrative Science Quarterly,* 1977, *22,* 310-339.

Blumberg, M., and Alber, A. "The Human Element: Its Impact on the Productivity of Advanced Batch Manufacturing Systems." *Journal of Manufacturing Systems,* 1982, *1,* 43-52.

Blumberg, M., and Gerwin, D. "Coping with Advanced Manufacturing Technology." In E. Rhodes and D. Wield (eds.), *Implementing New Technologies.* Oxford: Basil Blackwell, 1985.

Chao, G. T., and Kozlowski, S. W. "Employee Perceptions on the Implementation of Robotic Manufacturing Technology." *Journal of Applied Psychology,* 1986, *71,* 70-76.

Clutterbuck, D., and Hill, R. *The Re-Making of Work.* London: Grant McIntyre, 1981.

Dupont-Gatelmand, C. "A Survey of Flexible Manufacturing Systems." *Journal of Manufacturing Systems,* 1981, *1,* 1-16.

Ettlie, J. E. "Technology Transfer—from Innovators to Users." *Industrial Engineering,* 1973, *5,* 16-23.

Ettlie, J. E. "Organizational Adaptations for Radical Process Innovators." Paper presented at the Academy of Management meeting, Los Angeles, Aug. 1985.

Ettlie, J. E. "Facing the Factory of the Future." In D. D. Davis and Associates, *Managing Technological Innovation: Organizational Strategies for Implementing Advanced Manufacturing Technologies.* San Francisco: Jossey-Bass, 1986a.

Ettlie, J. E. "The First-Line Supervisor and Advanced Manufacturing Technology." Paper presented at the Academy of Management meeting, Chicago, Ill., Aug. 1986b.

Ettlie, J. E. "Systemic Innovation." In D. Gray and others (eds.), *Strategies and Practices for Technological Innovation.* New York: North-Holland, 1986c.

Ettlie, J. E., and Rubenstein, A. H. "Social Learning Theory and the Implementation of Production Innovation." *Decision Sciences,* 1980, *11,* 648-668.

Fazakerley, G. M. "A Research Report on the Human Aspects of Group Technology and Cellular Manufacturing." *International Journal of Production Research,* 1976, *1,* 123–134.

Fossum, B. "A Survey of CIM Plants." Paper presented at the American Institute of Decision Sciences meeting, Las Vegas, Nev., Nov. 1985.

Gent, M. J., and Weinstein, A. G. "Effects of Auto Plant Technology Change on Worker Outcomes: A Path Analysis." Paper presented at the American Institute of Decision Sciences meeting, Las Vegas, Nev., Nov. 1985.

Graham, M., and Rosenthal, S. R. "Flexible Manufacturing Systems Require Flexible People." Paper presented at the Institute of Management Sciences/Operations Research Society of America meeting, Nov. 1985.

Hartmann, G.; Nicholas, I.; Sorge, A.; and Warner, M. "Computerized Machine Tools, Manpower Consequences, and Skill Utilization: A Study of British and West German Manufacturing Firms." *British Journal of Industrial Relations,* 1983, *21,* 221–231.

Hazlehurst, R. J.; Bradbury, R. J.; and Corlett, E. N. "A Comparison of the Skills of Machinists on N-C and Conventional Machines." *Occupational Psychology,* 1969, *43,* 169–182.

Hedberg, B., and Mumford, E. "The Design of Computer Systems: Man's Vision of Man as an Integral Part of the System Design Process." In E. Mumford and H. Sackman (eds.), *Human Choices and Computers.* New York: North-Holland, 1975.

Huber, V. L., and Hyer, N. L. "The Human Factor in Cellular Manufacturing." *Journal of Operations Management,* 1985, *5,* 213–228.

Hwang, S., and Salvendy, G. "Effect of Allocation of Functions and Size of Flexible Manufacturing Systems on Human Supervisory Performance." Paper presented at the Ninth Congress of the International Ergonomics Association, Sweden, Sept. 1985.

Hyer, N. L. "Management's Guide to Group Technology." *Operations Management Review,* 1984, *12.*

Jacobs, J. *The Training Needs of Michigan Automobile Suppliers: Interim Report.* Ann Arbor, Mich.: Industrial Technology Institute, 1985.

Leonard-Barton, D. "The Secondary Adoption Decision: Implementing A New Technology Within an Organization." Paper presented at the Academy of Management meeting, Chicago, Ill., Aug. 1986b.

Lusterman, S. *Education in Industry.* New York: Conference Board, 1977.

Lusterman, S. *Trends in Corporate Education and Training.* New York: Conference Board, 1985.

Majchrzak, A. "Changes to Work Resulting from CAD." Paper presented to the American Institute of Industrial Engineers meeting, Chicago, Ill., Dec. 1985a.

Majchrzak, A. "The Effect of CAM Technologies on Training Activities," *Journal of Manufacturing Systems,* 1986a, *5,* 203–211.

Majchrzak, A. "A National Probability Survey on Education and Training for CAD/CAM." *IEEE Transactions on Engineering Management,* 1986b, *33,* 197–206.

Majchrzak, A.; Collins, P.; and Mandeville, D. "Quantitative Assessment of Changes in Work Activities Resulting from CAD." *Behavior and Information Technology,* 1986, *5,* 259–271.

Majchrzak, A., and Cotton, J. "A Longitudinal Study of Adjustment to Technological Change: The Case of Job Transfers from Mass to Computer-Automated Batch Production." Paper presented at the Claremont Graduate School Colloquium, Claremont, Calif., Nov. 1986.

Majchrzak, A.; Nieva, V. F.; and Newman, P. D. "A National Probability Survey of Contemporary CAD/CAM Adoption." In D. D. Davis and Associates, *Managing Technological Innovation: Organizational Strategies for Implementing Advanced Manufacturing Technologies.* San Francisco: Jossey-Bass, 1986.

Majchrzak, A., and Paris, M. *Successful Management Infrastructures for Advanced Manufacturing Technology.* Chicago, Ill.: Michael Paris Associates, 1986.

Mosher, P., and Majchrzak, A. "Workplace Changes Mediating Effect of Technology on Individuals' Attitudes and Performance." Paper presented at the Academy of Management meeting, Chicago, Ill., Aug. 1986.

Nieva, V. F.; Gaertner, G. H.; Argoff, N. J.; and Newman, P. D.

Work in a Changing Factory: Interim Report. Rockville, Md.: Westat, Inc., 1986.

Nieva, V. F.; Majchrzak, A.; and Huneycutt, M. J. *Education and Training in Computer Automated Manufacturing.* Rockville, Md.: Westat, Inc., 1982.

Pullen, R. D. "A Survey of Cellular Manufacturing Cells." *Production Engineer,* Sept. 1976.

Riche, R. W. "Impact of New Electronic Technology." *Monthly Labor Review,* Mar. 1982, pp. 37–39.

Rothwell, S. "Supervisors and New Technology." In E. Rhodes and D. Wield (eds.), *Implementing New Technologies.* Oxford: Basil Blackwell, 1985.

Rouse, W. B. "Experimental Studies and Mathematical Models of Human Problem Solving Performance in Fault Diagnosis Tasks." In J. Rasmussen and W. B. Rouse (eds.), *Human Detection and Diagnosis of System Failures.* New York: Plenum Press, 1981.

Sharit, J. "Human Supervisory Control of a Flexible Manufacturing System: An Exploratory Investigation." Unpublished doctoral dissertation, Department of Industrial Engineering, Purdue University, 1984.

Susman, G. I.; Dean, J. W.; and Porter, P. S. "Departmental Interfaces in the Implementation of Advanced Manufacturing Technology." Center for the Management of Technological and Organizational Change. Working Paper Series 86–2. University Park: Pennsylvania State University, 1986.

Swamidass, P. M. "Manufacturing Process Innovation in Export Oriented Firms." Paper presented at the American Institute of Decision Sciences, Las Vegas, Nev., Nov. 1985.

Taylor, J. C. "Job Design Criteria Twenty Years Later." In L. E. Davis and J. C. Taylor (eds.), *Design of Jobs.* Santa Monica, Calif.: Goodyear, 1979.

U.S. Department of Labor, Bureau of Labor Statistics. *Occupational Projections and Training Data.* Bulletin 2052. Washington, D.C.: Government Printing Office, 1980.

U.S. Department of Labor, Bureau of Labor Statistics. *Outlook for Computer Process Control.* Washington, D.C.: Government Printing Office, 1970.

U.S. Department of Labor, Bureau of Labor Statistics. *Occupational Training in Selected Metalworking Industries.* R&D Monograph no. 53. Washington, D.C.: Government Printing Office, 1974.

U.S. Department of Labor, Bureau of Labor Statistics. *Technology and Labor in Four Industries.* Washington, D.C.: Government Printing Office, 1982.

U.S. General Accounting Office. *Report to the Congress: Manufacturing Technology: A Changing Challenge to Improved Productivity.* Library of Congress Document 75-436. Washington, D.C.: Government Printing Office, June 3, 1976.

Westcott, B. J., and Eisenhardt, K. M. "The Dynamics of Process Innovation in Manufacturing." Paper presented at the Academy of Management meeting, Chicago, Ill., Aug. 1986.

Research Reviews

Abbott, L. F. *Technological Development in Industry: A Survey of Social Aspects.* Manchester, England: Industrial Systems Research, 1981.

Barfield, W.; Chang, T.; Majchrzak, A.; Eberts, R. E.; and Salvendy, G. "Human Factors in the Design and Use of CAD Systems." In G. Salvendy (ed.), *Handbook of Human Factors.* New York: Wiley, 1987.

Belitsky, A. H. *New Technologies and Training in Metalworking.* Washington, D.C.: National Center for Productivity and Quality of Working Life, 1978.

Bishop, A. B. *A Comprehensive Research Program for Effective Design and Operation of Flexible Manufacturing Systems.* MS84-634. Dearborn, Mich.: Society of Manufacturing Engineers, 1984.

Blumenthal, M., and Dray, J. "The Automated Factory: Vision and Reality." *Technology Review,* Jan. 1985, pp. 29-37.

Boddy, D. and Buchanan, D. A. "New Technology with a Human Face." *Personnel Management,* 1985, *17,* 28-31.

Boddy, D., and Buchanan, D. A. *Managing New Technology.* New York: Basil Blackwell, 1986.

Chapanis, A. "On the Allocation of Functions Between Men and Machines." *Occupational Psychology*, 1965, *19*, 1–11.

Christensen, J. M., and Howard, J. M. "Field Experience in Maintenance." In J. Rasmussen and W. B. Rouse (eds.), *Human Detection and Diagnosis of System Failures*. New York: Plenum Press, 1981.

Davis, D. D. "Designing Organizations for Technological Innovation, Productivity, and Quality of Work Life: A Human Resource Perspective." In D. Grey, T. Solomon, and W. Hetzner (eds.), *Strategies for Technological Innovation*. Amsterdam: North-Holland, 1986a.

Davis, D. D. "Integrating Technological, Manufacturing, Marketing, and Human Resource Strategy." In D. D. Davis and Associates, *Managing Technological Innovation: Organizational Strategies for Implementing Advanced Manufacturing Technologies*. San Francisco: Jossey-Bass, 1986b.

Davis, D. D., and Roitman, D. "Technological Change in the Workplace: Labor and Management Issues." Unpublished paper. Norfolk, Va.: Old Dominion University, 1986.

Davis, L. E., and Wacker, G. J. "Job Design." In G. Salvendy (ed.), *Handbook of Human Factors*. New York: Wiley, 1987.

Fadem, J. A. "Automation and Work Design in the United States." In F. Butera and J. Thurman (eds.), *Automation and Work Design*. New York: Elsevier Science, 1984.

Fazakerley, G. M. "Group Technology: Social Benefits and Social Problems." *Production Engineer*, Oct. 1974, pp. 384–386.

Gerwin, D. "Do's and Don'ts of Computerized Manufacturing." *Harvard Business Review*, Mar.-Apr. 1982, pp. 107–116.

Ghosh, B. K., and Helander, M. G. "A Systems Approach to Task Allocation of Human-Robot Interaction in Manufacturing." *Journal of Manufacturing Systems*, 1986, *5*, 41–49.

Gold, B. "CAM Sets New Rules for Production." *Harvard Business Review*, Nov.-Dec. 1982, pp. 88–94.

Goldhar, J. D., and Jelinek, M. "Plan for Economies of Scope." *Harvard Business Review*, 1983, *61*, 141–148.

Hedberg, B. "Computer Systems to Support Industrial Democracy." In E. Mumford and H. Sackman (eds.), *Human Choice and Computers*. New York: North-Holland, 1975.

Hirschhorn, L. *Beyond Mechanization: Work and Technology in a Postindustrial Age.* Cambridge, Mass.: MIT Press, 1984.

Hulin, C. L., and Roznowski, M. "Organizational Technologies: Effects on Organizations' Characteristics and Individuals' Responses." *Research in Organizational Behavior*, 1985, 7, 39-85.

Hull, D. M., and Lovett, J. E. *Task Analysis and Job Descriptions for Robotics/Automated Systems Technicians.* Waco, Tex.: Center for Occupational Research and Development, 1985.

International Labor Office. *Workers' Participation in Decisions Within Undertakings.* International Labor Office: Geneva, 1981.

Jelinek, M. "Production Innovation and Economies of Scope: Beyond the 'Technological Fix.'" Paper presented at the Fourth International Working Seminar on Production Economics, Cleveland, Feb. 1986.

Jelinek, M., and Goldhar, J. D. "Economics in the Factory of the Future," forthcoming.

Kamali, J.; Moodie, C. L.; and Salvendy, G. "A Framework for Integrated Assembly Systems: Humans, Automation, and Robots." *International Journal of Production Research*, 1982, 20, 431-448.

Kaplan, R. S. "Measuring Manufacturing Performance: A New Challenge for Managerial Accounting Research." *Accounting Review*, 1983, 43, 686-705.

Kaplan, R. S. "Yesterday's Accounting Undermines Production." *Harvard Business Review*, July-Aug. 1984, pp. 95-101.

Kaplan, R. S. "Accounting Lag: The Obsolescence of Cost Accounting Systems." In D. B. Clark, R. H. Hayes, and C. Lorenz (eds.), *The Uneasy Alliance: Managing the Productivity-Technology Dilemma.* Boston: Harvard Business School Press, 1985.

Kaplan, R. S. "Must CIM Be Justified by Faith Alone?" *Harvard Business Review*, 1986, 64, 87-95.

Katz, H. C., and Sabel, C. F. "Industrial Relations and Industrial Adjustment in the Car Industry." *Industrial Relations*, 1985, 24, 295-315.

Kerr, S.; Hill, K. D.; and Broedling, L. "The First-Line Supervisor:

Phasing Out or Here to Stay?" *Academy of Management Review,* 1986, *11,* 103–117.

Kohler, C., and Schultz-Wild, R. "Flexible Manufacturing Systems—Manpower Problems and Policies." Paper presented at the World Congress on the Human Aspects of Automation, London, Aug. 1983.

Leonard-Barton, D., and Kraus, W. A. "Implementing New Technology." *Harvard Business Review,* 1985, *63,*102–110.

McDonald, J. L. "Making the Transition from CAD/CAM Systems Planning to Operation." In K. M. Dunn and B. Herzog (eds.), *CAD/CAM Management Strategies.* Pennsauken, N.J.: Auerbach Publications, 1984.

Macek, A. J. "Human Factors Facilitating the Implementation of Automation." *Journal of Manufacturing Systems,* 1982, *1,* 195–206.

Majchrzak, A. *Effects of Computerized Integration on Shopfloor Human Resources and Structure.* MS85–1080. Dearborn, Mich.: Society of Manufacturing Engineers, 1985b.

Majchrzak, A., and Klein, K. J. "Things Are Always More Complicated Than You Think: An Open Systems Approach to the Organizational Effects of Computer-Automated Technology." Forthcoming.

Majchrzak, A., and others. *Human Aspects of Computer-Aided Design.* London: Taylor & Francis, 1987.

Margulies, N., and Colflesh, L. "An Organizational Development Approach to the Planning and Implementation of New Technology." In D. D. Warrick (ed.), *Contemporary Organizational Development.* Glenview, Ill.: Scott, Foresman, 1985.

Markus, M. L. *Systems in Organizations: Bugs and Features.* Boston: Pitman, 1984.

Montgomery, G. "CAD/CAM Feasibility Assessment: A Systematic Approach." In K. M. Dunn and B. Herzog (eds.), *CAD/CAM Management Strategies.* Pennsauken, N.J.: Auerbach Publications, 1984.

Mumford, E., and Sackman, H. "International Human Choice and Computers: Conference Retrospect and Prospect." In E. Mumford and H. Sackman (eds.), *Human Choice and Computers.* New York: North-Holland, 1975.

National Ministry of Social Affairs and Employment. *The Impact of Chip Technology on Conditions and Quality of Work.* London: Metra Consulting Group, 1983.

Office of Technology Assessment. *Computerized Manufacturing Automation,* Library of Congress no. 84-601053. Washington, D.C.: Government Printing Office, 1984.

Parsons, H. M., and Kearsley, G. P. "Robotics and Human Factors: Current Status and Future Prospects." *Human Factors,* 1982, *24,* 535-552.

Piore, M. J. "Computer Technologies, Market Structure, and Strategic Union Choices." In T. A. Kochan (ed.), *Challenges and Choices Facing American Labor.* Cambridge, Mass.: MIT Press, 1985.

Roberts, M. "The Impact of Technology on Union Organizing and Collective Bargaining." In D. Kennedy, C. Craypo, and M. Lehman (eds.), *Labor and Technology: Union Response to Changing Environments.* University Park: Department of Labor Studies, Pennsylvania State University, 1982.

Salvendy, G. "Review and Reappraisal of Human Aspects in Planning Robotic Systems." *Behavior and Information Technology,* 1983, *2,* 263-287.

Seibt, D. "User and Specialist Evaluations in System Development." In E. Grochla and N. Szyperski (eds.), *Design and Implementation of Computer-Based Information Systems.* Oslo, Norway: Sijthoff & Noordhoff, 1979.

Shaiken, H.; Herzenberg, S.; and Kuhn, S. "The Work Process Under More Flexible Production." *Industrial Relations,* 1986, *25,* 167-182.

Sharit, J.; Chang, T.; and Salvendy, G. "Technical and Human Aspects of Computer-Aided Manufacturing." In G. Salvendy (ed.), *Handbook of Human Factors.* New York: Wiley, 1987.

Sheridan, T. B. "Understanding Human Error and Aiding Human Diagnostic Behavior in Nuclear Power Plants." In J. Rasmussen and W. B. Rouse (eds.), *Human Detection and Diagnosis of System Failures.* New York: Plenum, 1981.

Skinner, W. "The Focused Factory." *Harvard Business Review,* 1974, *52,* 113-121.

Skinner, W. "The Productivity Paradox." *Harvard Business Review*, 1986, *64*, 55–59.

Skinner, W., and Chakraborty, K. *The Impact of New Technology*. Elmsford, N.Y.: Pergamon Press, 1982.

Spenner, K. "Deciphering Prometheus: Temporal Change in the Skill Level of Work." *American Sociological Review*, 1983, *48*, 824–837.

Susman, G. I. and Chase, R. B. "A Sociotechnical Analysis of the Integrated Factory." *Journal of Applied Behavioral Science*, 1986, *22*, 257–270.

Teresko, J. "Automation and the Bottom Line." *Industry Week*, May 26, 1986, pp. 41–94.

Thompson, H., and Scalpone, R. "Managing the Human Resource in the Factory of the Future." Paper presented at the World Congress on the Human Aspects of Automation, Detroit, Mich., Aug. 1983.

Tombari, H. "Analyzing the Benefits and Costs of Computer-Aided Manufacturing Methods." In K. M. Dunn and B. Herzog (eds.), *CAD/CAM Management Strategies*. Pennsauken, N.J.: Auerbach Publications, 1984.

Tornatzky, L., and others. *The Process of Technological Innovation: Reviewing the Literature*. Washington, D.C.: Productivity Improvement Research Section, National Science Foundation, 1983.

Turner, J. A., and Karasek, R. A. "Software Ergonomics: Effects of Computer Application Design Parameters on Operator Task Performance and Health." *Ergonomics*, 1984, *27*, 663–690.

Walton, R. E. "New Work Technology and Its Work Force Implications: Union and Management Approaches." Harvard Working Paper 84-13. Boston, Mass.: Harvard University, 1983.

Warner, M. "New Technology, Work Organizations and Industrial Relations." *Omega*, 1984, *12*, 203–210.

Whitney, D. E. "Real Robots Do Need Jigs." *Harvard Business Review*, 1986, *64*, 110–116.

References

Abbott, L. F. *Technological Development in Industry: A Survey of Social Aspects*. Manchester, England: Industrial Systems Research, 1981.

Aguren, S., and Edgren, J. *New Factories: Job Design Through Factory Planning in Sweden*. Stockholm: Swedish Employers' Confederation, 1980.

Allred, J. K. *Computer-Integrated Robotic Assembly Systems and Their Potential for the Factory of the Future*. MS 85-533. Dearborn, Mich.: Society of Manufacturing Engineers, 1985.

Amber, G. H., and Amber, P. S. *Anatomy of Automation*. Englewood Cliffs, N.J.: Prentice-Hall, 1962.

Anderson, R. L. "Implementation of the Autonomous Group Model in a Unionized Plant: The Influence of Selected Process, Design, and Contextual Considerations on Participant Support." Unpublished doctoral dissertation, School of Management, University of Oregon, 1985.

Anshen, M. "Managerial Decisions." In J. T. Dunlop (ed.), *Automation and Technological Change*. Englewood Cliffs, N.J.: Prentice-Hall, 1962.

Argoff, N. J. *Report to the Office of Technology Assessment on Training for Programmable Automation*. Washington, D.C.: Office of Technology Assessment, 1983-84.

Argote, L., and Goodman, P. S. "Investigating the Implementation of Robotics." In D. D. Davis and Associates, *Managing Technological Innovation: Organizational Strategies for Implementing Advanced Manufacturing Technologies*. San Francisco: Jossey-Bass, 1986.

Argote, L.; Goodman, P. S.; and Schkade, D. "The Human Side of Robotics: How Workers React to a Robot." *Sloan Management Review*, 1983, *24*, 31–41.

Ayres, R. U., and Miller, S. M. *Robotics: Application and Social Implications*. New York: Harper & Row, 1983.

Barfield, W.; Chang, T.; Majchrzak, A.; Eberts, R. E.; and Salvendy, G. "Human Factors in the Design and Use of CAD Systems." In G. Salvendy (ed.), *Handbook of Human Factors*. New York: Wiley, 1987.

Belitsky, A. H. *New Technologies and Training in Metalworking*. Washington, D.C.: National Center for Productivity and Quality of Working Life, 1978.

Berman, P. "Thinking About Programmed and Adaptive Implementation: Matching Strategies in Situation." In H. M. Ingram and D. E. Mann (eds.), *Why Policies Succeed or Fail*. Beverly Hills, Calif.: Sage, 1980.

Billings, R. S.; Klimoski, R. J.; and Breaugh, J. A. "The Impact of a Change in Technology on Job Characteristics: A Quasi-Experiment." *Administrative Science Quarterly*, 1977, *22*, 310–339.

Birn, S. A. "Improving Motivation Through Job Design in the GT Work Cell." Paper presented at the Computers and Automated Systems Association/Society of Manufacturing Engineers Group Technology Seminar, Detroit, Mich., Aug. 1978.

Bishop, A. B. *A Comprehensive Research Program for Effective Design and Operation of Flexible Manufacturing Systems*. MS84–634. Dearborn, Mich.: Society of Manufacturing Engineers, 1984.

Blumberg, M., and Alber, A. "The Human Element: Its Impact on the Productivity of Advanced Batch Manufacturing Systems." *Journal of Manufacturing Systems*, 1982, *1*, 43–52.

Blumberg, M., and Gerwin, D. "Coping with Advanced Manufacturing Technology." In E. Rhodes and D. Wield (eds.), *Implementing New Technologies*. Oxford: Basil Blackwell, 1985.

Blumenthal, M., and Dray, J. "The Automated Factory: Vision and Reality." *Technology Review*, Jan. 1985, pp. 29–37.

Boddy, D., and Buchanan, D. A. "New Technology with a Human Face." *Personnel Management*, 1985, *17*, 28–31.

Boddy, D., and Buchanan, D. A. *Managing New Technology.* New York: Basil Blackwell, 1986.

Bowman, B. L. "Cross-Functional Collaboration: Teaming for Technological Change." In O. Brown and H. W. Hendrick (eds.), *Human Factors in Organizational Design and Management.* Vol. 2. New York: Elsevier Science, 1986.

Boynton, R. E. "Design Elements for a Human Resource Impact Statement." *Human Resource Planning*, 1979, *2*, 103–109.

Bright, J. R. "Does Automation Raise Skill Requirements?" *Harvard Business Review*, July/Aug. 1958, pp. 85–98.

Brody, H. "Overcoming Barriers to Automation." *High Technology*, May 1985, pp. 41–46.

Buss, D. "Winners and Losers: On the Factory Floor, Technology Brings Challenge for Some, Drudgery for Others." *Wall Street Journal*, Sept. 16, 1985, p. 1.

Butera, F. "Designing Work in Automated Systems: A Review of Case Studies." In F. Butera and J. E. Thurman (eds.), *Automation and Work Design.* New York: Elsevier Science, 1984.

Bylinsky, G. "The Race to the Automatic Factory." *Fortune*, Feb. 21, 1983, pp. 52–64.

Campion, M. A., and Thayer, P. W. "Development and Field Evaluation of an Interdisciplinary Measure of Job Design." *Journal of Applied Psychology*, 1985, *70*, 29–43.

Cascio, W. F. *Costing Human Resources: The Financial Impact of Behavior in Organizations.* Belmont, Calif.: Kent, 1982.

Chamot, D., and Dymmel, M. D. *Cooperation or Conflict: European Experiences with Technological Change at the Workplace.* Washington, D.C.: AFL-CIO, 1981.

Chao, G. T., and Kozlowski, S. W. "Employee Perceptions on the Implementation of Robotic Manufacturing Technology." *Journal of Applied Psychology*, 1986, *71*, 70–76.

Chapanis, A. "On the Allocation of Functions Between Men and Machines." *Occupational Psychology*, 1965, *19*, 1–11.

Chauvin, B. "Training NC Maintenance Personnel." In Numerical Control Society (ed.), *Striving for Technological Excellence in*

Manufacturing. Princeton, N.J.: Numerical Control Society, 1981.

Chen, K.; Eisley, J. G.; Liker, J. K.; Rothman, J.; and Thomas, R. J. *Human Resource Development and New Technology in the Automobile Industry: A Case Study of Ford Motor Company's Dearborn Engine Plant.* Ann Arbor, Mich.: University of Michigan, 1984.

Cherry, R. "The Development of GM's Team-Based Plants." In R. Zager and M. Rosow (eds.) *The Innovative Organization.* Elmsford, N.Y.: Pergamon Press, 1982.

Chervany, N. L., and Dickson, G. W. "An Experimental Evaluation of Information Overload in a Production Environment." *Management Science,* 1974, *20,* 1335-1344.

Child, J. "Organizational Structure and Strategies of Control: A Replication of the Aston Study." *Administrative Science Quarterly,* 1973, *18,* 1-17.

Christensen, J. M., and Howard, J. M. "Field Experience in Maintenance." In J. Rasmussen and W. B. Rouse (eds.), *Human Detection and Diagnosis of System Failures.* New York: Plenum Press, 1981.

Clark, J.; Jacobs, A.; King, R.; and Rose, H. "Industrial Relations, New Technology, and Divisions Within the Workforce." *Industrial Relations Journal,* 1984, *16,* 36-44.

Clayton, R. J. *Integration of CAD and CAM.* Dearborn, Mich.: Society of Manufacturing Engineers, 1982.

Clutterbuck, D., and Hill, R. *The Re-Making of Work.* London: Grant McIntyre, 1981.

Corlett, E. N., and Coates, J. B. "Costs and Benefits from Human Resources Studies." *International Journal of Production Research,* 1976, *14,* 135-144.

Cotton, J. L., and others. "Employee Participation: Diverse Forms and Different Outcomes," forthcoming.

Curley, K. F., and Pyburn, P. J. "'Intellectual' Technologies: The Key to Improving White-Collar Productivity." *Sloan Management Review,* Fall 1982, pp. 31-39.

Darlin, D. "Coping with Technofright." *Wall Street Journal,* Sept. 16, 1985, p. 90C.

Davis, D. B. "Apple: Harvesting the Macintosh." *High Technology*, May 1985a, pp. 39–40.

Davis, D. B. "Renaissance on the Factory Floor." *High Technology*, May 1985b, pp. 24–25.

Davis, D. D. "Designing Organizations for Technological Innovation, Productivity, and Quality of Work Life: A Human Resource Perspective." In D. Grey, T. Solomon, and W. Hetzner (eds.), *Strategies for Technological Innovation*. Amsterdam: North-Holland, 1986a.

Davis, D. D. "Integrating Technological, Manufacturing, Marketing, and Human Resource Strategy." In D. D. Davis and Associates, *Managing Technological Innovation: Organizational Strategies for Implementing Advanced Manufacturing Technologies*. San Francisco: Jossey-Bass, 1986b.

Davis, D. D., and Roitman, D. "Technological Change in the Workplace: Labor and Management Issues." Unpublished paper. Norfolk, Va.: Old Dominion University, 1986.

Davis, L. E., and Taylor, J. *Design of Jobs*, 2nd Edition. Santa Monica, Calif.: Goodyear, 1979.

Davis, L. E., and Trist, E. "Improving the Quality of Work Life: Sociotechnical Case Studies." In J. O'Toole (ed.), *Work and Quality of Life*. Cambridge, Mass.: MIT Press, 1974.

Davis, L. E., and Wacker, G. J. "Job Design." In G. Salvendy (ed.), *Handbook of Human Factors*. New York: Wiley, 1987.

Dawes, R., and Lofquist, L. *A Psychological Theory of Work Adjustment*. Minneapolis: University of Minnesota Press, 1984.

Dawson, P., and McLoughlin, I. "Computer Technology and the Redefinition of Supervision: A Study of the Effects of Computerization on Railway Freight Supervisors." *Journal of Management Studies*, 1986, *23*, 116–132.

DeYoung, H. G. "GE: Dishing out Efficiency." *High Technology*, May 1985, pp. 32–33.

Dickson, K. "Pet Foods by Computer: A Case Study of Automation." In T. Forester (ed.), *The Microelectronics Revolution*, Cambridge, Mass.: MIT Press, 1981.

Dudley, N. A. *Work Measurement: Some Research Studies*. London: Macmillan, 1968.

Dupont-Gatelmand, C. "A Survey of Flexible Manufacturing Systems." *Journal of Manufacturing Systems*, 1981, *1*, 1-16.

Ettlie, J. E. "Technology Transfer—from Innovators to Users." *Industrial Engineering*, 1973, *5*, 16-23.

Ettlie, J. E. "Organizational Adaptations for Radical Process Innovators." Paper presented at the Academy of Management meeting, Los Angeles, Calif., Aug. 1985.

Ettlie, J. E. "Facing the Factory of the Future." In D. D. Davis and Associates, *Managing Technological Innovation: Organizational Strategies for Implementing Advanced Manufacturing Technologies*. San Francisco: Jossey-Bass, 1986a.

Ettlie, J. E. "The First-Line Supervisor and Advanced Manufacturing Technology." Paper presented at the Academy of Management meeting, Chicago, Ill., Aug. 1986b.

Ettlie, J. E. "Systemic Innovation." In D. Gray and others (eds.), *Strategies and Practices for Technological Innovation*. New York: North-Holland, 1986c.

Ettlie, J. E., and Rubenstein, A. H. "Social Learning Theory and the Implementation of Production Innovation." *Decision Sciences*, 1980, *11*, 648-668.

Fadem, J. A. "Automation and Work Design in the United States." In F. Butera and J. Thurman (eds.), *Automation and Work Design*. New York: Elsevier Science, 1984.

Farnum, G. T. "An Experiment in Management." *Manufacturing Engineering*, Mar. 1986, pp. 91-92.

Farris, G. F. "The Technical Supervisor: Beyond the Peter Principle." *Technology Review*, 1973, *75*, 26-33.

Fazakerley, G. M. "Group Technology: Social Benefits and Social Problems." *Production Engineer*, Oct. 1974, pp. 384-386.

Fazakerley, G. M. "A Research Report on the Human Aspects of Group Technology and Cellular Manufacturing." *International Journal of Production Research*, 1976, *1*, 123-134.

Fischer, R. E. "Training Needs of Associate Degree Graduates." In Numerical Control Society (ed.), *Striving for Technological Excellence in Manufacturing*. Princeton, N.J.: Numerical Control Society, 1981.

Fisher, M. S. "Work Teams: A Case Study." *Personnel Journal*, 1981, *60*, 42-45.

Fossum, B. "A Survey of CIM Plants." Paper presented at the American Institute of Decision Sciences meeting, Las Vegas, Nev., Nov. 1985.

Foulkes, F. K., and Hirsch, J. L. "People Make Robots Work." *Harvard Business Review*, 1984, *62*, 94–102.

Fraade, D. J. "Some Aspects of In-House Training for Computer Control of Batch Processing." *Computer Control of Batch Processes*, Fall 1979, 38–39.

Freedy, A., and Lucaccini, L. F. "Adaptive Computer Training System (ACTS) for Fault Diagnosis in Maintenance Tasks." In J. Rasmussen and W. B. Rouse (eds.), *Human Detection and Diagnosis of System Failures*. New York: Plenum Press, 1981.

Gent, M. J., and Weinstein, A. G. "Effects of Auto Plant Technology Change on Worker Outcomes: A Path Analysis." Paper presented at the American Institute of Decision Sciences meeting, Las Vegas, Nev., Nov. 1985.

Gerwin, D. "Do's and Don'ts of Computerized Manufacturing." *Harvard Business Review*, Mar.-Apr. 1982, pp. 107–116.

Gerwin, D., and Tarondeau, J. C. "Case Studies of Computer Integrated Manufacturing Systems: A View of Uncertainty and Innovation Processes." *Journal of Operations Management*, 1982, *2*, 87–92.

Ghosh, B. K., and Helander, M. G. "A Systems Approach to Task Allocation of Human-Robot Interaction in Manufacturing." *Journal of Manufacturing Systems*, 1986, *5*, 41–49.

Gibson, J. E., and Richards, L. G. "Redirecting Engineering Education: Computer Graphics and CAD/CAM." In P. Wang (ed.), *Automation Technology for Management and Productivity Advancements Through CAD/CAM and Engineering Data Handling*. Englewood Cliffs, N.J.: Prentice-Hall, 1983.

Globerson, S., and Salvendy, G. "A Sociotechnical Accounting Approach to the Evaluation of Job Performance." *International Journal of Operations and Production Management*, 1984, *4*, 36–42.

Gold, B. "CAM Sets New Rules for Production." *Harvard Business Review*, Nov.-Dec. 1982, pp. 88–94.

Goldhar, J. D., and Jelinek, M. "Plan for Economies of Scope." *Harvard Business Review*, 1983, *61*, 141–148.

Graham, M., and Rosenthal, S. R. "Flexible Manufacturing Systems Require Flexible People." Paper presented at the Institute of Management Sciences/Operations Research Society of America meeting, Nov. 1985.

Griffin, R. W. *Task Design*. Glenview, Ill.: Scott, Foresman, 1982.

Groebner, D., and Merz, C. M. "An Empirical Study of the Benefits óf Japanese Manufacturing Techniques to Hewlett-Packard." Paper presented at the American Institute of Decision Sciences meeting, Las Vegas, Nev., Nov. 1985.

Guest, R. H. "Tarrytown: Quality of Work Life at a General Motors Plant." In R. Zager and M. Rosow (eds.), *The Innovative Organization*. New York: Pergamon Press, 1982.

Gulowsen, J. "A Measure of Workgroup Autonomy." In L. E. Davis and J. C. Taylor (eds.), *Design of Jobs*, 2nd ed. Santa Monica, Calif.: Goodyear, 1979.

Gunn, T. "The Mechanization of Design and Manufacturing." *Scientific American*, 1982, *245*, 114–131.

Gyllenhammar, P. G. "How Volvo Adapts Work to People." *Harvard Business Review*, July-Aug. 1977, pp. 102–113.

Hackman, J. R.; Pierce, J. L.; and Wolfe, J. C. "Effects of Changes in Job Characteristics on Work Attitudes and Behaviors: A Naturally Occurring Quasi-Experiment." *Organizational Behavior and Human Performance*, 1978, *21*, 289–304.

Hanauer, G. "Bargaining for Jobs in the Automated Factory." *California Lawyer*, 1984, *4*, 28–31, 54.

Harris, P. R. *Management in Transition: Transforming Managerial Practices and Organizational Strategies for a New Work Culture*. San Francisco: Jossey-Bass, 1985.

Hartmann, G.; Nicholas, I.; Sorge, A.; and Warner, M. "Computerized Machine Tools, Manpower Consequences, and Skill Utilization: A Study of British and West German Manufacturing Firms." *British Journal of Industrial Relations*, 1983, *21*, 221–231.

Hauck, W. C., and Ross, T. L. "Volvo's New Solution at Kalmar: Multi-Factor Productivity Gainsharing." Paper presented at the American Institute of Decision Sciences meeting, Las Vegas, Nev., Nov. 1985.

Hayes, R. H., and Clark, K. B. "Exploring the Sources of Productivity Differences at the Factory Level." In K. B. Clark, R. H. Hayes, and C. Lorenz (eds.), *The Uneasy Alliance: Managing the Productivity-Technology Dilemma.* Boston: Harvard Business School Press, 1985.

Hazlehurst, R. J.; Bradbury, R. J.; and Corlett, E. N. "A Comparison of the Skills of Machinists on N-C and Conventional Machines." *Occupational Psychology,* 1969, *43,* 169–182.

Hedberg, B. "Computer Systems to Support Industrial Democracy." In E. Mumford and H. Sackman (eds.), *Human Choice and Computers.* New York: North-Holland, 1975.

Hedberg, B., and Mumford, E. "The Design of Computer Systems: Man's Vision of Man as an Integral Part of the System Design Process." In E. Mumford and H. Sackman (eds.), *Human Choices and Computers.* New York: North-Holland, 1975.

"High Tech to the Rescue." *Business Week,* June 16, 1986, pp. 100–108.

Hiltz, S. R. *Online Communities.* Norwood, N.J.: Ablex, 1984.

Hirschhorn, L. *Beyond Mechanization: Work and Technology in a Postindustrial Age.* Cambridge, Mass.: MIT Press, 1984.

Houtzeel, A., and Brown, C. S. "A Management Overview of Group Technology." Paper presented at the Computers and Automated Systems Association/Society of Manufacturing Engineers Westec 82 conference, Detroit, Mich., Mar. 1982.

Hoxie, G., and Shea, G. "Ten Hot Buttons Facing Management." *Infosystems,* Sept. 1977, pp. 60–100.

Huber, V. L., and Hyer, N. L. "The Human Factor in Cellular Manufacturing." *Journal of Operations Management,* 1985, *5,* 213–228.

Hulin, C. L., and Roznowski, M. "Organizational Technologies: Effects on Organizations' Characteristics and Individuals' Responses." *Research in Organizational Behavior,* 1985, *7,* 39–85.

Hull, D. M., and Lovett, J. E. *Task Analysis and Job Descriptions for Robotics/Automated Systems Technicians.* Waco, Tex.: Center for Occupational Research and Development, 1985.

Hwang, S., and Salvendy, G. "Effect of Allocation of Functions and Size of Flexible Manufacturing Systems on Human Supervisory

Performance." Paper presented at the Ninth Congress of the International Ergonomics Association, Sweden, Sept. 1985.

Hyer, N. L. "Management's Guide to Group Technology." *Operations Management Review*, 1984, *12*.

Hymowitz, C. "Manufacturing Change: Automation Experts Explore the Promise and Problems of the Factory of the Future." *Wall Street Journal*, Sept. 16, 1985, pp. 10C–12C.

International Labor Office. *Workers' Participation in Decisions Within Undertakings*. International Labor Office: Geneva, 1981.

Jacobs, J. *The Training Needs of Michigan Automobile Suppliers: Interim Report*. Ann Arbor, Mich.: Industrial Technology Institute, 1985.

Jaikumar, R. "Postindustrial Manufacturing." *Harvard Business Review*, 1986, *6*, 69–76.

Jasinski, F. J. "Adapting Organization to New Technology." *Harvard Business Review*, 1959, *37*, 79–86.

Jasper, W. A., and Vapor, J. C. "GT Approach Proves Out." *American Machinist*, Feb. 1979, pp. 86–89.

Jelinek, M. "Rethink Strategy or Perish: Technology Lessons from Telecommunications." *Journal of Production Innovation Management*, 1984, *1*, 36–42.

Jelinek, M. "Production Innovation and Economies of Scope: Beyond the 'Technological Fix'." Paper presented at the Fourth International Working Seminar on Production Economics, Cleveland, Feb. 1986.

Jelinek, M., and Goldhar, J. D. "Economics in the Factory of the Future," forthcoming.

Jones, G. R. "Task Visibility, Free Riding and Shirking: Explaining the Effect of Structure and Technology on Employee Behavior." *Academy of Management Review*, 1984, *9*, 684–695.

Julian, K. "Westinghouse: Building a Better Board." *High Technology*, May 1985, pp. 36–38.

Kamali, J.; Moodie, C. L.; and Salvendy, G. "A Framework for Integrated Assembly Systems: Humans, Automation, and Robots." *International Journal of Production Research*, 1982, *20*, 431–448.

Kaplan, R. S. "Measuring Manufacturing Performance: A New

Challenge for Managerial Accounting Research." *Accounting Review*, 1983, *43*, 686-705.

Kaplan, R. S. "Yesterday's Accounting Undermines Production." *Harvard Business Review*, July-Aug. 1984, pp. 95-101.

Kaplan, R. S. "Accounting Lag: The Obsolescence of Cost Accounting Systems." In D. B. Clark, R. H. Hayes, and C. Lorenz (eds.), *The Uneasy Alliance: Managing the Productivity-Technology Dilemma*. Boston: Harvard Business School Press, 1985.

Kaplan, R. S. "Must CIM Be Justified by Faith Alone?" *Harvard Business Review*, 1986, *64*, 87-95.

Katz, H. C., and Sabel, C. F. "Industrial Relations and Industrial Adjustment in the Car Industry." *Industrial Relations*, 1985, *24*, 295-315.

Kemp, N.; Wall, T.; Chris, C.; and Cordery, J. "Autonomous Work Groups in a Greenfield Site: A Comparative Study." *Journal of Occupational Psychology*, 1983, *46*, 271-288.

Kerr, S.; Hill, K. D.; and Broedling, L. "The First-Line Supervisor: Phasing Out or Here to Stay?" *Academy of Management Review*, 1986, *11*, 103-117.

Kiggundu, M. "Task Interdependence and Job Design." *Organizational Behavior and Human Performance*, 1983, *31*, 145-172.

Kinnucan, P. "Flexible Systems Invade the Factory." *High Technology*, 1983, *3*, 32-42.

Kinnucan, P. "IBM: Making the Chips Fly." *High Technology*, May 1985, pp. 34-35.

Knight, K. A. "Socio-Technical Engineering: An Approach to Technology Integration." Paper presented at the Society of Manufacturing Engineering Autofact Conference, Detroit, Mich., Nov. 1985.

Kohler, C., and Schultz-Wild, R. "Flexible Manufacturing Systems—Manpower Problems and Policies." Paper presented at the World Congress on the Human Aspects of Automation, London, Aug. 1983.

Kolodny, H., and Armstrong, A. "Three Bases for QWL Improvements: Structure, Technology, and Philosophy." Paper presented at the Academy of Management meetings, Los Angeles, Aug. 1985.

Kolodny, H., and Stjernberg, T. "The Change Process in Innovative Work Design: New Design and Redesign in Sweden, Canada and the USA." *Journal of Applied Behavioral Science*, 1986, *22*, 287–302.

Lansley, P. "AROUSAL: A Model to Match Reality." *Journal of European Industrial Training*, 1982, *6*, 17–21.

Lawler, E. E. "The Individualized Organization—Problems and Promise." *California Management Review*, 1974, *17*, 31–39.

Lawler, E. E. "Participation to Involvement: A Personal View of Workplace Change." Paper presented at the Academy of Management Meetings, Los Angeles, Aug. 1985.

Lawler, E. E., and Ledford, G. E. "Skill-Based Pay: A Concept That's Catching On." *Personnel*, Sept. 1985, pp. 30–37.

Leonard-Barton, D. *Interpersonal Influences of Innovation Adoption Within Organizations Under Conflictive and Compatible Conditions.* HBR Working Paper no. 9-787-004. Boston: Harvard Business School, 1986a.

Leonard-Barton, D. "The Secondary Adoption Decision: Implementing A New Technology Within an Organization." Paper presented at the Academy of Management meeting. Chicago, Ill., Aug. 1986b.

Leonard-Barton, D., and Kraus, W. A. "Implementing New Technology." *Harvard Business Review*, 1985, *63*, 102–110.

Levin, D. P. "Pitfalls of High-Tech Field." *Wall Street Journal*, May 14, 1984, p. 16C.

Lewin, K. *Field Theory and Social Science.* New York: Harper & Row, 1951.

Liker, J., and Thomas, R. J. "Prospects for Human Resource Development in the Context of Technological Change: Lessons from a Major Technological Renovation." In D. Kocacglu (ed.), *Handbook of Technology Management.* New York: Wiley, 1987.

Lipstreu, O., and Reed, K. A. "A New Look at the Organizational Implications of Automation." *Academy of Management Journal*, 1965, *8*, 24–31.

Love, J. H., and Walker, J. "Problems of New Technology Deployment in the Mechanical Engineering and Printing

Industries: A Case Study." Paper presented at the Managing Advanced Manufacturing Technology conference, London, Jan. 1986.

Lusterman, S. *Education in Industry*. New York: Conference Board, 1977.

Lusterman, S. *Trends in Corporate Education and Training*. New York: Conference Board, 1985.

McDonald, J. L. "Making the Transition from CAD/CAM Systems Planning to Operation." In K. M. Dunn and B. Herzog (eds.), *CAD/CAM Management Strategies*. Pennsauken, N.J.: Auerbach Publications, 1984.

Macek, A. J. "Human Factors Facilitating the Implementation of Automation." *Journal of Manufacturing Systems*, 1982, *1*, 195–206.

MacGregor, D. *The Human Side of Enterprise*. New York: McGraw-Hill, 1960.

Mackulak, G. T. "Planning Techniques for Computer-Integrated Manufacturing." *National Productivity Review*, Summer 1984, pp. 315–333.

McLoughlin, I.; Rose, H.; and Clark, J. "Managing the Introduction of New Technology." *Omega*, 1985, *13*, 251–262.

Macy, B. "The Bolivar Quality of Work Life Program: Success or Failure?" In R. Zager and M. Rosow (eds.), *The Innovation Organization*. New York: Pergamon Press, 1982.

Mahoney, T. A.; Jerdee, T. H.; and Carroll, S. I. "The Job(s) of Management." *Industrial Relations*, 1965, *4*, 97–110.

Majchrzak, A. "Changes to Work Resulting from CAD." Paper presented to the American Institute of Industrial Engineers meeting, Chicago, Ill., Dec. 1985a.

Majchrzak, A. *Effects of Computerized Integration on Shopfloor Human Resources and Structure*. MS85-1080. Dearborn, Mich.: Society of Manufacturing Engineers, 1985b.

Majchrzak, A. "The Effect of CAM Technologies on Training Activities." *Journal of Manufacturing Systems*, 1986a, *5*, 203–211.

Majchrzak, A. "A National Probability Survey on Education and Training for CAD/CAM." *IEEE Transactions on Engineering Management*, 1986b, *33*, 197–206.

Majchrzak, A.; Chang, T.-C.; Barfield, W.; Eberts, R. E.; and Salvendy, G. *Human Aspects of Computer-Aided Design*. London: Taylor & Francis, 1987.

Majchrzak, A.; Collins, P.; and Mandeville, D. "Quantitative Assessment of Changes in Work Activities Resulting from CAD." *Behavior and Information Technology*, 1986, 5, 259–271.

Majchrzak, A., and Cotton, J. "Western Electric Feedback Results." Unpublished document. West Lafayette, Ind.: Purdue University, 1985.

Majchrzak, A., and Cotton, J. "A Longitudinal Study of Adjustment to Technological Change: The Case of Job Transfers from Mass to Computer-Automated Batch Production." Paper presented at the Claremont Graduate School Colloquium, Claremont, Calif., Nov., 1986.

Majchrzak, A., and Klein, K. J. "Things Are Always More Complicated Than You Think: An Open Systems Approach to the Organizational Effects of Computer-Automated Technology," forthcoming.

Majchrzak, A.; Nieva, V. F.; and Newman, P. D. "A National Probability Survey of Contemporary CAD/CAM Adoption." In D. D. Davis and Associates, *Managing Technological Innovation: Organizational Strategies for Implementing Advanced Manufacturing Technologies*. San Francisco: Jossey-Bass, 1986.

Majchrzak, A., and Paris, M. *Successful Management Infrastructures for Advanced Manufacturing Technology*. Chicago, Ill.: Michael Paris Associates, 1986.

Mann, F. C. "Psychological and Organizational Impacts." In J. T. Dunlop (ed.), *Automation and Technological Change*. Englewood Cliffs, N.J.: Prentice-Hall, 1962.

Mann, F. C., and Williams, L. K. "Observations on the Dynamics of a Change to Electronic Data Processing Equipment." *Administrative Science Quarterly*, 1960, 5, 217–256.

Manufacturing Studies Board, Committee on the Effective Implementation of Advanced Manufacturing Technology, National Research Council, National Academy of Sciences. *Human Resource Practices for Implementing Advanced Manufacturing Technology*. Washington, D.C.: National Academy Press, 1986.

Manz, C. C., and Sims, H. P. "Searching for the 'Unleader':

Organizational Member Views on Leading Self-Managed Groups." *Human Relations,* 1984, *37,* 409-424.

Margulies, N., and Colflesh, L. "An Organizational Development Approach to the Planning and Implementation of New Technology." In D. D. Warrick (ed.), *Contemporary Organizational Development.* Glenview, Ill.: Scott, Foresman, 1985.

Markey, R. "New Technology, the Economy and the Unions in Britain." *Journal of Industrial Relations,* 1982, *24,* 557-577.

Markus, M. L. "Implementation Politics: Top Management, Support and User Involvement." *Systems, Objectives, Solutions,* 1981, *1,* 203-215.

Markus, M. L. *Systems in Organizations: Bugs and Features.* Boston: Pitman, 1984.

Mintzberg, H. *The Nature of Managerial Work.* New York: Harper & Row, 1973.

Mintzberg, H. *The Structuring of Organizations: A Synthesis of Research.* Englewood Cliffs, N.J.: Prentice-Hall, 1979.

Montgomery, G. "CAD/CAM Feasibility Assessment: A Systematic Approach." In K. M. Dunn and B. Herzog (eds.), *CAD/CAM Management Strategies.* Pennsauken, N.J.: Auerbach Publications, 1984.

Morse, J. J. "Person-Job Congruence and Individual Adjustment." *Human Relations,* 1975, *28,* 841-861.

Mosher, P., and Majchrzak, A. "Workplace Changes Mediating Effect of Technology on Individuals' Attitudes and Performance." Paper presented at the Academy of Management meeting, Chicago, Ill., Aug. 1986.

Mumford, E., and Sackman, H. "International Human Choice and Computers: Conference Retrospect and Prospect." In E. Mumford and H. Sackman (eds.), *Human Choice and Computers.* New York: North-Holland, 1975.

Mumford, E., and Weir, M. *Computer Systems in Work Design— The ETHICS Approach.* New York: Wiley, 1979.

Nadler, D., and Tushman, M. "A Congruence Model for Diagnosing Organizational Behavior." In D. Kolb, I. Rubin, and J. McIntyre (eds.), *Organizational Psychology,* 3rd ed. New York: Prentice-Hall, 1980.

Nag, A. "Automakers Discover Factory of the Future Is Headache Just Now." *Wall Street Journal,* May 13, 1986, pp. 1, 26, and 27.

National Center for Productivity and Quality of Working Life (NCPQWL). *Productivity and Job Security: Retraining to Adapt to Technological Change.* Washington, D.C.: National Center for Productivity and Quality of Working Life, 1977.

National Ministry of Social Affairs and Employment. *The Impact of Chip Technology on Conditions and Quality of Work.* London: Metra Consulting Group, 1983.

Nieva, V. F.; Gaertner, G. H.; Argoff, N. J.; and Newman, P. D. *Work in a Changing Factory: Interim Report.* Rockville, Md.: Westat, Inc., 1986.

Nieva, V. F.; Majchrzak, A.; and Huneycutt, M. J. *Education and Training in Computer Automated Manufacturing.* Rockville, Md.: Westat, Inc., 1982.

"No Automation Additives." *Automation News,* March 11, 1985, p. 2.

Nulty, L. E. "Case Studies of IAM Local Experiences with the Introduction of New Technologies." In D. Kennedy, C. Craypo, and M. Lehman (eds.), *Labor and Technology: Union Response to Changing Environments.* University Park: Department of Labor Studies, Pennsylvania State University, 1982.

Office of Technology Assessment. *Computerized Manufacturing Automation,* Library of Congress no. 84-601053. Washington, D.C.: Government Printing Office, 1984.

Parsons, H. M., and Kearsley, G. P. "Robotics and Human Factors: Current Status and Future Prospects." *Human Factors,* 1982, *24,* 535–552.

Pava, C. *Managing New Office Technology.* New York: Free Press, 1983.

Pearce, J., and Ravlin, E. "The Design and Activation of Self-Regulating Work Groups." Forthcoming.

Perrow, C. "A Framework for the Comparative Analysis of Organizations." *American Sociological Review,* 1967, *32,* 197–208.

Perrow, C. "The Organizational Context of Human Factors Engineering." *Administrative Science Quarterly,* 1983, *28,* 521–541.

Perrow, C. *Normal Accidents.* New York: Basic Books, 1984.

Pierce, J. L.; Dunham, R. B.; and Blackburn, R. S. "Social System Structure, Job Design, and Growth Need Strength." *Academy of Management Journal,* June 1979, pp. 223–240.

Piore, M. J. "Computer Technologies, Market Structure, and Strategic Union Choices." In T. A. Kochan (ed.), *Challenges and Choices Facing American Labor.* Cambridge, Mass.: MIT Press, 1985.

Poza, E. "Twelve Actions to Build Strong U.S. Factories." *Sloan Management Review,* Fall 1983, pp. 27–38.

Poza, E., and Markus, L. "Success Story: The Team Approach to Work Restructuring." *Organizational Dynamics,* Winter 1980, 1–20.

Pugh, D. S., and Hickson, D. J. *Organizational Structure in its Context.* Westmead, England: Saxon House, D. C. Heath, 1976.

Pullen, R. D. "A Survey of Cellular Manufacturing Cells." *Production Engineer,* Sept. 1976.

Reibstein, L. "More Firms Use Personality Tests for Entry-Level Blue-Collar Jobs." *Wall Street Journal,* Jan. 16, 1986, p. 25.

Riche, R. W. "Impact of New Electronic Technology." *Monthly Labor Review,* Mar. 1982, pp. 37–39.

Risch, R. P. "NC Is a Business Tool." In M. A. DeVries (ed.), *Management Guide to NC.* Princeton, N.J.: Numerical Control Society, 1971.

Roberts, M. "The Impact of Technology on Union Organizing and Collective Bargaining." In D. Kennedy, C. Craypo, and M. Lehman (eds.), *Labor and Technology: Union Response to Changing Environments.* University Park: Department of Labor Studies, Pennsylvania State University, 1982.

Robey, D. "Individual Moderators of the Task Design, Job Attitude Relationship." *Journal of Management Studies,* 1978, *15,* 68–76.

Robey, D., and Zeller, R. L. "Factors Affecting Success and Failures of an Information System for Product Quality." *Interfaces,* 1978, *8,* 70–75.

Rogers, E. *Diffusion of Innovation.* New York: Free Press, 1983.

Roitman, D., and Gottschalk, R. *Job Enrichment, Sociotechnical Design, and Quality Circles: Effects on Productivity and Quality of Worklife.* Washington, D.C.: National Science Foundation, 1984.

Roitman, D.; Liker, J. K.; and Roskies, E. "Birthing a Factory of the Future: When is 'All at Once' Too Much?" In R. H. Kilmann and T. M. Covin (eds.), *Corporate Transformation: Revitalizing Organizations for a Competitive World.* San Francisco: Jossey-Bass, 1987.

Rothwell, S. "Supervisors and New Technology." In E. Rhodes and D. Wield (eds.), *Implementing New Technologies.* Oxford: Basil Blackwell, 1985.

Rouse, W. B. "Experimental Studies and Mathematical Models of Human Problem Solving Performance in Fault Diagnosis Tasks." In J. Rasmussen and W. B. Rouse (eds.), *Human Detection and Diagnosis of System Failures.* New York: Plenum Press, 1981.

Rousseau, D. M. "Assessment of Technology in Organizations: Closed vs. Open Systems Approach." *Academy of Management Review,* 1979, *4,* 531–542.

Rubenowitz, S.; Norrgren, F.; and Tannenbaum, A. "Some Social Psychological Effects of Direct and Indirect Participation in Ten Swedish Companies." *Organization Studies,* 1983, *4,* 243–259.

Saari, L. M. "Human Resource Issues at Two Computerized Sawmills." Paper presented at the Academy of Management meeting, Los Angeles, Aug. 1985.

Salvendy, G. "An Industrial Engineering Dilemma: Simplified Versus Enlarged Jobs." Proceedings of the twenty-ninth annual conference of the American Institute of Industrial Engineers, Toronto, May, 1978a.

Salvendy, G. "An Industrial Dilemma: Simplified vs. Enlarged Jobs." In R. Murumatsu and N. A. Dudley (eds.), *Production and Industrial Systems.* London: Taylor & Francis, 1978b.

Salvendy, G. "Review and Reappraisal of Human Aspects in Planning Robotic Systems." *Behavior and Information Technology,* 1983, *2,* 263–287.

Salvendy, G. *Handbook of Human Factors.* New York: Wiley, 1987.

Schaffer, G. "Implementing CIM." *American Machinist,* Aug. 1981, pp. 71–93.

Schoonhoven, C. B. "Sociotechnical Considerations for the Space

Station's Development: Autonomy and the Human Element in Space." *Journal of Applied Behavioral Science*, 1986, *22*, 271–286.

Schreiber, C. T. "Using Demographic and Technological Forecasts for Human Resource Planning." In G. Mensch and R. J. Niehaus (eds.), *Work, Organizations and Technological Change.* New York: Plenum Press, 1982.

Seibt, D. "User and Specialist Evaluations in System Development." In E. Grochla and N. Szyperski (eds.), *Design and Implementation of Computer-Based Information Systems.* Oslo, Norway: Sijthoff & Noordhoff, 1979.

Sepheri, M. *Just-in-Time, Not Just in Japan: Case Studies of American Pioneeers.* Falls Church, Va.: American Production and Inventory Control Society, 1986.

Shaiken, H. *Automation and the Workplace: Case Studies on the Introduction of Programmable Automation in Manufacturing.* Cambridge, Mass.: MIT Press, 1983.

Shaiken, H. *Work Transformed.* New York: Holt, Rinehart, and Winston, 1984.

Shaiken, H.; Herzenberg, S.; and Kuhn, S. "The Work Process Under More Flexible Production." *Industrial Relations*, 1986, *25*, 167–182.

Sharit, J. "Human Supervisory Control of a Flexible Manufacturing System: An Exploratory Investigation." Unpublished doctoral dissertation, Department of Industrial Engineering, Purdue University, 1984.

Sharit, J.; Chang, T.; and Salvendy, G. "Technical and Human Aspects of Computer-Aided Manufacturing." In G. Salvendy (ed.), *Handbook of Human Factors.* New York: Wiley, 1987.

Sheridan, T. B. "Understanding Human Error and Aiding Human Diagnostic Behavior in Nuclear Power Plants." In J. Rasmussen and W. B. Rouse (eds.), *Human Detection and Diagnosis of System Failures.* New York: Plenum Press, 1981.

Skinner, W. "The Focused Factory." *Harvard Business Review*, 1974, *52*, 113–121.

Skinner, W. *Manufacturing in the Corporate Strategy.* New York: Wiley, 1978.

Skinner, W. "The Productivity Paradox." *Harvard Business Review*, 1986, *64*, 55–59.

Skinner, W., and Chakraborty, K. *The Impact of New Technology.* Elmsford, N.Y.: Pergamon Press, 1982.

"Small Is Beautiful Now In Manufacturing." *Business Week*, 1984, *22*, 152–156.

Smyth, A. "Injury by Repetition—The Costs Are High." *Work and People*, 1982, *8*, 42–43.

Spenner, K. "Deciphering Prometheus: Temporal Change in the Skill Level of Work." *American Sociological Review*, 1983, *48*, 824–837.

Strauss, G. "Participative Management: A Critique." *International Labor Relations Research*, Nov. 1966, pp. 4–10.

Stricharchuk, G., and Winter, R. E. "Second Thoughts: Experience with Robots Shows They Can Be More Costly and Complicated Than Expected." *Wall Street Journal*, Sept. 16, 1985, p. 14C.

Susman, G. I., and Chase, R. B. "A Sociotechnical Analysis of the Integrated Factory." *Journal of Applied Behavioral Science*, 1986, *22*, 257–270.

Susman, G. I.; Dean, J. W.; and Porter, P. S. "Departmental Interfaces in the Implementation of Advanced Manufacturing Technology." Center for the Management of Technological and Organizational Change Working Paper Series 86-2. University Park: Pennsylvania State University, 1986.

Swamidass, P. M. "Manufacturing Process Innovation in Export Oriented Firms." Paper presented at the American Institute of Decision Sciences, Las Vegas, Nev., Nov. 1985.

Taylor, C. "Building a Bit of Fun in a Bomb Film." *Los Angeles Times*, May 6, 1986, p. C1.

Taylor, J. C. "Job Design Criteria Twenty Years Later." In L. E. Davis and J. C. Taylor (eds.), *Design of Jobs*. Santa Monica, Calif.: Goodyear, 1979.

Teresko, J. "Automation and the Bottom Line." *Industry Week*, May 26, 1986, 41–94.

Thompson, D. A. "Commercial Air Crew Detection of System Failures: State of the Art and Future Trends." In J. Rasmussen and W. B. Rouse (eds.), *Human Detection and Diagnosis of System Failures*. New York: Plenum Press, 1981.

Thompson, H., and Scalpone, R. "Managing the Human Resource in the Factory of the Future." Paper presented at the World Congress on the Human Aspects of Automation, Detroit, Mich., Aug. 1983.

Thompson, J. *Organizations in Action*. New York: McGraw-Hill, 1967.

Tombari, H. "Analyzing the Benefits and Costs of Computer-Aided Manufacturing Methods." In K. M. Dunn and B. Herzog (eds.), *CAD/CAM Management Strategies*. Pennsauken, N.J.: Auerbach Publications, 1984.

Tomeski, E. A., and Lazarus, H. *People-Oriented Computer Systems*. New York: Van Nostrand Reinhold, 1975.

Tornatzky, L., and others, *The Process of Technological Innovation: Reviewing the Literature*. Washington, D.C.: Productivity Improvement Research Section, National Science Foundation, 1983.

Trist, E. L.; Susman, G. I.; and Brown, G. R. "An Experiment in Autonomous Working in an American Underground Coal Mine." *Human Relations*, 1977, *30*, 201-236.

Tucker, J. B. "GM: Shifting to Automatic." *High Technology*, May 1985, pp. 26-29.

Turner, J. A., and Karasek, R. A. "Software Ergonomics: Effects of Computer Application Design Parameters on Operator Task Performance and Health." *Ergonomics*, 1984, *27*, 663-690.

U.S. Department of Labor, Bureau of Labor Statistics. *Outlook for Computer Process Control*. Washington, D.C.: Government Printing Office, 1970.

U.S. Department of Labor, Bureau of Labor Statistics. *Occupational Training in Selected Metalworking Industries*. R&D Monograph no. 53. Washington, D.C.: Government Printing Office, 1974.

U.S. Department of Labor. *Dictionary of Occupational Titles*. (4th ed.) Washington, D.C.: U.S. Government Printing Office, 1977.

U.S. Department of Labor, Bureau of Labor Statistics. *Occupational Projections and Training Data*. Bulletin 2052. Washington, D.C.: Government Printing Office, 1980.

U.S. Department of Labor, Bureau of Labor Statistics. *Technology and Labor in Four Industries.* Washington, D.C.: Government Printing Office, 1982.

U.S. General Accounting Office. *Report to the Congress: Manufacturing Technology: A Changing Challenge to Improved Productivity.* Library of Congress Document 75-436. Washington, D.C.: Government Printing Office, June 3, 1976.

Van Nostrand, R. C. "CAD/CAM Justification and Follow-Up: Simmonds Precision Products Case Study." In K. M. Dunn and B. Herzog (eds.), *CAD/CAM Management Strategies.* Pennsauken, N.J.: Auerbach Publications, 1984.

Wagner, J. A. "Pay Formulas." Paper presented at the American Institute of Decision Sciences meeting, Las Vegas, Nev., Nov. 1985.

Walker, C. R., and Guest, R. H. *The Man on the Assembly Line.* Cambridge, Mass.: Harvard University Press, 1952.

Walton, R. E. "New Work Technology and Its Work Force Implications: Union and Management Approaches." Harvard Working Paper 84-13. Boston, Mass.: Harvard University, 1983.

Walton, R. E., and Schlesinger, L. A. "Do Supervisors Thrive in Participative Work Systems?" *Organizational Dynamics,* Winter 1979, pp. 25-38.

Walton, R. E., and Vittori, W. "New Information Technology: Organizational Problem or Opportunity?" *Office: Technology and People,* 1983, *1,* 249-273.

Warner, M. "New Technology, Work Organizations and Industrial Relations." *Omega,* 1984, *12,* 203-210.

Westcott, B. J., and Eisenhardt, K. M. "The Dynamics of Process Innovation in Manufacturing." Paper presented at the Academy of Management meeting, Chicago, Ill., Aug. 1986.

White, S.; Dittrich, J.; and Lang, J. "The Effects of Group Decisionmaking Process and Problem-Situation Complexity on Implementation Attempts." *Administrative Science Quarterly,* 1980, *25,* 428-440.

Whitney, D. E. "Real Robots Do Need Jigs." *Harvard Business Review,* 1986, *64,* 110-116.

"Why Technical Training Will Prosper in the '80's." *Training/HRD,* 1982, *19,* 60-61.

Wilkinson, B. *The Shopfloor Politics of New Technology*. London: Heinemann Educational Books, 1983.

Williams, R. "Snakco: Negotiation over the Introduction of High-Speed Equipment." In E. Rhodes and D. Wield (eds.), *Implementing New Technology*. Oxford: Basil Blackwell, 1985.

"A Work Revolution in U.S. Industry." *Business Week*, May 16, 1983, p. 108.

Zager, R. "Introduction and Overview." In R. Zager and M. Rosow (eds.), *The Innovative Organization*. New York: Pergamon Press, 1982.

Zaltman, G.; Duncan, R.; and Hobek, J. *Innovations and Organizations*. New York: Wiley, 1973.

Zuboff, S. "New Worlds of Computer-Mediated Work." *Harvard Business Review*, 1982, *60*, 142–152.

Zukowski, R. "Retraining Existing Human Resources to Meet Tomorrow's Technology Needs." Paper presented at the National Science Foundation conference on Industrial Science and Technological Innovation, Raleigh, N.C., May 1984.

Index